KT-476-099

The Roots of Christian Freedom

THE RESOURCE ROOM
CHURCH HOUSE
9 THE CLOSE
WINCHESTER
SO23 9LS

WINCHESTER SCHOOL OF MISSION

06773

ALISTAIR KEE

The Roots of Christian Freedom

THE THEOLOGY OF
John A. T. Robinson

First published in Great Britain 1988
SPCK
Holy Trinity Church
Marylebone Road
London NW 1 4DU

Copyright © Alistair Kee 1988
All rights reserved. No part of this book may be
reproduced or transmitted in any form or by any means,
electronic or mechanical, including photocopying, recording
or by any information storage and retrieval system, without
permission in writing from the publisher.

British Library Cataloguing in Publication Data

Kee, Alistair
    The roots of Christian freedom : the
    theology of John A. T. Robinson.
    1. Robinson, John
    I. Title
    230'.092'4   BX4705.R56/

    ISBN 0–281–04338–8

    Photoset by Deltatype Ltd, Ellesmere Port
    Printed in Great Britain by
    Anchor Brendon Limited
    Tiptree, Essex

Contents

Preface

Two of my former teachers were personal friends of Dietrich Bonhoeffer, and contributed to a volume of essays entitled *I Knew Dietrich Bonhoeffer*. Although like many others of my generation I was intensely interested in some of Bonhoeffer's enigmatic sayings, I found the cult of personality which came to surround him distasteful. This is probably reflected in an article which I later wrote, 'I Did Not Know Dietrich Bonhoeffer'. Perhaps I should begin this book with the disclaimer, 'I Scarcely Knew John Robinson'. He was kind enough to contact me soon after the publication of my first book, the only theologian of standing to write to me about it, and I shall always be grateful for the encouragement he gave me at that stage. But even by that time, 1971, he was back in Cambridge and working on New Testament themes again. Soon after that I went on to political theology, and latterly we had little contact. I am therefore writing to assure the reader that this is not hagiography.

The idea of writing on John Robinson's work came from correspondence with Eric James, his friend and literary executor. Eric had just finished his biography, and mentioned that he had not attempted any systematic treatment of the content of John's writings. He also sent me a copy of a plan which John Robinson himself had drawn up as a suggestion to anyone who wished to write on his work. He had divided his books, some twenty-four in all, into three sections, adding some indications of how they might be treated and of the major themes running through them. I have used this division of the books, but since my interests were not entirely expository, I have not used any of his other suggestions.

I have always been puzzled by John Robinson's work. As an undergraduate I attended the lectures of the Shakespearean scholar Peter Alexander. It was at that time that I first heard the theory that Shakespeare's plays had not been written by William Shakespeare – but by someone of the same name. The two matters came together to suggest the following scenario. It seemed possible that at some time in the next century a research student might be trawling listlessly through a data base of publications from the second half of the twentieth century, and might come across a collection of books on New Testament themes published by a Cambridge scholar, John

Robinson. They would turn out to be in general conservative, even ultra-conservative, on many issues. At the same time he would come across another collection of books on theology, which were in general radical, even dangerously radical on many issues. He would conclude that the theological works were not written by John Robinson, but by someone of the same name.

Approaching the twenty-fifth anniversary of the publication of *Honest To God*, I therefore decided to settle the matter once and for all, at least to my own satisfaction. Writing about John Robinson's work is therefore in the first instance motivated by personal interest. I wished to get this matter straight in my own mind. However, that would not be a sufficient reason for publishing the results. Nor I suspect would it have been a reason of which John Robinson himself would have approved. However, it is only when his works are taken together that we can begin to understand what he was attempting to do. In fact he was trying to do two things at once: to recover the truly biblical roots of the Christian faith, and on this basis to indicate how Christian faith might develop in this time of constant change.

When I began to read or re-read his books I was not sure what I should find; it soon became evident, however, that there were not two John Robinsons, but one. He was neither conservative nor radical in the conventional meanings of these terms. His work is a very distinctive integration of the two. I have pursued this conservative–radical dialectic through his biblical studies, into his theological and social writings. What emerged was a fascinating and coherent position which I for one had not been aware of when reading his books spaced out over the years. Ironically the most important work, for those who would understand his thought, is the one which he never published, his doctoral dissertation. Few people have had the opportunity of reading it, yet all of his later books are based on it, exploring and pushing forward the frontiers on issue after issue.

I have therefore used this image of exploration as the key to understanding the unity and coherence of his work. It is original and exciting, and quite the opposite of aimless wandering. He writes as a man who has roots, roots in the Bible and in Christian experience, but he is so secure in these foundations that he is thereby liberated to explore what it means to be a Christian in a new world which is daily changing. And this is finally the reason for writing the book: not to get straight something which is already in the past, but to continue the exploration which he began and which is even more urgently needed today.

In the light of this there are a few explanatory notes to be made. The first is that I have not dealt with every article or lecture which John Robinson wrote. The unity and coherence of his work become clear from his major publications. Secondly, when I have criticized him, it is when he has not been true to his own method, when he has not explored issues as he promised to do. I have not entered into a general discussion of issues or sought to evaluate his treatment of them by comparison with other scholars. That would require a very different book. I am not assuming that his detailed work is beyond criticism, but it is beyond my more strictly defined treatment of his thought. Thirdly, I have quoted John Robinson continually and extensively so that the reader might know that it is his thought and not mine which is being presented. When I have added a comment or illustration on my own account I have tried to make this clear. In consequence I should have been writing his name every few lines throughout the book. Instead I have adopted a convention of using his very distinctive initials, JATR.

It will be clear that I am indebted to Eric James for his many kindnesses. I should like to congratulate him on his biography, which is beautifully written, producing a flowing narrative from what must have been a momentous task of sifting through thousands of printed pages, and, even worse, JATR's hand-written documents. Nor does he lapse into hagiography. JATR did not need that, and in view of what I have discovered in writing this book, I think it entirely appropriate that Eric was so secure in their friendship that he has been able to present a very honest and at times critical picture. The biography is not only a good read, it has proved an invaluable aid in understanding the context in which JATR's works appeared. It seemed clear that if he would be willing to write a very brief outline of JATR's life, this would be a great addition to my book. I am grateful that he agreed to produce a *cursus vitae*, and I realize that to write a very little about a subject on which he is so well informed must have been very demanding.

Finally I should like to thank SPCK for agreeing to my proposal to write this book. I hope that it will encourage a new generation to examine JATR's works, and to continue the explorations which he so courageously began.

Abbreviations

Unless indicated otherwise, abbreviations refer to books by John Robinson. Extracts from these books are reproduced with the permission of the publishers.

BTICB   *But That I Can't Believe!* (Collins Fontana, 1967)
CFPS   *Christian Freedom in a Permissive Society*
             (SCM Press, 1970)
CMT   *Christian Morals Today* (SCM Press, 1964)
CWT   *Can We Trust the New Testament?* (Mowbrays, 1977)
DBCT   *The Difference in Being a Christian Today*
             (Collins Fontana, 1972)
EIG   *Exploration into God* (SCM Press, 1967)
EJ   Eric James, *A Life of Bishop John A. T. Robinson: Scholar,*
             Pastor, Prophet (Collins, 1987)
HFG   *The Human Face of God* (SCM Press, 1973)
HTG   *Honest to God* (SCM Press, 1963)
HTGD   David L. Edwards (ed.), *The Honest to God Debate*
             (SCM Press, 1963)
IEG   *In the End God* (Collins Fontana, 1968)
JHC   *Jesus and His Coming: The Emergence of a Doctrine*
             (SCM Press, 1957)
LCL   *Liturgy Coming to Life* (Mowbrays, 1960)
NR   *The New Reformation?* (SCM Press, 1965)
OBCW   *On Being the Church in the World* (SCM Press, 1960;
             Penguin Books, 1969)
PJ   *The Priority of John* (SCM Press, 1985)
RD   *Redating the New Testament* (SCM Press, 1976)
RR   *The Roots of a Radical* (SCM Press, 1980)
TB   *The Body: A Study in Pauline Theology* (SCM Press, 1952)
TMNTS   *Twelve More New Testament Studies* (SCM Press, 1984)
TNTS   *Twelve New Testament Studies* (SCM Press, 1962)
TTE   *Truth is Two-Eyed* (SCM Press, 1979)
TWA   *Thou Who Art*, unpublished PhD Dissertation, University
             of Cambridge, 1945
WR   *Wrestling with Romans* (SCM Press 1979)
WTWM   *Where Three Ways Meet* (SCM Press, 1987)

The Life of
John A. T. Robinson

Eric James

It was a joy to me when I heard from Alistair Kee that he wanted to write a book on the work of Bishop John A. T. Robinson – whose literary executor and biographer I am privileged to be.

I so well remember, in the autumn of 1971, after the publication of Alistair's *The Way of Transcendence*, John sharing with me the review of it he had written for the American journal *The Christian Century*. John was bubbling with enthusiasm, and asked me what I knew of this 'young Scotsman' (then a member of the Iona Community and Lecturer in Theology at Hull University). John felt that he had found a friend in Alistair – someone who really understood the author of *Honest To God* and why he had written the book. In his review, John wrote 'I can think of no better introduction to and critique of the main movements of the past ten years'; and I know that John immediately invited Alistair to visit him and, after that, to preach for him in Cambridge.

I am glad that Alistair has written this introduction to and critique of John Robinson's thought, for I could think of few, if any, that John himself would more have wanted to do that.

There are certain facts about John Robinson's earliest years which are important. Arthur William Robinson, John's father, was sixty-two when he married Mary Beatrice Moore, John's mother. John was born 15 June 1919, the year after their marriage, in the Precincts of Canterbury Cathedral. A brother and sister soon followed.

Both John's father and his mother's father were Canons of Canterbury and scholars. John's father was a DD of Cambridge University and the author of a dozen books. Six of his uncles were ordained, including Armitage Robinson, Dean of Westminster and, later, of Wells, and Forbes, author of the spiritual classic *Letters to His Friends*.

John was nine, and already away at preparatory school, when his father died.

A Foundation Scholar of Marlborough College, his career there was not noteworthy; but in his last years he was introduced to Berdyaev's *The Destiny of Man* and to the poetry of Hopkins, Housman and Eliot.

He was awarded a Rustat Exhibition to Jesus College, Cambridge, and won the Burney Prize, and the Burney Scholarship, for 1942/3 to Trinity College. His thesis *Thou Who Art*, which gained him his PhD in 1946, was judged by Professor John Baillie, his examiner, 'the best ever to have come my way'.

At the beginning of 1944 John met Ruth Grace, a nineteen-year-old undergraduate at Newnham, where he was leading an SCM Group on C. S. Lewis's *The Problem of Pain*. (John had been President of the Cambridge SCM.) Ruth had come up to Cambridge from Liverpool to read Modern Languages. (She would gain a 'First' in French and Spanish.) During the previous vacation her father, a clerk in a tea merchant's office, had died. In May 1944 Ruth and John were engaged.

That September, John's uncle, Bishop Alfred Moore, died. John's mother had been housekeeping for him at Horspath Vicarage, Oxfordshire. (He had retired from his episcopate in South India.) Horspath Vicarage had been home for John in those wartime years. Ruth was never to see the grief-stricken John cry again. But, a month later, Archbishop William Temple also died. It was another personal bereavement. John had been training for ordination at Westcott House, though he lived for a term with the Presbyterians at Westminster College. It was Temple who had accepted John for ordination.

George Bell, Bishop of Chichester (who had befriended the family from his days as Dean of Canterbury), advised John not to pursue the possibility of becoming Assistant Professor in the Philosophy of Religion at Swarthmore College, Pennsylvania, USA, but to be ordained to a parish. So it was that John became curate of the inner-city parish of St Matthew Moorfield's, Bristol, in 1945, with Mervyn Stockwood as his vicar.

It was in 1947 that John married Ruth. Their first child, Stephen, arrived while they were at Bristol. Catherine, Elizabeth ('Buffy'), and Judith were to follow.

John had already written articles for *Theology* at Cambridge ('Agape and Eros', *Theology* 48, 1945) and Bristol ('The Temptations', *Theology* 50, 1947); but it was at Wells Theological College, where he was Chaplain from 1948 to 1951, that he wrote his first book, *In the End, God. . . : A Study of the Christian Doctrine of the Last Things* (James Clarke 1950; re-issued by Collins Fontana, 1968, as *In the End God*.

Made Fellow and Dean of Clare College, Cambridge, in 1951, John pioneered the liturgical revision described in *Liturgy Coming to Life*

(Mowbrays 1960). His second book, *The Body: A Study in Pauline Theology* (SCM Press, 1952), was much acclaimed. His third, *Jesus and His Coming: The Emergence of a Doctrine* (SCM Press, 1957), was delivered first as lectures at Harvard University – the beginning of John's many lecture journeys around the world. John wrote most of his *Twelve New Testament Studies* (SCM Press, 1962) while he was at Clare.

In 1953, Geoffrey Fisher, Archbishop of Canterbury, made him his Examining Chaplain and, in 1958, one of the Six-Preachers of Canterbury.

Articles were now beginning to flow from John's pen – like his contributions on 'The Christian Hope' to *Christian Faith and Communist Faith*, edited by Donald MacKinnon (Macmillan, 1953), and on 'Kingdom, Church and Ministry' to *The Historic Episcopate in the Fulness of the Church*, edited by Kenneth M. Carey (Dacre Press, 1960).

In 1958, Mervyn Stockwood, by now Vicar of Great St Mary's, Cambridge, was nominated Bishop of Southwark by the then Prime Minister, Harold Macmillan. Stockwood invited his erstwhile curate to become his suffragan Bishop of Woolwich. Despite contrary advice from fellow academics at Cambridge and from the then Archbishop of Canterbury, Geoffrey Fisher, John accepted, and was consecrated Bishop of Woolwich on 29 September 1959 in Canterbury Cathedral. Twelve days before the consecration Ruth had a subarachnoid brain haemorrhage and was still seriously ill in hospital on the consecration day.

After his consecration, John immediately began to pioneer the Southwark Ordination Course, a 'theological college without walls'. In 1960 he was elected a Proctor of the Convocation of Canterbury. He spoke in Convocation and the Church Assembly on the ordination of women, pastoral reorganization, the deployment and payment of the clergy, crown appointments, synodical government, inter-communion, the sharing of churches ecumenically, suicide, capital punishment, etc., and was soon recognized as the leading radical of the Church of England. *On Being the Church in the World* (SCM Press, 1960) confirmed his stature. His leadership of the radical Keble Conference Group was clear from his contribution to *New Ways with the Ministry* (Faith Press, 1960), and what being a bishop meant to him was equally clear from what he wrote for *Bishops: what they are and what they do*, edited by Glyn Simon, Bishop of Llandaff (Faith Press, 1961).

It was in fact 1960 which made John notorious. Till then he was simply a Cambridge scholar become a South London bishop. But he appeared in court to defend the publication of the unexpurgated edition of D. H. Lawrence's *Lady Chatterley's Lover* (Penguin Books, 1960), claiming that Lawrence 'tried to portray this relationship as . . . an act of holy communion' and provided several field-days for the Press. The Archbishop of Canterbury publicly censured him; but John did not regret what he said. He had simply said what he believed. He was both vociferously supported and attacked.

In the autumn of 1961 the back trouble began which was to be with John for the rest of his life. It was lying on his back – with Ruth reading aloud to him Tillich's *The Shaking of the Foundations* (SCM Press, 1949) and discussing as they read – that the idea of a book emerged which would eventually become *Honest to God* (SCM and Westminster Press, 1963). John was becoming acutely aware in South London of the need for reform. A year after *Honest to God* he would write a book with the title *The New Reformation?* (SCM Press, 1965); but however much the Church needed reformation in its liturgy and in its structures, however inappropriate so many of the church buildings were for their purpose, it was clear to John that the first and fundamental question which needed interpreting afresh to the people of the world which now surrounded him was the question of God himself. In June 1962 he shared the draft manuscript of *Honest to God* with several friends and asked them for their comments. Publication in March 1963 was preceded by a summary article in the *Observer* headed 'Our Image of God Must Go' – the headline inserted by the *Observer*. Life for the Robinsons was never the same after 19 March 1963. *Honest to God* sold over a million copies and was translated into seventeen languages. Opinions were again violently divided. John received over four thousand letters. Many who spoke for and against had never read the book. But henceforth there were always those who wanted to meet John and talk with him. With liberal quotations from Bonhoeffer, Bultmann and Tillich, John argued that the imagery in which God was presented made him unreal to people of a secular scientific world. He argued this not only in the book but in TV programmes, broadcasts, articles, interviews, sermons and in study groups.

The new Archbishop of Canterbury, Michael Ramsey, censured John, much as his predecessor had done. But Michael Ramsey admitted in *Canterbury Pilgrim* (SPCK, 1974) his 'initial error in reaction'.

In February 1963 John broadcast a talk, 'On Being a Radical', which was reprinted in *The Listener* (and in *Christian Freedom in a*

Permissive Society, SCM and Westminster Press, 1970). It was an important analysis of where he stood. In October 1963 *The Honest to God Debate* (SCM Press) was published, with John as co-editor; and he developed the chapter in *Honest to God* entitled 'The New Morality' into three much publicized lectures, *Christian Morals Today* (SCM Press, 1964 and reprinted in *Christian Freedom in a Permissive Society*). Lectures at Hartford Seminary, Connecticut, and at Cornell University occasioned *The New Reformation?*, and lectures at Stanford University, California, afforded further opportunity for *Exploration into God* (SCM Press, 1967).

Robinson the radical reformer – the programme of doctrinal, ethical and pastoral reform he adumbrated, alongside Mervyn Stockwood, was dubbed by the media 'South Bank Religion' – was at the same time the diligent diocesan pastor, awkwardly shy, incapable of malice, of profound faith and of childlike integrity. He was made BD of Cambridge University in 1962 and DD in 1968. His articles continued to pour forth – especially from October 1965 in the new fortnightly radical journal *New Christian*. John the journalist could write with brilliant simplicity, and did so in *But That I Can't Believe!* (Collins Fontana, 1967). But after ten punishing years as Bishop of Woolwich, and with the invitation to deliver the Hulsean Lectures in 1970 – *The Human Face of God* (SCM and Westminster Press, 1973) – he decided to return to Cambridge in 1969 as Fellow, Dean of Chapel, and Lecturer in Theology at Trinity College.

As soon as John returned to Cambridge, he gathered together in a book the fruits of the Woolwich decade, *Christian Freedom in a Permissive Society*. It is an important book; not least, it makes abundantly clear that John was not the 'high priest of the permissive society' his enemies made him, neither were his episcopal utterances made without being conscious of the 'additional responsibility which it seems to me that a bishop should reasonably be expected to show'.

There were only eight months between his move to Cambridge and his Hulsean Lectures – which were supposed to be 'the big book on Christology he had in him' – so there was much work to be done before he delivered them in Cambridge in Autumn 1970. He added to them material from lectures to Lancaster and Aberystwyth Universities in 1971 to become *The Human Face of God*. In May 1970 John was present in Westminster Abbey as a translator of the New Testament of the New English Bible. Eight months after his Hulsean Lectures, John gave four University Sermons to a crowded University Church in Cambridge. He expanded these as the lectures he gave in Buenos Aires in July 1971, *The Difference in Being a Christian Today* (Collins

Fontana and Westminster Pess, 1972). In 1976 John produced a *magnum opus, Redating the New Testament* (SCM and Westminster Press). He dedicated it to his father and mother. The latter had died in 1975, in her ninety-sixth year, and had been an important influence in his life. His New Testament scholarship also led him to concern himself with the Turin Shroud. In 1977 he put the fruits of *Redating the New Testament* into popular form as *Can We Trust the New Testament?* (Mowbrays).

The appointment to Trinity enabled John to tour the world. He visited the USA to lecture in 1973, 1976, 1978, 1980, 1982 and 1983. He lectured in South and Central America in 1971; South Africa in 1975; South Africa, Israel, India, Sri Lanka, Hong Kong, Japan and the USA in 1977/78 – *Truth is Two-Eyed* (SCM and Westminster Press, 1979), on the Buddhist-Hindu-Christian dialogue, was the product. In 1979 he lectured in New Zealand and Australia – *The Roots of a Radical* (SCM Press and Crossroad Publishing, 1980) being the result. In 1979, his lectures on St Paul's Epistle to the Romans were published as *Wrestling with Romans* (SCM and Westminster Press). In 1980 he was made an Hon. DCL of the University of Southern California. In 1981 he visited Israel again to do preparatory work on his second New Testament *magnum opus, The Priority of John* (SCM Press, 1985 and Meyer-Stone, 1987). In 1982 he was able to do more preparation as Visiting Professor at McMaster University, Hamilton, Ontario, Canada, where he was also able to pursue his longstanding concern with nuclear disarmament.

Some of John's travels were sabbatical leave given by his College; some for the preparation of the books that Trinity hoped he would produce; but Trinity were unhappy that they did not see more of him, and Cambridge University was unable to give him the lectureship or the professional chair which some thought he deserved.

In June 1983 it was diagnosed that John was suffering from a pancreatic tumour. He lived with cancer courageously for the next six months, preparing *Twelve More New Testament Studies* (SCM Press, 1984), and gathering material for *Where Three Ways Meet* (SCM Press, 1987). He preached his last sermon, on 'Learning from Cancer', to a packed College Chapel on 23 October 1983, and died 5 December 1983 at his home in Arncliffe, Yorkshire. John's friend of many years, Professor C. F. D. Moule, delivered his Bampton Lectures, *The Priority of John*, in St Mary's, Oxford, in 1984.

PART ONE

Biblical Exploration

Introduction

In 1962 JATR collected some previously published essays on New Testament themes. They were issued as *Twelve New Testament Studies*. In the Preface he indicated the basis of the choice: 'What unity they have is provided by an unsatisfied curiosity to push behind commonly accepted positions of New Testament study, and to explore and test alternative hypotheses' [TNTS, 7]. This particular statement could be taken in a more general sense to indicate one of the characteristic features of his New Testament research. One of the most difficult exercises to perform is to identify our own assumptions, to become aware of what we have taken for granted. By definition such matters seem uncontentious to us. Of all the questions which we might ask, of all the problems which occur to us, we are for the most part oblivious to the often quite unfounded assumptions which we make. Nor are these assumptions about peripheral things. They are so fundamental that they provide the context of our thinking and the parameters of our inquiries. Once having made them, our assumptions guarantee that any originality will be considerably curtailed. There are few more intellectually stimulating experiences than listening to the first few words of a public lecture when the speaker, by his lecture title, by the first sentence, by a phrase or even a word, makes it clear that he has identified as problematic what we have so far taken for granted. Then there is indeed the real possibility that something new might be discovered. And this is a constant feature of JATR's writings, that again and again by his choice of topic, or perhaps by his starting-point, he calls in question the 'accepted positions of New Testament study'. As he says, there is seldom any new material – that is unlikely in a subject contained within the ancient world – and yet he enters each discussion at an unconventional and often unfashionable point. Concerning his motivation, he does not try to reassert a conservative, traditional position. That would be to succumb to assumptions once again, though possibly different assumptions. He brings no philosophical position to the task, but the single-mindedness is reminiscent of Husserl's motto for phenomenology: 'To the things themselves.' For JATR we could say, *mutatis mutandis*, that his motto was 'To the texts themselves', rather than to the text through the filtering of the assumed and the taken for granted.

Yet we must be selective. He published some eight books on New

3

Testament themes and dozens of articles. It would be both tedious and unproductive to reproduce the arguments of these books. That would require setting out hundreds of particular positions on technical textual matters, together with the evidence for them and the arguments against counter-positions. Nor would it be useful to summarize everything he wrote on any particular theme. Our interests are altogether more specific than this. What would strike the general reader immediately is the conservatism of JATR's New Testament writings. If he was considered to be theologically radical, he was certainly not regarded in textual matters as a radical. At a time when radical theology and radical textual criticism shared an attitude of scepticism towards historical traditions, JATR occupied a position diametrically opposed. To anticipate somewhat, as we examine his writings we shall see certain recurring tendencies. One is scepticism about scepticism. He did not adopt an uncritical acceptance of texts, but neither did he uncritically accept the fashionable scepticism of the day which was not well founded. A related tendency is for him to accept traditions as at least counting for something, until firm evidence called them in question. A third tendency, by way of conclusion, is that although in many instances he came to positions normally considered conservative, he did so by an entirely different route. His was not a frenetic radicalism, but a conservative radicalism. Alternatively, his position was not quiescent conservatism, but a radical conservatism.

It will be clear already that the word 'radical' is commonly used in several loose and imprecise ways. After we have examined other aspects of JATR's thought, in Parts Two and Three, we shall see that he considered himself to be a radical – in a very particular sense. It would, however, be impracticable to reserve the term only for his position either in biblical studies or in theology. At the outset, therefore, we shall be content to suggest on the basis of selected topics from his writings where he might be placed on the spectrum. In reviewing JATR's New Testament work we shall therefore have a very specific interest before us, the illustration of this complex dialectical position: conservative radicalism and radical conservatism. He cannot be understood either as a conservative or a radical, in the conventional usages of these terms. But, before my good Anglican friends swoon with relief, let me say that it would be just as false to represent JATR as *both* conservative *and* radical. Only if we see the genuine dialectic inherent in his biblical writings shall we understand his position.

It is with relief, therefore, that we decline to reproduce or summarize all of JATR's New Testament works. Nor shall we constantly attempt to evaluate them. We shall bring out those points which illustrate the dialectic to which we have just pointed. But we shall not feel it necessary to question or analyse the grounds on which he came to hold his various views, except when he seems to depart from his own method and premises. The criticism that he has not said what others have said will be regarded as gratuitous. His chacteristic approach to and treatment of issues will soon emerge. And if there is one thing above all that will become clear in this as in later contexts, it is that JATR was not a liberal. If we place him on a spectrum, then it cannot be that linear form which sets radical and conservative at opposite ends from each other. They are agreed on too many points, not least a rejection and distaste for liberalism.

We can illustrate the process from the broad spectrum of his writings, beginning with studies from the synoptic tradition. Next we shall take up his highly original and controversial views on the fourth Gospel. Thereafter and more briefly we shall consider his two books on aspects of Paul's theology. We shall then deal with the more ambitious survey in which he sought to establish a completely new chronology for the literature of the whole of the New Testament. Finally we shall deal with those writings which exhibit an important tension and transition, as JATR seeks to bridge over from biblical studies to theology.

1 The Gospels as record

We can begin our examination of the biblical studies of JATR with his writings on the synoptic Gospels. The matters which are to be central to our concerns can be well illustrated in this field, and nowhere better than in his treatment of that difficult and daunting subject of eschatology, the doctrine of the last things. Paradoxically JATR's first publication was on the last things. In 1950 he wrote a book entitled *In the End, God. . . : A Study of the Christian Doctrine of the Last Things*. We shall deal with it in Chapter 7, for it is a theological work in which JATR attempted to deal with the meaning and relevance of the subject for the twentieth-century Church. But a few years later he came to see that it was founded not on the text but on assumptions about the text. In 1955 he delivered the William Belden Noble lectures at Harvard, later published under the title *Jesus and His Coming: The Emergence of a Doctrine*. In these lectures he claimed that the question, What does the doctrine mean for today? could be answered only on the basis of a proper investigation of the New Testament. His earlier work had tried to do this. 'But it makes the assumption, like most other writing at the doctrinal level, that it is possible to accept the New Testament teaching about the Second Coming more or less as it stands and then to build upon it,' [JHC, 11]. This assumption is shared by two very different approaches to the matter. Biblical fundamentalists put together a collage of references to produce a picture of the last things. But critical scholars accept the same picture, though they classify it as myth. 'This procedure, as much as that of the Fundamentalists, enables us to evade the critical and historical questions' [JHC, 10].

We see, therefore, an early example of the directness with which JATR goes to the text, cutting through assumptions of both conservatives and radicals. These two groups contend with each other over the question whether the picture is to be taken literally or interpreted mythologically. In contrast JATR uncovers their common assumptions about what constitutes 'the picture'. The question, although apparently obscure, has of course profound significance for the Christian faith, in two respects. The first is whether what is taken to be the Christian view comes from Jesus himself and his promises, or whether it is a later development which attributes to Jesus an eschatology to which he did not subscribe. The second consideration follows from this, because since the revival of interest in eschatology, initiated by H. S. Reimarus at the end of the eighteenth century, the doctrine in its developed form has seemed to many to undermine the credibility of Christianity. JATR therefore draws an interesting parallel:

> But this book is written with more than a purely academic interest. For, if I am right in the analysis of my earlier book, the Church finds itself today in much the same position in regard to its doctrine of the Last Things as our grandfathers did a century ago in relation to the First Things. It is here that obscurantism, whether in regard to the Biblical criticism or to the perspectives of contemporary science, can most easily provide the occasion for rejecting the whole Christian scheme of thought. [JHC, 14–15]

JATR distinguishes his position from the other two, but without accepting their premises. He does not accept the fundamentalist position, not because it is offensive to the modern scientific world-view, but rather because it is not well founded in the New Testament. He does not accept the commonly agreed position of critical scholarship, not because it is critical, but because it is not critical enough. It does not proceed from the text either.

What then does the text say in particular about the parousia, the coming again of Jesus Christ with power?

> Provisionally, we may describe the distinctive element that concerns us by defining it as *the expectation of the coming of Christ from heaven to earth in manifest and final glory*. It is this we shall refer to by the term *Parousia*, and it forms the distinctively Christian centre of the New Testament hope. Associated with it, however, are other elements in the traditional eschatology, or picture of the End, which in origin are distinct but which in Christianity have been merged in it. [JHC, 18]

That is to say, there are eschatological beliefs common to Jesus, the early Church and Judaism, concerning the day of the Lord, the last judgement, the ingathering of the elect and the end of the world, but the return of Christ in glory is something quite new, and the question arises as to how it enters the faith of the Church. In passing we might note a characteristic to which we shall have occasion to refer from time to time, namely JATR's readiness to accept the basic historicity of the New Testament until there are good critical grounds for doubting it. Unlike many critical scholars he is prepared to use the early speeches in Acts in forming a historical picture of the primitive Church. 'But I am convinced that the theology and vocabulary of the earlier speeches do afford confidence that there is here genuinely primitive material, from which it is possible to reconstruct a reasonably trustworthy picture of the earliest Apostolic preaching' [JHC, 27]. Acts does not base the hope of the parousia on the promise of Jesus himself. It first appears in 1 Thessalonians 1.10, which JATR dates about the year AD 50, but it is not regarded as a peculiarly Pauline doctrine. JATR examines the speeches in Acts and comes to the conclusion that they present 'a fully *inaugurated* eschatology' [JHC, 29–30]. Everything has already been set in motion by the messianic act, and no second messianic act is anticipated. Paul's introduction of a second messianic moment causes problems which cannot be resolved. JATR quotes Oscar Cullmann with approval: 'It is, then, the *present* Lordship of Christ, inaugurated by his resurrection and exaltation to the right hand of God, that is the centre of the faith of primitive Christianity' [JHC, 32]. There is no confessional statement corresponding to the phrase in the Apostles' Creed, 'whence he shall come again' until the second century. JATR therefore seems committed to the conclusion that if the doctrine does not arise in the earliest days of the Church, it must be a late development. However, as we shall have occasion to note from time to time, he never rushes towards such a critical conclusion. He will certainly not avoid it if the textual evidence points in that direction, but even at this stage he prefers to take the more conservative line: 'But there is one answer which, though nowhere suggested in these documents, would so obviously account for the phenomena, that it must be presumed the most probable until it is proved otherwise. That is that the disciples expected Jesus because he himself had led them to expect him' [JHC, 36].

JATR may be too critical for the conservatives, but he will not adopt the fashionable assumptions of critical scholarship, for example on the self-consciousness of Jesus. Indeed on this question he adopts a very conservative position at all times:

> The unique position in relation to the final purpose of God in which Jesus thus claimed to stand would present itself to a Jew as near to blasphemy. But in the actual categories of the End we have so far mentioned there was nothing that would not have been common ground, at any rate to every Pharisee. [JHC, 38]

He does not assume with many critical scholars that every text in which Jesus speaks of his own significance must be an example of the faith of the Church written back with hindsight. Even so, the question is whether in the midst of the eschatology which he shared with other Jews, or in addition to it, Jesus anticipated a parousia.

In the Gospels Jesus speaks of the coming crisis and of his part in it. JATR considers these carefully under two headings before drawing his conclusion. The first concerns Jesus' vindication, that the same events which will mean suffering and defeat, will in the providence of God be seen to be glory and victory: 'There is no suggestion in any of these sayings, which together form an impressive testimony, of any moment other than or separate from this climax, at once of deepest humiliation by man and of most certain vindication by God' [JHC, 43]. Thus JATR adopts a position which is at the same time conservative on the self-consciousness of Jesus, and critical on the emerging difference between the teaching of Jesus and the beliefs of the early Church.

As we indicated at the outset, it is not our intention to present all of JATR's conclusions or the arguments he uses for them, but rather to concentrate on the relationship between conservative and critical elements in his work. Of particular interest in this context are the words attributed to Jesus at his trial, in answer to the question of the high priest: ' "Are you the Christ, the Son of the Blessed?" And Jesus said, "I am; and you will see the Son of man sitting at the right hand of Power, and coming with the clouds of heaven" ' (Mark 14.61–2). The words of Jesus combine images from a coronation psalm (Ps. 110.1) and the book of Daniel (Dan. 7. 13). Radical critical scholarship would maintain that these words, supposedly from a trial carried out in secret, reflect the beliefs of the early Church rather than of Jesus himself. JATR goes directly to the text for his interpretation rather than to pre-established assumptions about what Jesus could or could never have said. Yet what he finds in the text does not confirm the conservative position either, for it too is based on assumptions which come from the position of the early Church. JATR quotes T. W. Manson with approval: 'It cannot be too strongly emphasized . . . that what Daniel portrays is not a divine, semi-divine, or angelic figure coming down from heaven, to bring deliverance, but a human figure going up to heaven to receive it' [JHC, 45]. The reference is normally assumed to be to the parousia, but that is to interpret it not in its original context, but in the context of the beliefs of the early Church. JATR in drawing attention to Manson's statement comes to the following conclusion:

> And the context in which Jesus makes the allusion fits this meaning like a glove. In other words, the two predictions of 'sitting at the right hand of God' and 'coming on the clouds of heaven' are to be understood as parallel expressions, static and dynamic, for the same conviction. Jesus is not at this point speaking of a coming *from* God: in whatever other sayings he may refer to the coming of the Son of man in visitation, here at any rate he is affirming his vindication. [JHC, 45]

In the midst of his humiliation Jesus speaks of his vindication, but in none of the synoptic accounts is there ever a suggestion that Jesus enters his triumph only at some second coming.

JATR has therefore avoided the assumptions of both conservative and radical positions. Not for the first time he exposes the common premises adopted by these apparently opposed groups. As we have seen, he comes to hold a conservative view of the self-consciousness of Jesus, though as a conclusion and not as an initial premise. But having established it he is prepared to be as radical if not more radical than the critical tradition. Yes, Jesus believed that he occupied a special place in God's purpose and that in spite of appearances would be vindicated. But on closer inspection what he believed in this matter was not determinative for the Church: 'Indeed, what is remarkable is that the Evangelists should still preserve traces of a different conception, which evidently they did not share' [JHC, 52]. Not surprisingly this other tradition, of a second coming, is also represented in the Gospels, but JATR is now confident that he has established a critical criterion which arises from the text itself and on this basis he does not hesitate to make the kind of evaluation associated with radical scholarship: 'There are, indeed, some sayings which speak of a coming in glory that may be attributed without hesitation to the work of the Church' [JHC, 52]. Under the first heading, of vindication, he is therefore confident in drawing the following conclusion: 'As far as his own words are concerned, there is nothing to suggest that he shared the expectation of a return in glory which the Church entertained and ascribed to him' [JHC, 57].

Turning to the second matter, visitation, JATR refers to the prophecy of Malachi, 'Behold, I send my messenger to prepare the way before me, and the Lord whom you seek will suddenly come to his temple . . .' (Mal. 3.1) As before, JATR adopts a conservative position on the self-consciousness of Jesus: 'There can be no doubt that Jesus set his own "coming" in the light of such expectations. The whole of his ministry, and particularly its climax, was seen by him, one could almost say staged by him, as a deliberate coming of the representative of God to his people' [JHC, 59]. The series of 'I came' sayings in the synoptics is parallel to the 'I am' sayings of the fourth Gospel. He is even prepared to claim that 'all Jesus' work may be comprehended as "the coming of the Son of Man" to "this generation"' . . . [JHC, 64]. But it is at this point that the more critical perspective re-enters. The treatment of the many and varied references to the Son of Man is very complicated, but by contrast the issue of time is quite clear. In their treatments of the parables of the Kingdom, both Dodd and Jeremias demonstrate that the themes of delay and watching had very different meanings for Jesus and for the early Church. It is on this one matter that JATR concentrates:

> But what, I believe, is clear is that there is in his teaching no 'coming of the Son of man' which does *not* refer to this ministry, its climax and its consequences. The visitation in judgement of which he spoke would indeed merely be *set in motion* by his rejection. Its outworking, like his own vindication, would take place 'from now on'. As in glory, so in visitation, we must speak, not of a realized, but of an inaugurated eschatology, of the Son of man 'coming to his own' . . . [JHC, 81]

There is no evidence that Jesus thought of a two-stage messianic act with an interval between the present and its consummation.

JATR finally turns to the problem of the origin of belief in the parousia, if indeed it cannot be traced back to Jesus himself. Briefly, his solution is that Jesus stands in a prophetic tradition, the early Church in an apocalyptic tradition. There was a very close relationship between these two traditions, so much so that it is possible to mistake one for the other, or at least to read examples of one as if they should be understood within the context of the other. If the prophetic tradition is fundamentally concerned with morality, the apocalyptic is characterized by its concern with chronology. The difference in interpretation is illustrated in the two understandings of such references as 'this day' or 'this generation'. In the prophetic mode these phrases convey the directness of the divine judgement, but this is not so when read from the perspective of apocalyptic:

> Then the focus of attention is subtly shifted, and whether the twenty-four hours is up or the requisite number of years has elapsed makes all the difference. In the first case, the mere passage of time cannot affect the truth of the judgement; in the second, if the day or generation goes by and nothing happens, the statement is discredited. [JHC, 88]

So the teaching of Jesus, originally prophetic and concerned with the judgement of God, is read as if it were concerned with the prediction of a future event. In Mark we read: 'And he said to them, "Truly, I say to you, there are some standing here who will not taste death before they see that the kingdom of God has come with power" ' (Mark 9.1). In the prophetic mode this refers to the crisis set in motion by the coming of Jesus. But in the apocalyptic mode attention is focused on what are taken to be the chronological parameters of an event which is predicted for the future. This is naturally conducive to the usual speculation about how long and when – matters which intrigued apocalypticists in general. An indication of this may be found in the closing verses of the fourth Gospel, that a particular disciple would not die before the predicted end would come (John 21.23). It is not difficult to see how the events surrounding Jesus which were the focus of his prophetic teaching could become of secondary interest to the early Church as they awaited future events reckoned to bring the fulfilment of his predictions.

It is, however, possible, I believe, to detect a fairly clear process of development by which the accent of finality comes to be lifted from the ministry of Jesus itself and its consequences and laid upon a second event expected after it, at whatever interval. To this event are transferred those warnings and promises in which Jesus sought originally to define the crisis that his presence involved. The really decisive 'coming of the Son of man' is projected into an imminent but ever receding future. [JHC, 93]

Nor is this a matter of adding chronology to morality. The 'events' which interest the apocalyptic tradition are not historical events at all. They take place outside of human history and are in a real sense quite independent of human actions, motives or intentions. Whereas the prophetic is concerned with present events in which people are caught up, apocalyptic deals in mythological events which are quite unrelated to the present. 'The "ethics" of Jesus come to be separated out, detached from their eschatological setting, and adapted to the ordered life of the Church. In the same way, the eschatological elements are assembled and schematized to provide a map for the future and a programme for its hope' [JHC, 98]. According to JATR, Albert Schweizer in his influential study of eschatology failed to make this distinction. He followed Reimarus in taking Christian eschatology in a purely apocalyptic sense, in which failure of fulfilment falsified the basis of Christian faith. Schweitzer's radicalism has been shown to be quite unsatisfactory simply because it was not founded on a sufficiently careful textual study. And Bultmann's radicalism, which required the demythologization of the first-century Christian message might have been unnecessary had he cared to include the teaching of Jesus himself within his exposition of New Testament faith. It is significant that Bultmann declared that the teaching of Jesus was presupposed by the Church. On closer inspection, on JATR's view, what the early Church presupposed was not – at least in this matter – what Jesus actually believed and taught. Bultmann shared an assumption with the early Church, and as we have seen it is the distinguishing feature of the work of JATR that he will not make such assumptions. At the same time, if radicalism was not radical enough in the sense of not going to the text itself, the more conservative position has been guilty of reading the teaching of Jesus – still remarkably preserved in the midst of a fundamentally transposed message – from the perspective of the early Church.

We have already referred to the collection of shorter writings which JATR issued in 1962 as *Twelve New Testament Studies*. Most of the essays had been published in the 1950s, though one was as early as 1947. When he came to prepare his Bampton Lectures, which were to have been delivered in 1984, JATR made a second collection of essays to which he wished to be able conveniently to refer. It was published with the accurate and entirely uncontroversial title, *Twelve More New Testament Studies*. The two collections provide numerous illustrations of the general theme which we are examining. Once again we shall not reproduce all of JATR's arguments or conclusions, but simply bring forward examples of the complex relationship of conservative and radical elements in his work.

We shall refer to essays which are of particular interest, but relevant material can be found throughout the two volumes in the course of treating a wide variety of subjects. The article on 'The Temptations' was published in 1947, but even at that time JATR was rejecting the assumptions of what he refers to as 'liberal theology'. In the temptations concerning changing of stones into bread it was assumed that the issue was the appropriate form of the messianic programme. JATR goes first of all to the text. It is necessary to get the order right. If we assume that we know what constituted the temptation then we shall interpret the answer given by Jesus in this light. But if we begin with the answer which Jesus gave this will guide us in discovering what was actually at stake. 'What, then, was this first temptation? It was the incitement to Jesus to tempt God, by putting to the proof what must rest on the conviction of faith – namely, that he was the Son of God' [TNTS, 55]. After examining each of the three temptations he comes to the conclusion that 'the result of the foregoing exegesis has been to establish that the Temptation narrative as we have it is the record of a struggle, not about the programme of the Messiah, but about his person' [TNTS, 58]. In the article we have an early example of the identification of unfounded assumptions which distort the understanding of the subject, and by contrast a return to the text itself to establish the true position. However, we have included reference to the article not so much for what it exhibits, as for what is entirely missing, namely any corresponding critical dimension.

JATR does refer in passing to the suggestion that the form of the temptations is determined by the pattern of 'fulfilment'. That is, three passages from Deuteronomy are brought forward as types fulfilled in the life of the Messiah. But JATR declines to 'go as far as that'

[TNTS, 59]. More striking, however, is the fact that he simply takes the passage to be 'the record' of a struggle about the person of the Messiah. Did a supernatural being, Satan, address three specific propositions to Jesus, and did Jesus in turn quote Scriptures to Satan? As noted at the outset, we shall not take it upon ourselves to evaluate JATR's arguments: our interest is in the relationship between conservative and radical elements in his thought. But in the light of what is to follow in discussing his theology it is worth drawing attention to this article. To go to the text to establish the original meaning is one thing, but to assume (yes, an assumption) that it provides us with a 'record' of a historical event is quite another thing – especially when it includes reference to such supernatural appearances. Bultman's famous article on 'New Testament and Mythology' was written in 1941 and was probably not available to JATR in 1947, but the essay on 'The Temptations' was reissued in 1962, without amendment. The second striking feature is the assumption of messianic consciousness. The evangelists certainly believed that Jesus was the Messiah and knew himself to be so, but to be the record of a struggle Jesus must historically have believed this. Yet to begin the exegesis of the temptation narrative at this point probably means accepting in turn that the baptism is a 'record' – heavenly voice, dove and all. Although in this article JATR goes to the text itself, he makes nothing of the critical distinction between the experience of Jesus and the faith of the evangelists. We have to conclude that at this early stage his characteristic method was not yet complete.

JATR of course took up these matters later. Indeed one of his last public lectures in Cambridge was on 'The Last Tabu? The Self-Consciousness of Jesus' [TMNTS, 155–70]. In this he takes issue once again with Bultmann for dealing with the topic only in terms of titles, such as messianic self-consciousness. Bultmann in his *Theology of the New Testament* never cites the claim: 'All things have been delivered to me by my Father; and no one knows the Son except the Father, and no one knows the Father except the Son . . .' (Matt. 11.27). In this we see JATR going to the text to see what is said about the self-consciousness of Jesus, rather than adopting an indirect approach which involves putting predetermined choices to the text. But while this is what the text says, JATR does seem to be accepting it once again as a record. He makes an important concession here, which is repeated in several places. 'This does not mean that we may not catch the *ipsissima vox*, but it certainly does not commit us to claiming the *ipsissima verba*' [TMNTS, 166]. However it is a fine point of compromise as to why words would be changed at all if the overall effect did not affect that voice which spoke. The distinction reflects a tendency already noted, that JATR accepted the historicity of the texts until further notice. This he affirmed in an article written in 1982 on the question 'Did Jesus Have a Distinctive Use of Scripture?': 'But equally I believe, and the belief grows stronger rather than weaker the longer I spend on New Testament work, that the gospels afford good confidence that we can reach down to bedrock tradition about the historical Jesus' [TMNTS, 36].

Because of his determination to be honest to the text this 'bedrock tradition' sometimes leads to conclusions which are unpalatable, as can be seen in 'Hosea and the Virgin Birth' [TMNTS, 1–11], an article which JATR updated several times from its first appearance in 1948. Once again the procedure is not to begin with our questions about the text, for example whether Matthew knew of a tradition about a virgin birth, but with the text itself. The very subtle and powerful theological arguments which Matthew makes in his opening chapter presuppose that Jesus was born out of wedlock:

> Matthew in his genealogy was using the same argument for including Jesus himself, who as 'the descendent of an irregular union' (Deut. 23.2) was ineligible not only for membership of Israel but *a fortiori* for messiahship. It is interesting that in face of Jewish slanders of illegitimacy Matthew does not take the line that these are pure fabrications, like the later allegations that the disciples stole the body of Jesus (28. 13–15). [TMNTS, 5]

Joseph clearly does not see himself as the father of the child, and Matthew 'deliberately draws attention in his genealogy to four women of dubious sexual liaisons [TMNTS, 5]. The 'bedrock tradition' in this case tells us perhaps more than we should care to know: 'It does not prove anything historically about Jesus' parentage – though it is surely an approach that would not have been resorted to had Christians simply been able to dismiss out of hand the Jewish slurs, of which we find plentiful evidence in the Talmud [TMNTS, 5]. Although when dealing with the temptations the supernatural elements in 'the record' were accepted without difficulty, here it does not seem to occur to JATR that there might actually have been a virgin conception. Instead he adopts a theological position which he describes as a 'two-story' Christology (not to be confused with Bultmann's three-storey universe!). This enables him to distinguish between the historical events and their theological presentation. He can affirm both the illegitimacy of Jesus and also his unique place as Son of God. 'We shall never know humanly speaking who Jesus' father was' [TMNTS, 5]. Not surprisingly JATR sees that this statement could be as offensive as a parallel conclusion about the resurrection, which also follows from his two-story approach:

> There is a paradox here. On the one hand we can afford to be agnostic about what happened to the old body; for the truth of the Resurrection is not contained within it: we are speaking of a new order of being. For all we can be sure, as Ronald Gregor Smith scandalized many by insisting, the bones of Jesus may still be lying about somewhere in Palestine. And we must be *free* to say so. [TMNTS, 7–8]

The 'bedrock tradition' lies within 'the record' and sometimes leads to uncomfortable conclusions, but on the difficult question of how to pass from the record to the bedrock we must say that JATR has not set out a clear and consistent procedure. His intuitive conservatism encourages him to rest with a fudging of the issue which we may suspect he found more comfortable than a more radical attempt at eliminating the ambiguities inherent in these unresolved questions. But it cannot be satisfactory in the long run simply to assume (sic) the continuity between tradition and history, record and event, *verba* and *vox*.

The reference to the resurrection leads us to one of the least expected and most intriguing interests of JATR, namely the Turin Shroud. In 1978 he published a study entitled 'The Shroud and the New Testament' [TMNTS, 81–94]. As with so many other matters connected with the Gospels the tendency is to ask, Did it happen?, or in this case, Is it authentic? But here, as in examples to which we have already referred, JATR does not regard this as the proper place to begin. Many people were surprised that he showed such interest in the Shroud, but of course his concern was as ever with the gospel *texts* and any possible light which the Shroud might throw on them. JATR does not intend to link it with the resurrection or the grounds of Christian faith. In other words there is nothing at stake here. He begins with an initial indication of why it is worth paying attention to the Shroud at all:

> One of the things that shook my natural predisposition to scepticism about the Turin Shroud was precisely that it could not at all easily be harmonized with the New Testament accounts of the grave-clothes. I am not saying that it is incompatible with them but simply that no forger starting, as he inevitably would, from the gospel narratives, and especially that of the fourth, would have created the shroud we have. [TMNTS, 81]

If it is not genuine then it can be set aside: Christian faith certainly does not depend on such evidence. But if it were genuine JATR asks whether it helps to make sense of texts which are surprisingly difficult to interpret. Of the fourth Gospel he warns, 'The Greek is in fact extraordinarily elusive, considering the significance that the evangelist evidently attaches to the details' [TMNTS, 84].

There then follows a discussion of the significance and interpretation of the technical mortuary terminology of the Gospels (including reference to the raising of Lazarus) and how the image on the Shroud clarifies the situation. Eventually he comes to this conclusion: 'If . . . everything else were to prove positive, there must be a strong presumption that it belonged to this man. We cannot say more, but neither, I think, can we say less' [TMNTS, 89]. Once again he follows the logic of the evidence, regardless. But his interest is still on the subsequent question, Even so, what difference would it make? JATR claims firstly that it would undermine the theory that the story of the empty tomb was invented later by the early Church. However, that theory is based on textual studies and it would seem out of character for JATR simply to introduce a new element which had to be preferred to the textual evidence. Secondly, 'If genuine, the Shroud would also constrain us to take more seriously many details in the record which its image had confirmed' [TMNTS, 90]. But as we have seen, there are difficulties in taking the Gospels as providing a 'record' of events. If the Shroud were 'genuine' would that not mean simply that it dated from the first century AD and conveyed information about typical mortuary rites of the time? But JATR moves on to make a particular connection: 'Finally, though this is inevitably a subjective judgment, the image of the Shroud reveals a visage, like that of Hamlet's father, altogether "most majestical". It is surely a face that could credibly have commanded the loyalty and faith which the gospels describe' [TMNTS, 91]. By this time we seem to be well removed from anything that could be relevant to the interpretation of the text, and fast approaching that kind of pious commitment to the Shroud which at the onset we claimed JATR eschewed. This impression is furthered by two concluding passages:

> Yet, on what looks at present to be the most promising hypothesis, it does appear to record some moment, some burst perhaps of low-energy non-ionizing radiation, lasting but a fraction of a second. Otherwise it would have penetrated further than the surface of the fibres, which is what the microscope tests disclose. [TMNTS, 91]

And finally he does after all attempt to relate it to the resurrection:

> What it *could* show us might be, so to speak, a side-effect of its generation, a brief but intense discharge of some sort of physical radiation sufficient to have left marks of thermal discolouration on the cloth. It would be the last

trace, the final footprint, as it were, of the old body – corresponding more to the skin sloughed off by the snake except of course that it was nothing substantial but only an image. [TMNTS, 92]

What now of the bones of Jesus lying somewhere in Palestine? The evidence for the resurrection, for example in Paul, has nothing to do with the empty tomb. Is JATR not here in danger of making assumptions about the resurrection which do not arise from the texts? The article is of particular interest as it shows him beginning in line with his own characteristic method, but gradually departing from it as he becomes influenced by assumptions associated both with the Shroud and with the traditions of the empty tomb.

Our intention has not been to present an exhaustive account of all issues in the synoptic Gospels tackled by JATR, but rather to choose examples from the whole course of his writings which illustrate the way in which he combined conservative and radical elements in a distinctive way. But as we have seen, although he had a peculiar awareness of undeclared and unfounded assumptions which others commonly made – on both sides – his work was itself based on certain premises. He did not justify them: whether they could have been justified critically is an open question. On balance he operated on the assumption that the *onus probandi* lay with those who did not accept the historicity of the gospel texts. This does not mean, however, that he was simply a conservative. He could hold or come to hold positions regarded as conservative, but on grounds which were entirely critical. This is nowhere better illustrated than in his treatment of the Johannine corpus, evidently his favourite texts, and to these we now turn.

2 John and Judaism

To anyone familiar with New Testament scholarship it might seem odd that the Gospel of John is to be treated at this point. It is referred to as the fourth Gospel not simply because it comes after the synoptics in the traditional order of the New Testament but because it is assumed to be the latest in order of writing. Indeed it is often regarded as so late that it might seem more appropriate to discuss the Johannine tradition after every other New Testament work had been examined. But as soon as it appears that this view is based on an assumption, we should not be surprised to find that it is vigorously challenged by JATR.

No area of New Testament scholarship is more subject to assumptions than the question of the origins and order of writing of the Gospels. From the eighteenth century onwards the proponents of the various solutions to the synoptic problem have used essentially the *same* material to argue in favour of the priority of Mark, the priority of Matthew – or even the priority of Luke. The observer often has the impression that reputations are at stake and that winning the argument has overtaken examination of the text. JATR in his accustomed way does not begin with any 'agreed' position, and subsequently finds that the texts cannot be fitted into the various Procrustean beds without distortion: 'I believe that at this point the conclusion must be faced that none of our existing gospels as it stands is the source of the written tradition they have in common. In other words, we are back at some *Grundschrift* or Ur-gospel that lies behind them all' [TMNTS, 27]. JATR in several places makes the point that so far as he can judge none of the synoptic Gospels is the main source of the other two, though he does not normally go so far as to posit an *Ur*-gospel. Nor does he develop this theory, though presumably it would *not* in any case be along the lines originally suggested by Lessing.

The question of priority therefore illustrates JATR's typical approach, which is more critical than critical scholarship, but reaches conclusions often more traditional than conservative scholarship – though not with the intention of arriving at conservative goals. But on priority there is more to be said, and that even more surprising. However much the various theories have diverged, there has at least been general agreement – a common assumption – that the earliest tradition is represented in one of the synoptic Gospels. The Gospel of John is assumed to be later than the first Gospel, and indeed later than all of the other three. If JATR rejects the assumption of one Gospel – winner take all – he also rejects the widespread assumptions about the historicity and dating of the fourth Gospel. For reasons which we shall go on to review, he came to hold that regardless of when it reached its final form, the Gospel of John was actually the first Gospel to be written. It was therefore fitting that the last major piece of writing, his Bampton Lectures, should be *The Priority of John*, the first critical book since Schleiermacher to advocate this position. In this work he drew together arguments which he had developed over the previous thirty years:

> It has been the fate of many books on John to be left unfinished, for its interpretation naturally forms the crowning of a lifetime. I have myself been intending to write a book on the Fourth Gospel since the 'fifties, before I broke off (reluctantly) to be Bishop of Woolwich. [PJ, xiii]

To this fascinating parenthetic aside we shall certainly return, but there is no doubt that the Johannine tradition was the most important subject for his work as a New Testament scholar. Although in some conservative circles there has been a preference for the fourth Gospel, JATR is at pains to point out that he advocates the priority of John not on doctrinal presuppositions, but because of historical textual questions. 'Personally too I would claim not to come at them with any doctrinally conservative interest, as I hope that some of my other writings may show. It is simply that on historical grounds I find that they will not lie down or go away' [PJ, 6].

As early as 1957 JATR, in an article entitled 'The New Look at the Fourth Gospel' [TNTS, 94–106], was challenging what he identified as five unjustified assumptions about the Fourth Gospel. The first of these to be rejected was the assumption that the writer used the synoptic tradition as a primary source. He was encouraged in this revision by C. H. Dodd, to whom he later refers as his 'mentor' [PJ, ix]. Dodd had recently claimed that 'the presumption of literary dependence of John on the Synoptists no longer holds [TNTS, 96 note 7]. Throughout his career JATR was to argue that the Gospel of John was an independent source. He frequently quotes with approval the view of P. H. Menoud on the sovereign freedom and confidence which characterizes the writer of the Gospel. Far from relying on the recollections of others, the author seems to be saying, 'La tradition, c'est moi!' [e.g. PJ, 14]. He also approves of the claim of Pierson

Parker: 'It looks as though, if the author of the fourth Gospel used documentary sources, he wrote them all himself' [PJ, 19].

Those who look for evidence of literary dependence on the synoptics do so very often because of the second assumption which JATR identified, namely that the author of the Gospel of John was unacquainted with Palestine, Palestinian Judaism and the early traditions of the Church. Whether this was ever a reasonable assumption, JATR argued that it could not be held following the discoveries at Qumran: 'The Qumran material comes from the heart of southern Palestine before the Jewish war. Though certainly not supporting or establishing any *direct* contact with or influence upon John, it has killed any dogmatism that the fundamental Johannine categories must be Hellenistic and must be late' [RD, 284]. Another form of this assumption is the premise, taken as self-evident, that the Gospel of John is written from the Hellenistic world and is addressed to that world. That is to say, the assumption that the author was a Gentile, pursuing the Gentile mission of the Church out in the Hellenistic world of the Empire. JATR argues strongly against any such assumptions.

To settle this matter JATR returns to the text. In an article first published in 1960, entitled 'The Destination and Purpose of St John's Gospel' [TNTS, 107–25], he had pointed out that the term 'the Gentiles' never appears in the fourth Gospel. There is no contrast between the Jews and the Gentiles: the author shows no concern with the Gentiles, nor does he present Jesus as showing any. In this Gospel Jesus, the Jew, comes to 'his own'. He is the revelation of the cosmos, but that does not contrast the Jewish world and the Greek world: 'The contrast for John is always between light and darkness, not between Jew and Gentile. There is no agony, as there is for Paul, about the relation between these latter as groups . . .' [TNTS, 113]. Although Jesus is presented in the prologue as the Logos, throughout the body of the Gospel itself he is referred to as 'the Christ'. The title is used more often than in Matthew, more often than in Mark and Luke taken together. The challenge of the fourth Gospel is for the true Jew to recognize Jesus. 'But for the Jew who would remain loyal to his traditional faith, "How can this be?" (3.9)' [TNTS, 115]. Nicodemus illustrates the issue. Circumcision and the law are not issues between the Jews and the Gentiles, as for Paul, but within Judaism itself: 'For John they are what must be transcended by Judaism within its own life, because they belong to the level of flesh and not spirit, *whether a single Gentile wanted to enter the Church or not*' [TNTS, 116]. In John there is a distinction between Jew and Greek, but attention to the text reveals that these are two groups *within* Judaism, namely, the Jews of Palestine, especially Judaea, and the Jews of the Greek diaspora. The Judaean Jews ask, 'Does he intend to go to the Dispersion among the Greeks and teach the Greeks?' (John 7.35). It is the prayer of Jesus that 'they all may be one'. There are many instances when John explains Aramaic-speaking Judaism to those who are of another language and ethos.

As we shall see later, JATR relates the Gospel to the disciple John. In this context it is therefore significant that when in Galatians 2.9 Paul speaks of the division of the apostolic mission, James, Cephas and John are to pursue the mission to the Jews. The disciples with Greek names, Andrew and Philip, who come from the Hellenized city of Bethsaida, bring to Jesus 'Greeks' who have come for the Passover. When that happens, Jesus announces that 'the hour has come' (John 12.23). By a careful examination of the text JATR exposes as quite false an assumption shared by many conservative as well as radical scholars. The Gospel is not a late work by someone alienated from and ignorant of Palestinian Judaism, but by someone with an intimate knowledge of and appreciation for it.

This leads us to the third assumption uncovered and rejected by JATR, that the Gospel of John provides us with no information about the historical Jesus, as contrasted with the Christ of faith. There are in fact several assumptions here which together lead to a circular argument. It is assumed, as we have seen, that the synoptic tradition is older than the Johannine and that John knew and used the synoptics. It is further assumed, therefore, that whenever there is a disagreement between John and the synoptics it can be accounted for by saying that John has no interest in historical accuracy. The conclusion is therefore that the fourth Gospel is not guided by history but by theology. Yet the grounds for this conclusion are assumptions which JATR came to reject. Consequently he rejected also the conclusion. His starting-point, as already noted, is the material which has come to light at Qumran. JATR judged that words attributed to John the Baptist in the fourth Gospel, far from being late and anachronistic inventions of the early Church, place him in the mainstream of Palestinian Judaism in the time of Jesus. In an article written almost twenty years previously, JATR had argued for a close relationship between 'The Baptism of John and the Qumran Community' [TNTS, 11–27]. He sought to use the theology of baptism, repentance and redemptive suffering as found in Qumran to explain not only the preaching of John but also the mission of Jesus:

In other words, the final object of all the sect's discipline, repentance and purification is that the Community itself may become the embodiment of the Servant ideal, the Elect of God for atoning work (cf. Isa. 43. 10; 53. 12). And in Jesus this ideal is *already declared* by the divine voice to have found its fulfilment . . . [TNTS, 23]

We have already noted that JATR adopts a very conservative position with regard to the self-consciousness of Jesus, but if here he is conflating the synoptic account of the baptism of Jesus with John the Baptist's testimony to Jesus in the fourth Gospel, then he appears to be accepting as history the highly mythological account of the descent of the dove and the audible voice from heaven. In a later chapter we shall return to the significance of the fact that JATR as a New Testament scholar seems to find entirely unproblematic elements which were to exercise him deeply as a theologian.

Ironically, the problematic reference comes not from the fourth Gospel, but from the synoptic tradition. John the Baptist may well have had the kind of theology and expectations indicated by JATR, but they are not expressed in the objective mythological form of the synoptics. This would be an illustration of another associated theme, namely that JATR claims that the fourth Gospel actually throws light on the synoptics historically. For example, he argues 'that while the Johannine chronology cannot be fitted into the Markan because the latter is too fragmentary, the Markan can be fitted into the Johannine' [PJ, 124].

A fourth assumption which JATR questions is that the theology of the fourth Gospel comes from the very end of the first century. Although this is a considerable rehabilitation from the more extreme views which placed the work in the middle of the second century, it still depends on an assumption about the interests of the writer. In drawing attention to this assumption JATR is conscious that once again he is taking on both radicals and conservatives, who are in agreement at this point.

Yet the picture of John looking back through the mists of time upon the events of his youth is perpetuated almost without question in conservative circles, and, as we shall see, is reflected in the assumption by the other side read into the interpretation of John 21.23, 'that that disciple would not die'. [PJ, 68]

We have to some extent already dealt with such assumptions in considering the question of the intended readership. As we have seen, JATR goes back to the text itself to discover that the typical controversies which were prominent even by the time of Paul had not yet emerged when the first form of this Gospel was composed. We need not repeat these arguments, but instead turn now to the matter of eschatology. In the previous chapter we saw that for JATR there is a significant difference between the eschatology of Jesus and that of the early Church, including the writers of the synoptic Gospels themselves. On this important issue JATR argues that the fourth Gospel still reflects the original, prophetic position of Jesus. It avoids the 'progressive apocalypticization of the message of Jesus' [TNTS, 103] which characterizes the synoptics:

> The fourth Gospel . . . represents a form of the tradition which has never seriously undergone this process at all. While, in the Synoptists, elements in the eschatological teaching of Jesus were gradually detached from the supreme crisis in which he stood to his own generation and referred to a second separate moment, in the fourth Gospel the original unity is not broken; its picture of the vindication and the visitation of the Son of man is still essentially that, I believe, of Jesus himself and of the most primitive tradition, however immeasurably it may have been deepened by the recognition that it was in the Cross and not merely in the Resurrection that, in the terminology also of the earliest preaching, God 'glorified' and 'lifted up' his Son. [TNTS, 103]

The fifth assumption identified by JATR is that the author of the fourth Gospel was not the apostle John, nor an eyewitness of the events recorded. This seems a very reasonable assumption, if only because it would be impossible to demonstrate authorship. It looks like another winner-takes-all situation. The assumption runs that if apostolic authorship cannot be demonstrated then the Gospel has no apostolic connection at all. Arguments have certainly been less than conclusive. 'Their opponents found this link too weak to sustain. But having, as they felt, broken it, they tended to assume that there was no link . . .' [TNTS, 105]. But it will have been noticed that JATR tends to write of 'the Johannine tradition'. The fourth Gospel was composed over a period of time, perhaps latterly the responsibility of a school, but did the tradition itself go back to the most primitive source of all? We may note in passing that if JATR considers that biblical references to people and places should be accepted till proved otherwise, he is also inclined to accept early traditions in the Church until proved untenable. Thus, for example, he accepts the tradition that the author of the Gospel lived in his old age in Ephesus, even if the tradition is not clear on which John is intended. 'But that there were *no* Johns at Ephesus and that the entire tradition connecting it with the Gospel is groundless would seem quite improbable. It is worth emphasizing this, because it is merely uncritical to dismiss ancient tradition without due cause' [PJ, 47]. The possibility that there were no Johns in ancient Ephesus might give us pause for thought, but we see here the same challenge to radical scholarship, to be critical on a scientific and not merely a fashionably sceptical basis.

Since JATR has rejected the assumption that everything in the fourth Gospel is dictated by theological motives, he can look again at the wealth of detail in the text, especially at the many references to people and places which seem to serve no theological purpose whatsoever. It is at this point that we see one of the most conservative criteria used by JATR in his reading of texts in general. In an article entitled 'How Small was the Seed of the Church?' [TMNTS, 95–111] he spells out this principle: 'It is perfectly legitimate to begin by presuming the validity of details and interrelationships until proved otherwise and then to assess them by the coherence and convincingness of the picture they provide and by the data which this picture then enables us to explain' [TMNTS, 97]. For example, the call of two pairs of disciples has no context in Mark, but the Johannine tradition makes sense of it. In Luke, John and Jesus were related through their mothers. JATR adds the hypothesis that if Mary, the mother of Jesus, and Salome were sisters, John the son of Zebedee was a first cousin of Jesus and also related to John the Baptist. There are indications that Capernaum was the home of Jesus, Peter and John. The group is closely knit before the story begins. At the crucifixion Jesus gives responsibility for his mother to one who would then in any case be a close relative. JATR accepts C. H. Dodd's translation in John 1.15,30, 'There is a man in my following', meaning that Jesus was first a disciple of John. He quotes Dodd with approval:

> We are reaching back to a stage of tradition scarcely represented elsewhere in the gospels . . . namely, that Jesus was at one time regarded as a follower or adherent of John the Baptist. If, as the Synoptic Gospels report, he accepted baptism at his hands, how else should he be regarded? [PJ, 183]

JATR is arguing that the writer of the Gospel was very well informed about the smallest group from which the whole sequence of events arose, although he is selective about what is relevant to his main purpose. Some information emerges in passing. For example, given the possible priestly line of the families, it is of interest that a disciple, presumably John, is able to enter the court of the high priest along with Jesus, because he 'was known to the high priest' (John 18. 15), while Peter had to stand outside.

Radical scholarship seems to take for granted that any gifted thinker could have written a Gospel, as if the Church was so large and well endowed that anonymous geniuses composed its primary literature, which was then readily accepted by all. This is an unlikely scenario. As JATR warns us, 'Geniuses, like entities, are not to be multiplied beyond necessity' [PJ, 118]. Nor is this a reversion to the traditional view of authorship. Once again we find JATR criticizing radical scholarship for not being critical enough: 'I believe it is unscientific to invent unknown characters such as the author of this major contribution to New Testament literature and theology who have left no other trace behind them' [PJ, 117]. The author would be a Palestinian Jew, Aramaic-speaking, but sufficiently educated to write in correct Greek. He would belong to the original small community close to Jesus, perhaps related to him. He had connections with the high priest and came to have a special mission to the Jews of the diaspora:

> The evidence therefore for the person we are seeking, so far from ruling out a relatively poor and uneducated Palestinian, points suspiciously towards the kind of man that John, son of Zebedee, might have been. There is in fact no reason to suppose that his family was particularly poor and uneducated. [RD, 300]

JATR does not propose this as more than a hypothesis, but he is concerned that if there is evidence it should be properly evaluated and not dismissed out of hand because of ill-founded assumptions and prejudices.

We can end this discussion of the fourth Gospel with two further points. The first concerns JATR's reconstruction of the chronology of the ministry of Jesus. This in itself may seem a rather eccentric project, and if it does, that has its own significance. JATR is concerned not only with reconstructing the chronology, but with the very idea that the sources are sufficiently trustworthy to make such a project viable. As we have seen, many would assume that to attempt it on the basis of the evidence of the fourth Gospel is a contradiction in terms. 'I believe that this scepticism is unwarranted by the evidence and requires to be challenged' [PJ, 123]. He is concerned for the more general effects of this attitude: 'And, finally, I do not accept that excessive scepticism is a matter of indifference. It is corrosive, at this and many other points, of our confidence in possessing any firm knowledge about the Jesus of history . . .' [PJ, 124]. In various places he refers to historians of the same period, notably the Roman historian A. N. Sherwin-White, who are frankly amazed at the scepticism shown by New Testament scholars towards what in the wider context would be regarded as both excellent and well-informed sources. As usual we shall not reproduce the arguments used, but it is worth setting out the tentative result:

Summary of the Ministry of Jesus

AD 27	autumn (?)	Appearance of John the Baptist
AD 28	March (?)	Baptism of Jesus
	April	In Cana and Capernaum
		In Jerusalem before, and during, Passover and the feast of Unleavened Bread (April 28–May 5)
	May	In Judaea baptizing
		Arrest of John the Baptist
		Departure for Galilee
	June–October	In Galilee
	October 23–31	In Jerusalem for Tabernacles
	November–April	In Galilee
AD 29	early (?)	Death of John the Baptist
	April	Desert feeding, before Passover (April 18)
	May–September	In Phoenicia, Ituraea and Galilee
	October 15	In Jerusalem for Tabernacles (October 12–19)
	November–December	In Judaea and Peraea
	December 20–27	In Jerusalem for Dedication
	January–February	In Bethany beyond Jordan
AD 30	February (?)	In Bethany in Judaea
	March	In Ephraim
	April 2–6	In Bethany and Jerusalem
	April 7	Crucifixion

[PJ, 157]

For anyone brought up on form criticism and deeply suspicious of any quest of the historical Jesus the effect of reading through the chapters in which the chronology is developed is disconcerting but at the same time thrilling. If we set aside for the moment received assumptions about the unhistorical character of the fourth Gospel, the exposition has a dramatic total impact. The evangelist is well-informed about persons, relationships, topography, technical terminology, the Judaism of the period, and was acquainted with the city of Jerusalem at the time. These matters cannot be accounted for either as the exercise of imagination or historical guesswork on the part of the author, nor can they be explained as being motivated by the intention

27

of achieving what would have been a contrived theological effect, since for the most part they serve no obvious theological purpose. Perhaps we can refer to one instance, the claim that on the afternoon of 19 October, AD 29, Jesus was teaching in the treasury of the Jerusalem temple, and that in John 8 we have an account of what he taught on that particular occasion. What would Roman historians give to be able to say how Tiberius spent the day!

Nothing of course, depends on the chronology: it is an attempt to demonstrate what is possible when the various assumptions already discussed are identified and challenged. But it also leads to the final point, namely the relationship between fact and faith in the fourth Gospel, what at one point JATR can even call history and 'meta-history' [PJ, 297]. From the second century there has been a tendency to see the fourth Gospel as a 'spiritual' Gospel. It is of course a profound spiritual document, concerned that those who are illuminated by Christ will understand spiritual things. It is all too easy, but misleading, to see this in Pauline terms, as a contrast with the things of the flesh. But it does not at all follow, as is often assumed, that the writer of a spiritual work is not concerned with the words and deeds of Jesus during his lifetime. It is after all he who claims that 'the Word became flesh' (John 1.14). If it is in the flesh that the Word was made known, then these historical events are of fundamental importance to the evangelist. In taking this as his starting-point JATR passes beyond another assumption which radicals and conservative share. The fourth Gospel is often approached through a curious reversal, as if certain timeless religious truths were being illustrated by the evangelist by references only tenuously related at best to the life of Jesus, 'in much the same way that Hegel saw the Christian stories as picture-book presentations of what is eternally valid in the realm of ideas' ['The Relation of the Prologue to the Gospel of St John'; TMNTS, 75]. In passing we might observe that JATR might have referred to Strauss rather than Hegel. It was Strauss who suggested that already existing ideas, from the Old Testament, were given objective (i.e. mythological) form in the Gospels by the invention of historical events. For Hegel, for the truths to be eternal the events would need to have happened much as reported. But JATR's point is clear enough:

> If we are right, the timeless truths were not the matrix of the Gospel, but the fruit of meditation upon it. On this view the Gospel is no less theological. But the history has its own primacy, the facts are sacred – and the theology is given only in, with and under it [TMNTS, 75]

To hear the words and observe the deeds do not of themselves achieve anything. But to those who understand them aright they are the way, the truth and the life. And yet it is all the more necessary to attend to the actual words and deeds if their true meaning and significance is to be seen. As early as 1959 JATR was already clear on this point:

> It is, I believe, by taking the historical setting of St John's narrative seriously, and not by playing ducks and drakes with it, that we shall be led to a true appreciation of his profound reverence for the history of Jesus as the indispensable and inexpendable locus for the revelation of the eternal Logos itself. ['The "Others" of John 4.38'; TNTS, 66]

If the evangelist is both imaginative and creative it is in his capacity 'to evoke rather than invent' [PJ, 209]. His prologue, like most introductions, is written after the main work. It does not direct the course of the Gospel, it places the historical events in a cosmic setting which reveals their inner significance. Perhaps JATR's conclusion about the writer of the fourth Gospel throws light on his own distinctive method: 'Hence for this writer the relation between flesh and spirit, seeing and believing, theology and history, is always a dialectical one, never a simple either-or' [PJ, 345].

3 The Relevance of Paul

JATR produced many interesting and important studies of themes in the synoptic Gospels, and as we have seen he wrote with considerable scholarship and originality on the Johannine tradition. In the next two sections we shall examine another issue on which he challenged widely held assumptions, namely the chronology of the whole of the New Testament. And yet it was in none of these fields that he first became widely known.

In 1952 JATR published *The Body: A Study in Pauline Theology*. It was to establish his reputation internationally as a New Testament scholar, both for its careful treatment of the texts and also for its refreshing originality in dealing with a difficult and important subject. Indeed many who respected this work were puzzled by his later theological development. If we were to reverse the order of perspectives here, what might be particularly striking about the book to someone only familiar with his theological writings would be the ease with which JATR uses the most traditional Pauline terminology, as if it were entirely unproblematic in the modern world. This emerges in the Introduction, written against the background of a Europe bitterly divided by the claims of competing ideologies and philosophies: 'The redemption of man to-day means his release to become, not an individual – for in independence he is powerless in the face of the giant State – but a person, who may find rather than lose himself in the interdependence of the community' [TB, 8]. Faced with collectivism and existentialism, 'the alternative to the "They" is not the "I" but the "We" ' [TB, 8]. These thoughts and the language in which they are expressed may seem strange for a New Testament scholar, but as we shall see in considering JATR's theological writings, they carry over from his doctoral dissertation, which he had written only a few years before. To this point we shall return at the appropriate time, but it is against this background of the situation in Europe that he offers a study of what might otherwise have been regarded as an obscure matter. He assures us that 'in the Pauline concept of the body there is something of profound implication and relevance both for the understanding of this problem (which, it must be remembered, is nothing less than *the* social, political and religious problem of our age) and for its Christian solution' [TB, 8]. Not that JATR was the only

New Testament scholar to find in Paul a peculiar relevance for the day. By coincidence the English translation of Bultmann's *Theology of the New Testament* appeared in the same year. There could hardly have been two more contrasting treatments of Paul. The Marburg scholar made Paul comprehensible for the modern world – at least for that section of it who could first of all understand the existential analytic of his former colleague Martin Heidegger. JATR was conscious of what was at stake:

> Christians should be the last people to be found clinging to the wrecks of an atomistic individualism, which has no foundation in the Bible. For their hope does not lie in escape from collectivism: it lies in the resurrection of the body – that is to say, in the redemption, transfiguration, and ultimate supersession of one solidarity by another. This is Paul's gospel of the new corporeity of the Body of Christ, which itself depends on the redemptive act wrought by Jesus in the body of His flesh through death.
>
> One could say without exaggeration that the concept of the body forms the keystone of Paul's theology. [TB, 9]

We can already see our themes of conservatism and radicalism begin to emerge. Once again JATR goes back to the text to discover what is central to the message of Paul. He does not import into Paul assumptions and categories from elsewhere. This is a rejection of the presuppositions of an existentialist approach to Paul, the most radical of its day. But it is also a criticism of another kind of individualism, a conservative piety which has neither a doctrine of the Church nor an understanding of the communion of believers. In returning to the text JATR distances himself from both perspectives. However, as we saw in his treatment of the temptations, JATR can use terminology which has become problematic for many. Just as certain assumptions must be made before it is possible to describe the 'record' of a conversation with Satan, so other assumptions must be made before we can speak of 'the redemptive act wrought by Jesus in the body of His flesh through death'. Those who felt comfortable with such statements when the book first appeared may well have been disturbed by JATR's later theological developments. Conversely, those who were attracted to this theology might be surprised to find that he regarded such traditional language as unproblematic. It is somehow comparable to the assumption that the beliefs of the evangelists recorded the experience of Jesus. 'A Study in Pauline Theology' is presumably intended to be more than the repetition of what Paul said. It involves clarification at least. While Bultmann can be criticized in certain respects, more for what he omits than for what he includes, he expressed the teaching of Paul with great insight and originality, especially in dealing with the concept of the body. But above all he was guided by the need to reinterpret assumptions which Paul and his first hearers took for granted. So far as JATR is concerned, we should have to say that at this point the radicalism of going directly to the text has not been carried through. Traditional doctrinal assumptions still govern the construction.

Although the author of 2 Peter found the writings of Paul heavy going – 'There are some things in them hard to understand . . .' (2 Peter 3.16) – we may assume that on the basis of a shared religious world-view Paul's theology was perfectly comprehensible to those who received his letters. Since we do not share that world-view today New Testament scholars have found it almost a full-time occupation to conduct modern people back into the ancient world. For the most part this is what JATR now does in respect of Paul's teaching on the body. It is impressively done, but we shall not rehearse the exposition since it takes us little further in examining the dual themes of conservatism and radicalism in JATR's thought. And if truth be told there is something missing in the book. We may well question whether it is the job of the scholar to take us back into the past, as if we could through information about those times become one with those of a previous age. Even if we could come to understand what they believed, it does not follow that we could believe what they believed – in the way in which they believed it. It may well be that such antiquarian scholarship is never more than the first part of a necessary hermeneutical process, but in any case, as we have seen, in the Introduction JATR promises more, claiming 'there is something of profound implication and relevance' in Paul's teaching on the body. This surely means not just that we must move towards Paul, but that Paul will be brought towards us. It is this second movement which is almost entirely missing in JATR's book.

The main argument of the book begins with the terminology used by Paul. Since he was writing in Greek he used terminology which had religious and metaphysical connotations, but JATR maintains that Paul's meaning is determined not by Greek anthropology but by the most fundamental assumptions of Hebraic thought about man:

> All the richness of Semitic terminology in respect of the body and its functions was devoted to expressing a deep understanding of the *theological* truth of man's nature.
>
> If these interests and presuppositions are borne in mind they will illuminate much of what Paul is saying and forearm us to some extent against false and anachronistic interpretations of his thought. [TB, 16]

Thus flesh (*sarx*) is the world organized in a way contrary to the will of God and alienated from him. What Paul condemns as being life according to the flesh is not physical life, including for example sexuality, but a life lived in disregard of God. In contrast the body (*soma*) is not praised because of its sensuousness, but as a life which is lived in consciousness of God and his purposes. Such expositions are helpful in understanding Paul's meaning, as are also the sections on death and sin. If Christians had always been aware of these careful distinctions and responsible in maintaining them, than religion would have made a very different contribution to the development of European society and culture. For example, it would have been a wholesome force in treating sexual neuroses instead of a means of institutionalizing them.

In these examples JATR goes directly to the text and then to its meaning beyond the surface level. It is a continuation of his method of combining conservative and radical elements. But they are followed by other sections in which only the conservative element is visible. We may illustrate this in what JATR describes as 'a forensic metaphor' as used by Paul, concerning the way in which God has in Christ dealt with sin:

> For God has done what the law, weakened by the flesh, could not do: sending his own Son in the likeness of sinful flesh and for sin, he condemned sin in the flesh, in order that the just requirement of the law might be fulfilled in us, who walk not according to the flesh but according to the Spirit. (Rom. 8.3–4)

Now what Paul is saying here is not at all clear to modern readers, as it would have been patently obvious to Paul's first readers. Quite properly JATR therefore attempts to explain not only this metaphor but other illustrations used by Paul:

> Now all these phrases depend for their understanding on a single assumption and mean nothing without it. It is the assumption that *Christians have died in, with and through the crucified body of the Lord* (have a share, that is, in the actual death that He died unto sin historically, 'once for all' (Rom. 6.10, R.V.M.) *because, and only because, they are now in and of His body in the 'life that he liveth unto God', viz., the body of the Church.* [TB, 46–7]

Now I am sure that anyone in Paul's time who understood what he said, would also understand what JATR now says. But are we not here simply being presented with alternative metaphors, and metaphors which can only function on the basis of the same premises as the original text? This may well be what Paul *says*, but it still does not tell us what Paul *means*. It is this final hermeneutical step which is missing. As it stands the book shares the common conservative assumption that to convey 'something of profound implication and relevance' it is only necessary to repeat and clarify what was said. Thereafter it will be possible to believe now what was believed then – in the way in which it was then believed. This is not only an unlikely scenario in practice, it is based on a truncated hermeneutical method. It is for this reason that the book seems incomplete and fails to maintain the conservative/radical dialectic.

Unfortunately the same criticism might be made of JATR's other work on Paul, *Wrestling with Romans*, published in 1979. Some years ago, in the Preface to a 'reader' which I had collected, I said that JATR had once told me that there were two things he would not do. The second was to edit a book. The first I had at that time unfortunately forgotten. I can now reveal that it was his determination never to write a commentary. (Nothing more untoward!) His reason was that in a commentary you are constrained to say something on everything, whether you have anything to say or not. Judging by the length of commentaries and the minutiae of their observations about sentences, subordinate clauses and even individual letters, having nothing to say is not the problem. But I think that by 'to say something' JATR meant to say something edifying, of religious or spiritual significance. This indicates something of the origins of the book. *Wrestling with Romans* was a lecture course no longer being offered, a 'discontinued line' as we are told in the Preface. As a book it was therefore intended for 'the educated layman', that endangered species so much sought after by religious publishers. In other words the motivation is similar to that behind *The Body*, and JATR intended that it would provide for those willing to 'wrestle with Romans', 'a sharpened appreciation of its contemporary relevance' [WR, vii].

Although the end product is intended to be edification, the study begins as always with the text, since only what is well-founded can eventually edify. As we have seen before, this apparently obvious starting-point can on occasion demonstrate that conservative and fundamentalist assumptions are quite unbiblical. An example is found as JATR deals with Romans 3.25, 'For God designated him to be the means of expiating sin by his sacrificial death, effective through faith' (NEB). In non-biblical Greek *hilastērion* meant a gift given to placate or propitiate an angry person, especially a deity, or to expiate sin. But assumptions have very often been brought to the text which distort what Paul actually says:

34

The *hilastērion* does something not to God but to the sin which distorts and sours the relationship. By way of contrast I would cite something that I heard Billy Graham once say: 'The lightning of the divine justice struck Jesus instead of us.' The cross is here viewed as a lightning conductor which draws to itself the divine anger against sin and earths it. The *hilastērion* is then seen as neutralizing God's attitude rather than neutralizing the power and effect of sin – and this, with all due respect, is what is unbiblical, however many times it may be introduced with the rubric 'the Bible says'. [WR, 45]

Once again we see JATR, in his adherence to the text, exposing the assumptions which some conservatives and in this case fundamentalists bring to it. This is entirely in line with the approach which we have seen illustrated in material already discussed. But does it not also fall under the same criticism with which we ended our comments on *The Body*? Having established what Paul actually said, are we any closer to what he actually meant? Now that we know how the word *hilastērion* was actually used, can it be assumed that the meaning of the passage is self-evident? Previously we were faced with a 'forensic metaphor', and in this later work the phrase is again used in commenting on Romans 8.33, 'Who will be the accuser of God's chosen ones? It is God who pronounces acquittal . . .' (NEB). But is it not equally metaphorical to say that 'God designated him to be the means of expiating sin by his sacrificial death, effective through faith'? When we are told what he in fact said, we may be no closer to what Paul actually meant. To fail to deal with the metaphor, we have already argued, is to make certain assumptions which in their own way exhibit a kind of fundamentalism and even literalism.

4 Redating the New Testament

Although it has not been our responsibility to reproduce every argument of JATR on the many and varied subjects on which he has written, yet it will be clear that the historicity of the New Testament documents is a fundamental concern underpinning his work as a whole. Not surprisingly therefore he undertook a systematic study, concentrating on the question of the date of each piece. *Redating the New Testament* published in 1976, is a long and technical book in which JATR allows himself the luxury of considering in full the evidence on which he came to a radical review of the whole question of when and in what circumstances each part of the New Testament was written. But as we shall see, it is radical in the now familiar way, that it challenges the ill-founded assumptions of critical scholarship, and by this route arrives at surprisingly conservative answers. He points out, rather apologetically, that questions about dating are often regarded with some irritation by those who wish to move directly to the weightier issues of New Testament theology. And yet that theology is not free-floating: it arises from specific situations, and its interpretation is often coloured by assumptions about place and time of origination. As JATR exposes these assumptions he is therefore contributing to the same goal of interpretation, except that he sees himself in the older tradition of Lightfoot and others who paid particular attention to questions of dating before attempting to construct a theology on these foundations.

At the outset JATR prepares us for the fact that although he will be using the most rigorous critical method, he will be arriving at very different and unexpected conclusions. He therefore takes time to argue that the commonly held critical consensus is not well-founded. As we have already noted, if JATR holds what otherwise appears as a traditional position, it is not because he begins with that view and uses the arguments of critical scholarship to justify conservative ends. He is peculiarly sensitive to presuppositions, from whichever direction. His redating of the New Testament does not derive from a longing for a traditional, pre-critical position, but rather from a deeper application of the very critical approach itself: 'It is that certain obstinate questionings have led me to ask just what basis there really is for certain assumptions which the prevailing consensus of critical orthodoxy would seem to make it hazardous or even impertinent to question' [RD, 2–3]. The questioning was encouraged by parallel developments in redating in the field of archaeology:

> . . . It provides an instructive parallel for the way in which the reigning assumptions of scientific scholarship can, and from time to time do, get challenged for the assumptions they are. For, much more than is generally recognized, the chronology of the New Testament rests on presuppositions rather than facts. [RD, 2]

Critical scholarship itself, consistently applied, uncovers the current agreed radical positions for 'the precarious constructions they are' [RD, 3]. The consensus of the nineteen and twentieth centuries, even when it avoids the most extreme scale suggested in German scholarship, is based on certain assumptions about the time required for cultural developments to unfold: 'The entire developmental schema (closely parallel to the "diffusionist framework" in archaeology), together with the time it is assumed to require, begins to look as if it may be imposed upon the material as arbitrarily as the earlier one of the Tübingen school' [RD, 8]. He looks in vain in modern scholarship for any serious wrestling with the evidence, external and internal, for the dating of individual books. Instead we are presented with 'an *a priori* pattern of theological development into which they are then made to fit' [RD 8–9].

It is when this sifting of evidence is performed that we discover how insecure are the foundations for conclusions which are constantly repeated in textbooks on the subject. If one stone is withdrawn from its place for any reason, the whole edifice is threatened. For JATR this took place as he considered again the traditional dating of the Gospel of John. We have already spent some time on JATR's arguments for the historicity of the fourth Gospel. It is an important topic in its own right, but beyond that it was the starting-point in his reassessment of the chronology and historicity of the whole of the New Testament.

When reviewing historical evidence in any area, especially if we have uncovered and rejected the assumptions governing the current consensus position, it is often useful to set up an alternative framework, provisionally. With some excitement we see the hypothesis, which originally looked quite absurd, withstand challenge after challenge, until it makes a fair bid to become the new agreed position: 'So, as little more than a theological joke, I thought I would see how far one could get with the hypothesis that the whole of the New Testament was written before 70' [RD, 10]. A rather 'in' joke one might think, not necessarily recommended for retelling in one's local, but certainly not a scenario to which one would expect a critical scholar to devote any serious attention, and certainly not a theologian who had acquired a particular kind of reputation: 'My position will probably seem surprisingly conservative – especially to those who judge me radical on other issues' [RD, 11].

Although a certain amount of cross-reference of events is possible within the New Testament, it is notoriously difficult to establish a correlation between the events concerning the life of Jesus and the early Church, and the history of the Roman Empire within which these events took place. We know of sequences either within the New Testament or within the Empire; the difficulty is in bringing the two together at a common agreed point. This may be less surprising than would first appear since the Church was of little importance to the Empire. Events which were of great and datable significance to the Empire may have mattered little to the Church, while those things which were of fundamental importance to the first Christians may not have registered on the imperial scale of things. The two histories would coexist without significantly intersecting. The obvious exception to this – we might reasonably assume – would be the destruction of Jerusalem in AD 70 by the Romans. Such was the historic importance of the city for Judaism, Jesus and the first Christians that its fall would be traumatic and would have called forth immediately one or more theological interpretations. It is for this reason that JATR in his theological jest concentrated on AD 70:

> One of the oddest facts about the New Testament is that what on any showing would appear to be the single most datable and climactic event of the period – the fall of Jerusalem in AD 70, and with it the collapse of institutional Judaism based on the temple – is never once mentioned as a past fact. [RD, 13]

In Mark we read of one of the disciples drawing the attention of Jesus to the magnificence of the temple. 'And Jesus said to him, "Do you see these great buildings? There will not be left here one stone upon another, that will not be thrown down." ' (Mark 13.2). His disciples naturally ask when this prophecy will be fulfilled: such is its importance. But the question is ignored. Critical scholarship has been quick to attribute varying degrees of imagination and creativity to the gospel writers. If the core of Judaism had been destroyed by the time the Gospels were written, in fulfilment of the prophecy by Jesus, would not something have been made of it? Similarly, Matthew has a parable of Jesus concerning a king who gave a marriage feast, but the invitations were rejected, and the servants who delivered them killed. 'The king was angry, and he sent his troops and destroyed those murderers and burned their city' (Matt. 22.7). This is the verse in the

New Testament which looks most like an indirect reference to the destruction of Jerusalem. And if this is the *most* explicit reference, that gives some idea of the problem. The emperors Nero and then Vespasian sent their legions not because an invitation had been declined, nor was the occasion the unlawful killing of imperial messengers. The destruction of Jerusalem and the dispersal of the Jewish people was to be a final response to their rebellion. If the evangelists wished to present Jesus as a true prophet then they would have written back into his words some of the specific details of that decisive and cosmic event. This is how critical scholarship assumes that the evangelists operated. Anyone who accepts this historical-critical view of their writings must therefore conclude that the event had not yet been fulfilled. That is the only critical explanation open.

Throughout this study of JATR's work I have tried to avoid entering any of the discussions on my own account. Perhaps, however, I could make an illustrative intervention at this point. In the third prediction of the Passion, Jesus tells his disciples what is to happen:

> Behold, we are going up to Jerusalem; and the Son of man will be delivered to the chief priests and the scribes, and they will condemn him to death, and deliver him to the Gentiles; and they will mock him, and spit upon him, and scourge him, and kill him; and after three days he will rise. (Mark 10.33–34)

The crucifixion and resurrection had already taken place before the Gospels were written, and critical scholarship assumes that the prophecy has been substantially filled out with hindsight, especially with regard to the details concerning the Romans. JATR does not use this example, but I think it operates as an *argumentum ad hominem* for critical scholarship. If the evangelists can be seen to do this with events which have already taken place, should we not assume they would have done it with reference to the fall of Jerusalem – if it had already taken place?

This conclusion, for which we have only provided a flavour of the argument, sets the scene for a redating of the New Testament much earlier than current scholarship would accept. But if it appears as support for a traditional position it must be stressed that it is achieved by two means. The first involves going back to the text itself, to look at internal and external evidences, without assumptions as to what must be the case. The second is that the conclusion is reached not by ignoring the historical-critical method, but rather through its more consistent application. *Redating the New Testament* is therefore based on the radical/conservative dialectic which we have attributed to JATR and illustrates the method throughout.

We shall not go through the many analyses and arguments of the book. It contains positions now familiar from JATR's other writings, including a tendency to accept the traditional view until critical reasons compel a revision: 'So we shall follow the procedure of trusting Acts until proved otherwise and allow this procedure to be tested by the results it yields' [RD, 33–4]. Ephesians is accepted as Pauline, the Epistle of James is attributed to the brother of Jesus, on the grounds that if it had been pseudonymous the author would have ensured apostolic legitimation by spelling out which James was meant. And Petrine authorship is affirmed at least for 1 Peter. Throughout the book he refers with approval to Edmundson's 1913 Bampton Lectures, *The Church of Rome in the First Century*, noting that, 'he proceeds to sift the various traditions and by careful historical methods reaches surprisingly conservative conclusions' [RD, 112–113].

JATR begins with a chronology of Paul: conversion (33), first visit to Jerusalem (35), second visit to Jerusalem (46); first missionary journey (47–8); council of Jerusalem (48); . . . imprisonment in Rome (60–2). Using this framework he dates the letters of Paul and then the rest of the New Testament. James (c. 47–8); 1 Thessalonians (early 50) 2 Thessalonians (50–1) 1 Corinthians (spring 55) . . . Revelation (late 68). All of the New Testament is therefore dated before 70, followed immediately by the sub-apostolic writings such as 1 Clement (70); The Epistle of Barnabas (c. 75) and The Shepherd of Hermas (c. 85). Having established these dates on internal and external evidence relevant to each, JATR is in a position to claim that his hypothesis actually explains why the production of literature in the Church ended abruptly, as we might expect in face of the shattering blow of the destruction of Jerusalem:

> The possibility, if not the probability, must indeed be faced that there was not a steady stream of early Christian writings but that an intense period of missionary, pastoral and literary activity, culminating in the desolation of Israel and the demise of all the 'pillars' of the apostolic church except John, was followed by one of retrenchment and relative quiescence. [RD, 312]

And if these dates are at first unacceptable, is it because of careful attention paid to the evidence, or simply the triumph of 'the manifold tyranny of unexamined assumptions'? [RD, 345]. One important assumption here is that it must have taken a much longer period for the doctrine of the Church to develop. But JATR quotes Hengel with approval, that the crucial stages in Christology took place in the explosive years between 30 and 35, and that more important developments in this doctrine took place in the period up to the council of Jerusalem than in the next seven hundred years. JATR sought to establish a chronology first. It is dangerous and misleading to set out limits based on the development of doctrine, since we have no idea what such constraints might reasonably be. And so in his Conclusion JATR reiterates the point which he made at the outset with respect to archaeology:

> Another factor which we have observed is the subjectivity in assessing the intervals required for development, distribution or diffusion. There is a close parallel here, as we saw, with what has been going on in archaeology. What Renfrew calls the 'archaeological bellows' can be moved in or out at will. And there is a kind of Parkinson's law that takes over; the intervals will contract or expand to fill the time available. [RD, 344]

Since our main concern is with JATR's method, it is of some significance that it is on this point which he ends:

> Just as the shrinking of the span from 50–150+ to one from 50–100+ resulted in discrediting some of the extreme forms of scepticism about the Christian tradition, so a further reduction in final datings by more than half from 50–70+ must tend to reinforce a greater conservatism. Yet it is important to define this rather carefully. The last inference to be drawn is that it renders otiose or invalid the critical work done on the documents of the New Testament over the past two hundred years. For it is by applying the same critical methods and criteria that the conclusions have been reached. [RD, 364]

By the more radical and consistent application of critical methods than had been hitherto attempted, he has arrived at conclusions in some respect closer to traditional positions than could have been derived from conservative assumptions. The book well illustrates the radical/conservative dialectic.

5 Trusting the Bible

In 1977 JATR published a short book which in many respects is a companion volumn to *Redating the New Testament*. Unlike the earlier work, intended for New Testament scholars, *Can We Trust the New Testament?* was written for a lay readership who would not be in a position to participate in such technical inquiries. It presupposes the detailed discussion of the longer book and tends merely to summarize the main points of the arguments before bringing forward their conclusions. This is not an unreasonable way to proceed, and JATR makes it quite clear to his readers when his own position differs from the consensus of critical scholarship. *Can We Trust the New Testament?* is therefore a 'popular' version, a redating without tears, or at least without Greek. Having examined the longer work in some detail, and since there is no substantial change of position between the writing of the two books, there is no need to discuss the shorter sequel considered as another survey of the New Testament. However, although it is not an important work of scholarship, it is of particular interest in *our* inquiries. Indeed it marks a point of tension and of transition between the biblical and theological dimensions of JATR's work.

Although in many respects the book presents us with now familiar features, the tension and transition – already present in the title itself – confronts us at the outset. In the Introduction to *Can We Trust the New Testament?* JATR draws attention to a number of texts in the New Testament which speak of trusting in the gospel, believing what is written, trusting and believing 'not a timeless prescription for good living but a person born at a moment of history. And trusting the New Testament is trusting it for a portrait of that person' [CWT, 7]. Attempting a portrait of Jesus went out of fashion earlier this century when the problems inherent in a 'quest of the historical Jesus' were highlighted by critical New Testament scholarship. Even in its more recent form the renewed quest had no expectations of being able to produce a portrait from the material which could be affirmed critically. JATR seems to be adopting a conservative and even pre-critical stance in setting out to uncover the picture of Jesus conveyed in the Gospels: 'You cannot "trust the New Testament" without trusting the claim at its very heart that it is not just an imaginary picture but a faithful portrait – full of faith, to be sure, but true also to fact' [CWT, 8]. It is precisely in the relationship of faith and fact that we see JATR combining conservative and radical elements in his own distinctive way. It is widely assumed in critical scholarship that the 'facts' of the Gospels were largely the creation of the faith of the early Church. Once again JATR recognizes that this is an assumption, and decides to go directly to the text. In reopening the issue he is calling in question something which seems so obvious to all but the most conservative scholars, a fixed point for many generations of students of the New Testament. He notes that this is not what might be expected of a critical scholar, but neither would it be expected by those who by that time knew him by his reputation as a theologian:

> This is somewhat against the stream of what I suppose would be called current critical orthodoxy in the field of New Testament scholarship. I would be more conservative – on some issues much more conservative – than most of my colleagues who are prepared to use the same methods. Since this may surprise many of my readers, who may regard me by reputation as a dangerous radical, let me try to describe, as I see it, the lie of the field. [CWT, 9–10]

This is one of several places where JATR shows that he is aware that he does not fit comfortably into either camp.

He can now proceed in the main body of the book to argue for early dating, objective evaluation of internal and external evidence, due attention to historical traditions, no undue scepticism and all the points we have met in works previously discussed. However, as indicated above, there is additionally a new element present both in the Introduction and even in the title of the book. *Can We Trust the New Testament?* is intended as a 'popular' work in two respects. In the first place many of the conclusions reached by careful textual analyses in *Redating the New Testament* are simply stated here without argument, as we have already noted. But there is another aspect to the work which relates to its intended readership: it is highly evangelical, in the sense that JATR is advocating Christian faith. The 'trust' and 'believing' which concern him are not simply matters of historicity. He wishes Christians to be reassured that their faith need not be undermined by the findings of modern New Testament scholarship. This in turn may surprise us, for three different reasons. The first is that many would take the view that such assurances are counter-productive. That is to say, the whole exercise would seem to consist in drawing the attention of the laity to problems raised by radical scholarship, only to assure them that they need not be concerned about these problems, problems which they did not know existed until being advised to ignore them. JATR knows this argument:

> For there are things that may be true for the cognoscenti – but the faithful must not be needlessly disturbed. This has been a feature especially of much liberal catholicism, both Roman Catholic and Anglican.
>
> Now this is not a position in which I find myself, and I do not think I could hold it for long if I did. [CWT, 11]

The second reason why this position might surprise us is that it echoes assurances given at the end of the last century by the Halle theologian Martin Kähler, and reiterated more recently by his pupil Paul Tillich, that in matters of faith ordinary people need have nothing to fear from the papal pretensions of the scholars. But it must be said that in this book JATR does not treat the issue theologically. He simply seeks to establish a trustworthy picture of the historical basis of Christian faith. In reducing the issue to a historical quest, with no consideration of the theological dimension, JATR seems to share conservative, traditional and even pre-critical assumptions about the relationship between the historicity of the text and the foundations of faith. These are assumptions which could not unthinkingly be made in the nineteenth century after the work of David Strauss, nor can they reasonably be made in the twentieth century after the impact of the work of Kähler and the influence of his pupils, including Bultmann. But it must be said that JATR displays little interest in New Testament *theology*, as opposed to historical criticism; a surprising deficiency in view of his high regard for my own former teacher, the American New Testament theologian John Knox.

Yet in the third place we might be surprised by this evangelical motivation, not by the manner in which it is undertaken, but, as Dr Johnson might have said, that it should be undertaken at all. Up till now we have on occasion noted the lack of theological concern. In Parts Two and Three we shall see a consistent evangelical or missionary concern, as it is appropriate in these areas. But such concern seems out of place in a purely New Testament context. Apparently re-establishing the historical trustworthiness of the sources will not be enough:

> But that does not mean that we may not need to rethink pretty drastically how we can make the New Testament tradition meaningful today. For instance, what does it really mean to say that Jesus is 'the son of God' or 'pre-existent' in a world like ours where those sort of categories are alien, *as they weren't in the first century*, to the way in which ordinary people think or talk? Just to go on repeating them as they stand may convey nothing – or something subtly different.

The corollary of this position is that I do *not* want to protect ordinary people from what the scholars are saying, but precisely to expose them. [CWT, 11]

And what are scholars saying about such questions? I do not think it would be unfair to say, 'Nothing at all.' The reason, as already observed, is that biblical scholars see their task as the understanding of the ancient world and establishing the meaning which texts had *within that world*. For the most part they would regard questions such as, And what does that mean for us today? as theological, evangelical or homiletical, and certainly not their responsibility. It is for this reason that it is surprising that JATR, *qua* New Testament scholar, should raise this issue.

There is therefore a tension and ambiguity in JATR's position at this point. The establishing of the historical will not be sufficient, but seems to be necessary. Yet as a biblical scholar he becomes so absorbed in the historical textual work that on its completion he assumes that all has been achieved: the foundations of the faith have been assured. We found the same ambiguity in *Wrestling with Romans*, when he undertook to demonstrate its relevance for today, but was content to reproduce the historical context of the 'forensic metaphor' of the death of Christ. The same unresolved problem is to be found in his long essay 'Interpreting the Book of Revelation', which was included in the recently published collection of posthumous papers entitled *Where Three Ways Meet*. C. H. Dodd apparently considered Revelation a sub-Christian work, and certainly in recent years it has received almost as much attention from psychiatrists as from theologians. It is an extraordinarily difficult text to understand in its own terms, but JATR, in eschewing the role of the historical commentator, set himself an even more difficult and evangelical task. The essay was originally material prepared in Cambridge for students and then lay audiences: 'It was addressed not to scholars, who will find little new here, but to men and women in the contemporary church who have seldom given their minds to this apparently remote and largely irrelevant appendix to their Bibles' [WTWM, 33]. As a student I was privileged to attend lectures given by William Barclay, a scholar with encyclopaedic knowledge of the ancient world, but known and loved as an outstanding and gifted communicator. Whatever his chosen subject for the day, he managed to convey the impression that this was the most important and exciting book in the New Testament. He could even find a claim to uniqueness for Philemon! JATR seems committed to the same *tour de force* in advocating The Book of Revelation to busy people in the modern world. 'It seemed to have little to do with the secular world in which they have to live their lives' [WTWM, 34]. Yet his evangelical motivation is only stimulated by the challenge. 'The Book of Revelation strikes the twentieth-century reader as the strangest and most remote in the New Testament. In fact it is in many ways the most modern' [WTWM, 35]. Who could leave the lecture hall early after that introduction!

The historical comments which JATR makes about selected chapters are as informed and informative as we should expect, but our interest in the essay concerns the evangelical question of the meaning of Revelation for today. But having been promised so much perhaps now the audience would sense that they were being confronted with a statement of the problem rather than a solution to it. For example, the writer of the book is dealing with the experience of the early Church within an Empire which was not only apparently all-powerful, but completely indifferent and insensitive to the God of the Christians. The theology of the Church, including the 'forensic metaphor', claimed that God had defeated sin and evil in Christ, and yet the world – what today we might call the secular world – seemed to be oblivious to this and by its continuation to contradict it. 'What is the significance of secularism in a redeemed world?' [WTWM, 58]. It is in tackling such questions that Revelation is judged to be 'modern', and JATR claims that it is the first book in the New Testament to attempt a 'Christian theology of power': 'The Book of Revelation was the first essay in coming to terms with the post-Christian situation, with the incredible assertion that the *telos*, the goal, of history had already taken place and that in consequence everything was henceforth different' [WTWM, 58]. But is this really an answer to the question of the meaning for today? Is it not rather an indication that however meaningful that theology was in its own time it does not describe modern experience at all? I fear that at this point JATR has fallen back into the ranks of those who have raised paradox to an art form and claimed the contradiction of experience as a religious virtue. It is the assertion that at a metaphysical level everything has been changed, when in our daily experience the world is as bad as it ever was. This is surely not evidence of great faith, but simply of bad theology.

The essay of Revelation illustrates the issue raised more extensively in *Can We Trust the New Testament?*, namely, the gulf between the credibility of textual sources and the foundations of religious belief, between historical trustworthiness and Christian faith. As we have seen, the book begins with what we have been calling evangelical motivation, in the broad non-sectarian meaning of this term. But it then moves directly to provide assurances about the historical-critical method used, and the chronology of the New Testament already established in JATR's previous scholarly works. But because of his underlying concern for the communication of the Christian faith and its defence he inevitably re-enters the area of ambiguity between fact and faith. The effect can be seen, for example, in the treatment of the birth and infancy accounts in Matthew. In the case of the narrative about the holy family's flight into Egypt, critical scholarship would regard this simply as a setting created by the writer, enabling him to claim that events in the life of Jesus fulfil prophecies or typologies of the Old Testament: 'Out of Egypt have I called my son' (Mat. 2.15, cf Hos. 11.1). From our previous studies we should expect JATR to decline to write the episode off entirely as the creation of the evangelist, and indeed he claims that there may well be historical elements in this as in the other accounts. But another criterion has now entered his approach to the texts: 'But to take it all, with the fundamentalists, as prose rather than poetry is to confound everything, and, these days, to put off a large number of intelligent people' [CWT, 97]. The evangelical concern means that what people today find credible or incredible, based on what is often and imprecisely referred to as 'the modern world-view', becomes a factor in assessing the historicity of the texts. Up till now JATR, as a New Testament scholar, has been confident about proceeding objectively and scientifically, but this new criterion introduces an element of subjectivity and cultural relativism. Previously, in discussing a reference by JATR to Hegel, we said that in this tradition the eternal verities could not be true unless the events in which they are incarnate occurred much as reported. Would this not be true also in the case of Matthew? The argument from 'prophecy' would only be an *argumentum ad hominem* to the Jewish readers/hearers if the flight to Egypt had actually happened. Otherwise Strauss would have been correct in claiming the narrative to be entirely mythological. JATR's evangelical motive seems to have displaced him from his conservative/radical dialectic into that vaguely critical liberalism against which he normally argues so forcefully and successfully.

Of course we have great sympathy for JATR at this point, but we should have to say that it is only now that he begins to face the kind of issues constantly raised by Bultmann in his proposals on demythologizing the New Testament. Up till now JATR has been content to remain within the circle of historical-critical research, the goal of which is to understand what the ancient writers actually said. We have had occasion to point out that this is not at all the same as establishing the meaning of the text, especially the meaning that it might have today. Although in those works examined in this section we have noted JATR's desire to bridge that hermeneutical gap, he has provided no criteria comparable to those carefully defined in his enunciation and defence of the truly historical-critical method.

Not surprisingly, another example of this ambiguous position concerns the resurrection: 'The historical evidence is not decisive in the sense that it is all that is required. Yet it is decisive in the sense that if it could be exploded there would be a hole in the heart of the Christian faith' [CWT, 121]. This is not at all the confident New Testament scholar dealing with what the texts actually say. Here the evangelical issue hovers in the background, inserting what we have described as a further criterion. On the historical basis for the resurrection he is confused, or at least confusing. On the one hand he can distinguish certain aspects of the tradition from the mythological embellishments: 'But I am not persuaded that it is so easy to explain away the other language, of spices and stones and sweat-bands. This was never part of a stock of symbolic imagery and would not have been taken for such' [CWT, 128]. How is that to be reconciled with the position referred to earlier, that 'the bones of Jesus *could* yet be lying around Palestine and the resurrection still be true' [CWT, 124]? Are we dealing here with what the texts actually say about resurrection (which on closer inspection is very little) or is JATR struggling to present the meaning of resurrection, a meaning which could be accepted today? As we have already hinted, the problem is that JATR is not willing to tackle the issue as a *theological* problem, rather than a historical one:

> If the resurrection story has a foot in *public* history (and to abandon that claim is to abandon something that has been central to the entire Christian tradition), then it must be open and vulnerable to the historian's scrutiny. Never let us suppose that we need not bother with his questions or that we are impervious to them. [CWT, 128]

But as Kähler saw, this is not a historical question.

More briefly, we can illustrate the problem by reference to the ascension: 'In fact most thinking Christians would now agree that (whatever its historical basis) the ascension *story* is primarily to be seen as a symbolic representation of the spiritual truth that Christ is not only alive but Lord' [CWT, 128]. The New Testament scholar is still present in this quotation, residually present in the parenthetical reference to a 'historical basis'. Is it simply out of habit? What could the historical basis be to Jesus disappearing up into the sky above Palestine? In the gallery of stained-glass windows in the Burrell

Collection there is one in which a small band of people standing in a circle are looking upwards. The viewer is just in time, because at the top of the picture are a pair of legs and the lower part of a robe, as the wearer disappears out of sight. In the middle of the circle of people is a set of footprints in the sandy soil. This is how the ascension is described in Acts and how it was conceived for most of the history of the Christian church. Do some people not so understand it today? Why does JATR not give the same warning as with reference to the resurrection, that is, 'to abandon that claim is to abandon something that has been central to the entire Christian tradition'? The reason is that the interpretation of the passage is not now determined by the historical scholar. The dominant figure in the foreground now is the one comfortingly referred to as the thinking Christian. That is to say, a Christian who has no intention of setting aside his knowledge of the natural and social worlds in order to make room for ancient doctrine. Such a person cannot find the meaning of the text in what it says. The irony, we might suspect, is that thinking Christians have even more difficulty with the resurrection than with the ascension. Apart from the actual going up into the sky most Christians have no trouble in thinking of Jesus sitting in a large chair in heaven. But surprisingly, in the end JATR does not seem altogether unhappy with this kind of inconsistency. He concludes the book with some praise for what he describes as 'the conservatism of the committed': 'It exhibits that self-rectifying balance and solidity which has enabled English scholarship, as well as English religion, to weather the extremes of Continental radicalism and Transatlantic fashion. I believe too that more often than not it has been proved right – even if for wrong or muddled reasons' [CWT, 132]. I leave it JATR's fellow countrymen to debate whether 'wrong or muddled' thinking is a national virtue or vice, but clearly this cannot be a satisfactory position to adopt.

At the beginning of this chapter we claimed that *Can We Trust the New Testament?* exhibits both tension and transition. In previous chapters we have claimed that JATR's approach to biblical studies exhibits a conservative/radical dialectic. In this final book which we have discussed, that dialectic, although present, has been compromised in many places. It would seem that other factors have begun to influence his work. In fact it is likely that we are observing a transition from biblical studies to theology. It is therefore time to move on to the next Part, to examine JATR's theological writings. However, as in this first Part, we shall not be reproducing all of his arguments, but rather attempting to pursue the questions of method and coherence. We shall have to consider whether his theological method can also be characterized as a conservative/radical dialectic. In particular we shall have to examine the possibility that even if it can be so described, the dialectic might have a different *meaning* and significance in the theological context. To be conservative on historical matters, in the biblical context, will not be the same as being conservative on doctrinal matters in the theological context. Nor will the term 'radical' necessarily have the same meaning in both contexts.

PART TWO

Theological Exploration

Introduction

In this Part we shall consider JATR's most famous book, *Honest to God*, published in 1963 when he was Bishop of Woolwich, in south London. He was already well enough known within certain circles in the Church of England and to members of the University of Cambridge and his court appearance in 1960 at the *Lady Chatterley's Lover* obscenity trial had brought him a passing notoriety, but it was this book which first brought him to national and international attention. Most readers of the book knew nothing of his earlier works, or of his reputation as a New Testament scholar. It often appeared to them as the attempt by a busy bishop to come to terms with the works of eminent contemporary theologians. The time to write it, as is well known, came about not by choice or planning but by back trouble and the necessity of having to lie down for extended periods. But it was still taken to be the work of a gifted amateur, a pastor grappling with material which he intuitively knew to be relevant, but which he had trouble digesting. This, as a matter of fact, was not true, but it is not surprising that those who knew nothing of him to that point should take this view. What is more surprising is that JATR himself fostered it, in two ways.

The first of these comes in a specific denial that he was competent to attempt a proper treatment of the subject: 'I am not writing this book as a professional theologian: indeed, this is not my own academic field' [HTG, 26]. And yet this was precisely the field of his early training at Cambridge, for which he was awarded a First in Theology. Whatever he meant by this unduly modest disclaimer, JATR was not at all unfamiliar with the issues raised in his book. Some have criticized *Honest to God* as philosophically naive, as if whatever his competence in theology, he was unaware of the implications of his arguments. This is even less likely, since before he was a doctrinal theologian, JATR trained in the philosophy of religion. In 1942 he won the Burney Prize and in the following session held the Burney Student-ship. The subject of the prize essay was 'Kant's Ethics and the Christian Moral Ideal' [EJ, 14]. This philosophical orientation is fundamental to his doctoral research. Historically therefore JATR began with philosophy of religion, proceeding to an examination of Christian doctrine. He had a classical education at Marlborough, and read classics at Cambridge. On this basis he was able to accept the invitation to become chaplain at Wells Theological College, and Lecturer in New Testament. Early in his career he began to suspect that theological doctrines might not be as well founded in the New Testament as is often assumed. It was for this reason that he went back behind theology to textual studies. This progression is acknowledged in one of his earliest works, to which we have already made mention, *Jesus and His Coming*. In the Introduction to that book he develops a rather elaborate metaphor concerning his investigations of the foundations of theology:

> For subterranean rumblings are heard most clearly by those who have their rooms on the ground floor, that is, at the New Testament level of the doctrinal construction. And they are the more noticeable to one who has recently moved downstairs, in the first instance from the floor of the philosophy of religion to that of systematic theology, and then from systematic theology to Biblical studies. [JHC, 10–11]

JATR was not therefore a classical scholar of New Testament application who strayed innocently into a theological maze or a philosophical minefield. We should not allow his modest disclaimer to lead us into thinking that he was incompetent to handle the issues which he placed on the agenda.

But there is a second way in which JATR might mislead the unsuspecting concerning the value of *Honest to God*. Throughout the book he makes extensive use, with long quotations, of the work of Tillich, Bonhoeffer and Bultmann. The fact that they belong in this order confirms our outline of JATR's intellectual biography. While the New Testament theologian Bultmann figures little in the book, it is Tillich's more philosophical approach, rather than the work of Bonhoeffer, which reaches to the heart of the argument. JATR's second disclaimer concerns his indebtedness to these writers: 'I am struggling to think other people's thoughts after them. I cannot claim to have understood all I am trying to transmit' [HTG, 21]. Once again, the impression is given that the bishop, under medical constraint, at last had time to read some modern theology, and published his ill-digested reflections on three positions which in some important respects are incompatible. But, equally, nothing could be further from the truth, in two respects. On closer inspection the book is not a theological chop-suey; it is not composed of chopped up ingredients from different sources, thrown into the same pot, stirred, warmed over and served with a little spice. Of course use is made of the three scholars indicated, and JATR is fulsome in his praise of them and his indebtedness to them. But what he does not specifically draw to the reader's attention is his own contribution – on which basis the selections from the others are made. Those who claim that JATR simply borrows from others and repeats, to the extent that he understands, not only misrepresent *Honest to God* but fail to discern that element in the book which is original to JATR and which guarantees that his position is still theology and unquestionably Christian. That element is found in all of JATR's theological writings and is unmistakable to those who know what to look for. To that extent, more important than any of his published works is the work he never published, his doctoral dissertation. Virtually no one who read *Honest to God* had had the opportunity of reading the dissertation, but this unpublished manuscript makes clear the perspective from which the best seller was written, and throws a good deal of light on JATR's own presuppositions about Christian faith and theology.

We begin our study of JATR's theology with an analysis of his doctoral dissertation, not because chronologically it was his earliest major piece of work, the work of a young scholar soon to be overtaken by more considered positions. To the contrary, it is dealt with first because its major themes appear consistently throughout the entire corpus of JATR's theological writings. In his Bampton Lectures a lifetime of New Testament research came to fruition. But in theology it was his earliest work – displaying exceptional discernment and sophistication in one so young – which laid the foundations for his later writings.

6 The Personality of God

We have already noted that JATR began by establishing himself as a promising young scholar in the field of philosophy of religion. He was subsequently elected by Trinity College to the Stanton Studentship for the session 1943–4, and after discussions with F. R. Tennant he proposed a research topic for his PhD, to be supervised by H. H. Farmer [EJ, 16]. The title of his dissertation was *Thou Who Art*, on the subject of: 'The notion of personality and its relation to Christian theology, with particular reference to (a) the contemporary 'I-Thou' philosophy, (b) the doctrine of the Trinity and the Person of Christ.' The work is substantial in both senses. It runs to some six hundred pages of typescript (160,000 words), and presents a daunting prospect to any reader. However, its real substance is in the quality of the argument, the originality of the thought and the single-minded and confident manner in which this twenty-four year old disposed of various theological traditions in the course of presenting his own proposed new directions. John Baillie of New College, Edinburgh, judged it the best PhD he had ever examined [EJ, 16]. No one who has read the dissertation could think of JATR in his published works as an amateur theologian straying into a field beyond his competence, nor could there be any doubt concerning his own originality, regardless of the acknowledged use he made of other theologians.

In referring to the metaphor of moving downstairs in the theological edifice we saw that JATR's interest ranged from philosophy to biblical studies, not departmentally but in an integrated manner. The Preface to the dissertation opens with a description of the project which indicates the interrelationship of the three academic departments:

> This essay is offered as a study in Biblical philosophy. It is an attempt to rethink the most fundamental theme of Christian metaphysics – that of the personality of God – in terms of the 'Hebraic' categories of Word and Will, of speech and action, with which the Biblical writers constantly work. [TWA, i]

The rethinking to which JATR here refers concerns the main theological tradition which he takes to be epitomized in the *Summa Theologica* of Thomas Aquinas, a theological tradition which relied heavily on Greek thought. It was inevitable that the early Church would attempt to make increasingly systematic theological statements expressing and expounding the faith, but these statements were influenced by categories and concepts of the time which contributed clarity to the task but also brought their own problems: 'But the categories of this philosophical tradition are not such as can do justice to the "living" God of the Biblical revelation' [TWA, ii]. We can see therefore at the outset that there is an acceptance of the need for theology, but that it must be an exposition and extrapolation of and not an imposition on the biblical tradition. There is a recognition of the important contribution of philosophy in this context, but it must not distort the message or import alien premises.

In order to bring out the distinctiveness of JATR's approach to the issue, perhaps I might briefly refer to my own experience, a generation later. As a student in Glasgow I was introduced to this issue from several directions. There have of course been many studies by New Testament scholars of the differences between Greek and Hebrew thought, and G. H. C. MacGregor had published in this area. At the same time John Macquarrie, translator of *Being and Time*, introduced Heidegger's critique of the Aristotelian tradition in which human beings were described by use of categories of substance. Heidegger substituted existentialia, or modes of existence, in his analytic of *Dasein*. Macquarrie then showed how these in turn were taken up by Bultmann in his programme of demythologizing, to which JATR refers in *Honest to God*. These, then, were two rather different ways in which Greek and Hebraic thought were distinguished in seeking to be true to biblical thought. We were fortunate however to be introduced to yet another approach. Ronald Gregor Smith had first read and subsequently translated Martin Buber's *I and Thou* as a theological student. Few would consider *I and Thou* to be philosophically in the same class as *Being and Time*. Heidegger's observations on the ontic and his analyses of existential structures offered a new and dynamic entry to ontology which was difficult to resist. And yet at one point, but perhaps the most significant point of all, Buber was able to free himself of the Western philosophical tradition more radically than Heidegger. Heidegger could not bring himself to assign any constitutive importance to authentic human relations. This was a defect in his existential analytic and it was carried on into his later ontology to render questionable a position which in other respects seemed to offer a new philosophical basis for theology.

After that digression I can resume my position in the background, but I wished to indicate that although the contrast of Greek and Hebraic thought was not new, JATR did not approach it through the obvious routes. He did not begin with religious differences between two cultures. His subject was not the nature of God, far less the very existence of God. What he identified as 'the most fundamental theme of Christian metaphysics' was 'the *personality* of God'. And to do this he turned from the Aristotelian tradition, not to its most famous contemporary critic, Heidegger, but to the profoundly different philosophy of Martin Buber. In doing this JATR was not offering another solution to a familiar problem – he was fundamentally reconceiving the problem itself: 'But the systematic elaboration and application of these ideas in connection with the philosophical concept of the personality of God and His relation to the world is a need which we feel has hitherto hardly been met' [TWA, iii].

This position, set out simply as early as the Preface to his dissertation, is presupposed throughout the rest of his entire career as a theologian, and precisely because it was presupposed many failed to understand his position in *Honest to God*, or to appreciate its originality.

Moving on now to the argument, we can begin with a familiar question: What is it that distinguishes human beings from everything else? Many answers have been given. The distinguishing feature is normally an attribute, such as reason or the capacity to make tools, to laugh, or to form a picture of the self. The self-subsisting individual has, in addition to attributes which he or she shares in common with other species, one which is distinctive. Whatever the specific feature or function, all these attempts to answer the question share the traditional starting-point, that human beings can properly be described by using a model appropriate to the material world. Attributes can be added on, like rooms to a house or properties to herbs. JATR in several places refers to the classical definition of Boethius, that a person is 'an individual substance of a rational nature' [e.g. TWA, 40]. JATR rejects this starting-point and focuses attention instead on a particular kind of relationship. That relationship is to be constitutive of personal being; it is not a further quality or attribute to be appended to an already existing entity. The personal relationship is the way in which all qualities and attributes are possessed and exercised. There are of course many forms of relationship, some of them purely functional or institutional. These are regarded as impersonal: in them the other person is treated as less than a person, often as a means to an end. Personality, on this new view, arises from certain relationships; they are not to be regarded as optional extras to an existence which is otherwise complete in itself. This will be the basis of JATR's discussion of the personality of God. Of course some religious systems, notably in ancient Greece, would deny that the gods could or should enter into such relationships. In such a context it would be a merit to declare a god to be impersonal. But this would not be the case in the biblical understanding of God: 'The assertion that He was impersonal would *mean* that He was not the sort of God whose very existence was existence-in-love' [TWA, 9]. Nor would the situation be changed by adding the attribute of being able to love: 'There are numerous systems of thought in which different personal properties are appropriated to the Supreme Being, which yet leave no room for belief in a personal God' [TWA, 9]. A personal God displays a 'peculiarly individuating love between God and man' [TWA, 12].

There is an element of anachronism here, because JATR discovered in the course of his research that the whole idea of personality, of God or man, is a relatively recent development: 'It was in the Trinitarian controversies of the eighteenth century that the idea of God as a "person" in the modern sense of the term began to undergo the process of its prolonged and difficult parturition' [TWA, 13–14]. One of the first writers consciously concerned with the philosophical questions involved was the Swedish historian E. G. Geijer, who in 1842 published a theory of personality in which he insisted on the impossibility of the existence of a person except in relation to other persons. JATR was struck by the extension of this view, when Geijer claimed that 'even the Divine personality is unthinkable in isolation; God can only be conceived as a person if He has from all eternity made His counterpart as free as Himself' [TWA, 24]. The God who is Love is unthinkable in isolation. This was in contrast to the impersonalism of the Aristotelian Absolute, even when some attributes or functions predicable only of persons were added: 'But the mere addition of personal qualities and functions is not, as we saw before, sufficient to establish a properly personalistic doctrine of God. What is required to be asserted is a genuinely 'personal' relation between God and each of His creatures. This, we shall maintain, Thomism cannot provide' [TWA, 29].

JATR is claiming that the historical evidence indicates that when the understanding of personality finally emerged in Western thought, it was not from the classical tradition, which did not have one, but from the biblical view of God. This is a God who numbers the hairs on the head of each individual, who is the Good Shepherd who knows his sheep. Although, like any other concept, personality develops from within a cultural context, yet it is because of the individuating love of a personal God that the understanding of the person arises: 'Love not only appreciates individuality, it bestows it' [TWA, 67]. Historically the understanding of the individual does not derive from a social, but a religious context. JATR refers to Kierkegaard's claim that it is the task of everyone to become 'an individual before God' [TWA, 16]. Although Kierkegaard is often accused of individualism, his position is profoundly different from that of Descartes, who, as the father of modern philosophy, still preserves the fundamental assumptions of the classical tradition about human existence and the divine being.

JATR therefore turns away from this tradition which could not do justice to the personality of God or to human personality. In its place he looks towards a personalist philosophy which not only gives a central place to human personality, but actually links it to the personality of God. In contrast to the classical tradition, and its modern expressions, Martin Buber asserts that 'There is no "I" taken in itself' [TWA, 74]. The real is not the rational, but the relational. 'What Buber is in fact saying is that the different relationships into which a man enters are not additional to the essence of personality but constitutive of it' [TWA, 74–5].

Although the phrase 'I-Thou' is now associated with the work of Buber, first published in 1923, it was central to the thought of three writers working independently in three countries, and three different languages, during the middle of the 1840s. We have already referred to Geijer, who claimed that there is 'no personality except in and through another. No Thou – no I' [TWA, 85]. There was also Ludwig Feuerbach, the first major critic of Hegel, who claimed: 'Man with man – the unity of I and Thou – is God.' He was critical of idealism in many of its aspects to which we have already referred. 'The true dialectic is no monologue of the solitary thinker with himself; it is a dialogue between I and Thou' [TWA, 87]. Feuerbach was regarded in his own day, by comparison, as a materialist, and certainly he paid a good deal of attention to experience. In this context he can therefore say that 'Where there is no love, neither is there any truth' [TWA, 87]. JATR considered Feuerbach's position at an important point inadequate, for all its interest in religion, since it turned away from 'a conception of a "Thou" wholly and transcendently "other", which disrupts the simple identification of theology with anthropology' [TWA, 88]. JATR is not entirely fair to Feuerbach here, since Feuerbach says, paradoxically, that anthropology is also theology. He was struggling, with an entirely inadequate ontology, to affirm truth existing independently of individuals but not alienated from them. However, at this point we can see JATR beginning to bring together various themes to express the constitutive nature of the I-Thou relationship for personality, both human and divine. The third writer was of course Kierkegaard. As we have seen, Kierkegaard took up the subject in dealing with the relationship between the individual and God. In contrast to the classical view, truth is encountered when the living individual meets the living God. Truth for Kierkegaard is a Person, Jesus Christ. It cannot be objectified and thereby made available to someone impersonally or in isolation, who does not base his life upon it. The individual does not possess the truth, but lives within it, as he lives in relationship to God. For that reason his relationship to the truth is one of faith. A final contribution comes from the end of the nineteenth century in the work of the Russian philosopher Vladimir Soloviev. All writers who deal with the constitutive place of the I-thou relationship face the transitional situation that no particular Thou can exert the absolute claim upon us necessary to break the bonds of egoism. But it is in the other that the divine Other is encountered: 'But this very act of faith presupposes (and herein lies its power for salvation) a radical revaluation of a man's own existence as having its centre not in himself but in the Divine "Thou" ' [TWA, 96–7].

The solitary figure of the classical and idealist tradition is therefore rejected as an abstraction. Instead the individual exists in and through a series of relationships with others. It is in and through these relationships that the I encounters other thous, but also the divine Thou. The individual exists in being addressed by others: at a more profound level he is created by the word of God addressed to him. JATR sees the contribution of Buber not simply in the analyses of various types of relationships, I-Thou and I-It, but in an ontological dimension:

> It is not until it is recognised that the 'proper' way of knowing, that is of existing towards, persons is but a part of a way of relating ourselves to the whole realm of nature, persons and values (a relation, if we may anticipate, which is fundamentally a recognition of 'responsibility', an 'obedience') – it is not until then that a true understanding is possible either of the personality of man or God. [TWA, 109–10]

Man is not alone, but neither is he at the centre of a world of his own making, existing as material for his manipulation: 'For Buber and the others are insistent that neither man's nature nor indeed the full truth even of these finite relationships can be understood without taking into account the most fundamental relation of all – that between man and the eternal personal "Thou" of God' [TWA, 135]. Individual relationships can be repudiated, but according to Buber there is one Thou from whom we cannot escape, and for this reason there is within each relationship the recognition of a deeper dimension of *Gabe* and

Aufgabe, of gift and task. The note of unconditionality comes not from the recognition of a principle but of a Person, a refuge and a strength as well as a consuming fire: 'Every contact of an "I" with a finite "Thou" points beyond itself to encounter with an infinite "Thou" ' [TWA, 143]. This means that every relationship can be an occasion in which the eternal is recognized as present. God is not outside and beyond relationships and is not to be found in turning away from others, least of all the neighbour, though Buber it will be recalled also dealt with relations with the natural world. God outside of relations is not God.

In the course of the various discussions JATR of course examines other contemporary works on the subject. At this point he deals with John Macmurray, who recognized man's responsiblity for three different types of relationships, those with the inorganic, the organic and the personal. But JATR finds no recognition here of 'an ultimate responsibility' [TWA, 184].

> There is no independent Divine 'Thou' transcending the nature and claims of the personal, with claims of its own capable of demanding the renunciation even, say, of the human love which mediates it. Macmurray's analysis in this matter, however, does not do justice to the accent on unconditionality which always attaches to the peculiarly religious awareness. [TWA, 184–5]

It lacks a further dimension, 'the dimension of the Supernatural, of the sense of the Holy, and the judgement of the Sacred' [TWA, 185].

Up till now JATR has concentrated for the most part on one side of the I-Thou relationship with God. He has dealt with human existence as essentially relational, and established that this governs not only relations with other thous, but also with God as Thou and the unconditional nature of that relationship. Man is not created complete, with a universal essence, but is made to respond to God in a special relationship. His value is not that he embodies some moral principle, in a Kantian sense, but because without any merit he is loved by God: 'Man is only one pole of a relationship, and that not the primal determinative pole. The principle of his being lies outside him; he is essentially one who is called into being by Another, and whose life from beginning to end is a *responsive* existence' [TWA, 256]. All this can be said, and could be expanded, but it will be recalled that the subject of his dissertation, beyond consideration of the implications of the I-Thou philosophy was to be a rethinking of the 'personality of God'. The application of the philosophy, replacing the classical metaphysical base, was to deal not only with one side of the relation, but with the implications for Christology and the doctrine of the

Trinity. To this other 'pole' JATR now turns his attention.

The I-Thou philosophy has immediate relevance to Christology, to the doctrine of the incarnation. The Chalcedonian formula of the two natures of Christ provides a good example of a theological doctrine based on the premises of the classical metaphysical position. On this view the eternal Logos takes on impersonal humanity and a body. In its kenotic form, the doctrine identifies certain divine attributes which can be set aside during the incarnation. But on the new theory the uniqueness of Christ must lie in his relationship to God: 'He was man simply because He stood in the human relation to God, other men and the world. And yet He who existed in this relation was none other than God Himself. God constituted Himself man by assuming the "Thou" relation to God' [TWA, 227]. We might pause here to ask whether JATR has not fallen into the trap of attempting to solve someone else's problem. Is he not trying to use the personalist philosophy to solve a dilemma deriving from the premises of the classical position? The same danger can be seen in his treatment of the *kenosis*: 'We do not think that any Christology can fit the Biblical facts which does not start from a genuine and consistent limitation of the Divine knowledge and powers of the Incarnate within the bounds of the human organs as their sole channels of expression' [TWA, 228]. He is more consistent when dealing with what it means for Christ to become man: 'The relations are no longer external to, but constitutive of, His essence as human' [TWA, 237]. He adopts a Kierkegaardian mode in saying that to the objective glance there should be nothing extra-ordinary about the incarnate One, only to the subjective eye of faith. The suspicion remains, however, that he is still reinterpreting at the level of classical assumptions and has not managed to return to the Bible itself. Similarly in dealing with the work of Christ he insists that Christ must have been *a* man and not in some sense *Man*: 'Only if Christ had conquered thus – as a historical individual – could his victory have any relevance to ourselves' [TWA, 251]. But again, is he not offering in personalist terms the solution to a problem which only arises because of objectifying assumptions which he should uncover to reject? He is probably more consistent in claiming, 'He is the type of humanity in that he as an "individual" does what every man must as an "individual" himself do' [TWA, 252]. However that might be, it illustrates just how difficult it is to make a radical break with an all-pervasive model of thinking.

In Part II of the dissertation JATR considers the implication of the new philosophy for the doctrine of God. The divine attributes must now be understood not as predicates of the divine being as such and without reference to any other person or thing. God is love:

> Comprehended in these monosyllables is the whole of the Hebraic conception of the One whose Being *is* a completely personal relationship to every single part of creation, who has no other existence except existence in a relation of this quality, and whose every attribute is but a way of working of a single, infinite, eternal, holy and omnipotent Love. For the Bible, the attributes of God are not a sum of separable qualities definable in terms of themselves (e.g. power, knowledge, goodness, etc.) and inhering in a neutral and undifferentiated 'substance' of Pure Being. [TWA, 258]

In this Part of the dissertation JATR will therefore undertake to show how the traditional attributes are actually modes of the divine love at work. Other traditional topics, such as divine freedom and necessity, can be properly discussed only in this context. God's love for his creation represents not an insufficiency or imperfection, as a need might have been regarded in the ancient world, but the overflowing of his love. More generally, what is revealed is not the being of God, but his will. This is a further criticism of the classical tradition: 'What God revealed Himself as having *done* was fitted as best as it could be into an already existent picture of what He *was*. *Will* was subordinated to *Being* and *ont*ological rather than *thelemat*ological categories have dominated the formulation of Christian metaphysics' [TWA, 285]. (The neologism 'thelematological', concerning that which refers to 'the will', JATR ascribes to Quick).

How then is the doctrine of God affected if the premises of the classical traditions are replaced with those of the personalist philosophy, which JATR takes to be closer to the Hebraic understanding? He considers first of all the divine attribute of omnipotence. In his first letter to the Church in the Greek city of Corinth, Paul deals with the power of God. What he says on the subject would contradict all that they had hitherto assumed. His gospel is of Christ crucified, 'the power of God and the wisdom of God' (1 Cor. 1.23–4). He is not saying that in the crucified Christ there is neither divine power nor divine wisdom, but to the contrary this is precisely where they are revealed. And if what is revealed is 'folly to Gentiles' it must be because what Paul is claiming as divine wisdom and divine power is completely different from the traditional understanding of omnipotence and omniscience. 'Yet', as JATR asks with justification,

> what Christian metaphysics has in fact started here? On the contrary, the wisdom of Greece has been too much for the foolishness of the preaching. The attributes concerned have been defined without reference to the Cross, in terms of an infinity of potency and knowledge which has no place

64

within it for the total constriction of both which Calvary presents. [TWA, 287]

Christian theology which has relied on the classical metaphysical position has taken on board an understanding of God and the divine attributes. These not only pre-date the incarnation and the crucifixion but are in no way rejected, challenged or even modified by them. JATR criticizes the Thomistic position. 'The facts of revelation neither determine in advance, nor modify in retrospect, the categories in which the nature of the Godhead are described' [TWA, 292]. The wisdom of men, epitomized in Greek metaphysics, established by reason the attributes of God. What happened in Christ must therefore be fitted into this framework. It can be done, but at what cost! The revelation must not be of God disclosing himself for the first time, but merely how what was already known by human reason and assumptions is confirmed. How could the omnipotent, omniscient God be present in such events? That is a considerable metaphysical problem. But the alternative approach is to ask, If God was indeed present in these events, how should we now understand the divine attributes? 'The Bible testifies to an omnipotence of a very different kind – a power in God which is at its most effective in the weakness and impotence of a dying man' [TWA, 293]. In the classical tradition the omnipotence of God is clearly not present in the Crucified One, therefore he must have set it aside during his sojourn on earth. But if, according to the gospel proclaimed by Paul, the omnipotence of God *is* revealed in Christ, then it must be a completely new understanding of power and how it operates. Whatever is 'set aside', it is not the divine nature. That nature is revealed in Christ the servant, obedient even to death. According to JATR, as he applies the personalist perspective there is no other nature of God, separate from Christ and from the world. That belongs to the classical metaphysic. 'The fundamental statement is not that God is "Actus Purus" but that "God is Love" ' [TWA, 297]. God is revealed in Christ because he takes the form of a servant, not in spite of this fact. JATR is critical of Thomism at this point. 'There is a strain of docetism ineradicable from its Christology. It sees the flesh always as what veils, rather than what reveals the Deity' [TWA, 304].

The classical tradition maintained in its understanding of omnipotence that there could be no limit to the divine power. But this cannot be the way to approach the divine activity when God is love, when the divine Thou seeks the human I: 'For an infinite love *must* reveal itself through limitation, since to respect the frontier of the "other" is involved in the very idea of love' [TWA, 310]. Divine omnipotence should not be approached ontologically, with assertions about a power which can perform any act which is not logically self-contradictory. Divine omnipotence must begin from God's will, and what love wishes to achieve.

Omnipotence as traditionally understood has meant that God must have the last word, either by justly condemning sinners to damnation, or by a universalism in which all are saved, regardless. But neither way owes anything to the love of God revealed in Christ. Love must allow for the possibility that it will be flouted: it is not love if it seeks to hide behind justice, refusing to forgive. Nor can love coerce the other. What then is omnipotence when God is love? In the I-Thou relationship omnipotence means that there is no insurmountable barrier between God and the individual, nor any finally impregnable defence against the love of God shown in Christ. Paul's words can refer to both positions. 'For I am sure that neither death, nor life, nor angels, nor principalities, nor things present, nor things to come, nor powers, nor height, nor depth, nor anything else in all creation, will be able to separate us from the love of God in Christ Jesus our Lord ' (Rom. 8.38–9).

JATR goes on to consider the attribute of eternity and the question of God's relationship to time, in which there is an even more marked contrast between the new and traditional positions. Theology has been dominated by Greek assumptions: 'God is absolutely immutable, and temporal succession or duration cannot enter into His experience. To postulate a real "not yet" in His apprehension would be to ascribe "potentiality" to Him' [TWA, 342]. On this view God is unchanging, unaffected by events in history. He is therefore above and beyond time, without motion and not participating in it. But this is not the biblical understanding of God. He is unchanging in the sense that his love and faithfulness remain the same, no matter the sins and failings of men. He is Lord of history, not by dissociating himself from it, but by pursuing his purposes within it. Once again we see the contrast of the ontological and the thelematological perspectives.

Even the two Greek words for time, *chronos* and *kairos*, illustrate the contrast in the positions: 'The difference in their meaning corresponds exactly to the difference between the "It" and the "Thou" view-points' [TWA, 376]. God's time, as Lord of history, is not marked by the even ticking of a cosmic clock, but the urgency of decision. He sets before his people times when they must choose. God's time is related to his purposes: 'But do not ignore this one fact, beloved, that with the Lord one day is as a thousand years, and a thousand years as one day' (2 Pet. 3.8). JATR takes this to mean that

God's will will be done in his time, and its fulfilment cannot be measured chronologically.

But there is an even more striking difference between the two positions. When the traditional attributes of omniscience and eternity are taken together, God already knows the outcome of all events: the future is therefore determined. But if God is understood in terms of I-Thou relationships, then this cannot be so. If God wishes to enter into actual relations with others then this can only be real if it includes freedom. The future cannot have already been determined: that would destroy I-Thou relationships and reduce God's relationship to history to an objective I-It. 'If the reality of the "Thou" of freedom, decision and responsibility, is to be maintained, this absolute non-existence of the future must at all costs be insisted upon' [TWA, 358].

JATR is highly critical of Thomism at this point and claims that it cannot take seriously the biblical presentation of God as the *living, personal* God. Indeed the issue is so fundamental as to be writen into the very title of the dissertation itself. *Thou Who Art* stands in deliberate contrast to the Thomistic work of Eric Mascall, *He Who Is*.

> Nothing is more significant than the different treatment accorded to the Biblical statement about the ultimate name and nature of God – the 'I AM THAT I AM'. It is the foundation of both the Hebraic and of Hellenistic theology. But for the latter, it is transformed into a substantival, impersonal, timeless 'It-existence'. The Original 'I am', that primal Word of deep calling unto deep, is transposed into the third person, into the relationless 'He who is' . . . [TWA, 363–4]

As we come to the end of this second Part of the dissertation JATR draws his argument together. He claims that Thomism and the classical tradition in theology begin with necessary divine attributes which derive from Greek metaphysical thinking. They not only describe the divine being in some particular, but in forming a systematic account, must be logically compatible with each other. This presents an objective picture of God which determines his relationship with the world and precludes any revision in the light of events in history:

> In the course of this section an attempt has been made to adumbrate some of the lines along which an adequate conception of the personality of God can be wrought out. The traditional theology, with its categories of substance and causality, its analysis of pure being and its attempted 'proofs', has left us with an 'It-God, a 'God of the third person', between whom and the 'Thou' of religious faith there is fixed an impassable gulf. [TWA, 403–4]

By contrast JATR is confident that the new personalist philosophy can assist the exposition of a more truly biblical faith. 'In this matter, the "I-Thou" philosophy has proved itself a true "handmaid of theology" ' [TWA, 410]

JATR then concludes Part II with a programmatic indication of how he sees the future for theology. In the Preface he claimed that the application of the personalist perspective had not been systematically attempted. He clearly considered that he had made a start:

> What is needed is, indeed, a new 'Summa' – one which will interpret the Biblical revelation in terms of a philosophy that has allowed the Bible's categories to come to their own. But this is something for which we may have to wait many years, perhaps generations. We stand as yet only at the opening of the vista that lies ahead. [TWA, 410]

With these words the young scholar draws to an end over two hundred and fifty pages of impressive analysis and argument. I can imagine, therefore, that the original examiners might have observed with a certain heaviness of heart that the text then continues for another three hundred pages. And worse, that the subject of Part III is the application of the new philosophical perspective to the doctrine of the Trinity! Those who now wish to enter this territory must do so without their present guide! The treatment of this issue is impressive not only for its historical scholarship but for the confident and incisive way in which the new perspective is applied, but our purpose in all this is already well served. We have examined the formation of a position which was to be presupposed throughout the rest of JATR's theological writings. Perhaps because of his practical involvement in the life and administration of the Church and the development of his New Testament work, JATR never attempted to carry out his own programme to produce a new Summa. By comparison with his massive and scholarly dissertation his subsequent theological works seem occasional and fragmentary, but of the need for such a fundamental rethinking of theology he was never in any doubt. The responsibilities of a bishop and the enforced immobility of a bad back coincided, in the providence of God, to enable him to take up the issue in a more direct, comprehensible and accessible form, issuing in the publication of *Honest to God*.

7 Honest to God

In Part One we discussed JATR's New Testament writings. As a classical scholar his motto could have been: 'To the texts themselves.' His lifelong concern was to get behind presuppositions about various subjects and to establish what the New Testament actually says. Indeed such was his narrow concern with this goal that we had cause to question whether in concentrating on what the text said he sometimes failed to continue the hermeneutical task to establish what the texts *meant*. It was, however, in his theological works that JATR took up this point, carrying it forward with the evangelical concern for what it means for today. The pattern of his theological writings has already emerged in his dissertation. For JATR the norm of Christian faith is the Bible, particularly the New Testament. Writing now as a Christian theologian and not simply as a classical scholar, he wishes to communicate the faith to his contemporaries. But fewer and fewer accept it, at least in the form in which it is presented. The conclusion often drawn from this observation is that modern man is sinful, hard of heart and that he has deliberately and wilfully closed his ears to the Good News in Christ Jesus. No doubt in every age there are many of whom that is true, but there are other indicators which suggest that this generation is no more evil than its predecessors, and indeed in at least some respects a good deal more humane. JATR, in face of widespread and increasing alienation from religion, makes a very different assumption. If the truth is put before man in the Bible and large numbers of good and reasonable people today do not respond to it, the blockage must lie in the medium, that is in theology. If there is one thing which characterizes everything which JATR wrote it is his deep commitment to the Bible as the word of God. As an evangelical, in the broad sense in which we have been using this term, he assumes that this word is addressed to everyone, and that if they can hear the word they will believe. His theological writings are therefore a consistent attempt to bring the Bible to modern man. He is confident that if the two can be brought together then modern man will respond to God's truth in Christ. The primary obstacle to this happening is not sin, though sin is present in the world now as in any other time. The problem in the first instance is not bad faith but bad theology. For JATR it is bad theology which has prevented modern man from being addressed by the word of God. His aim as a theologian is to reinterpret theology so that it is true to the Bible – but true not simply to what the Bible says, but to what it means. In this JATR the evangelical theologian goes beyond JATR the classical New Testament scholar. And here, as in Part One, we find him radically criticizing tradition when it is not traditional enough, that is when it is not biblical.

We have already observed at least part of this pattern in *Thou Who Art*. It begins with the assumption that Christian faith should be rooted in and guided at all points by the Bible. The dissertation was therefore a sustained critique of traditional theology where it is based on assumptions and guided by criteria which are incompatible with the biblical understanding of God. Perhaps because it was an academic dissertation JATR did not go on to display the third element, the evangelical concern for the communication of the faith to modern man. However, that was clearly his intention in the long term, and it becomes a central feature of his own theological writings.

The three elements – of biblical norm, communication with modern man, and criticism of traditional theological formulations – all come together in the first theological book which JATR wrote, entitled *In the End God. . . : A Study of the Christian Doctrine of the Last Things*, first published in 1950. It appeared in a series entitled 'Theology for Modern Men'. The doctrine of the first things was the centre of fierce controversy in the nineteenth century, but at last with considerable effort a reconciliation was reached between religion and the modern (scientific) world-view. The doctrine of the last things is, if anything, more incredible to modern man and more incompatible with the modern world-view. Yet although the doctrine has become central in theology and especially biblical studies in the twentieth century, it 'has hardly stirred a ripple of controversy. The entire Christian eschatological scheme has simply been silently dismissed without so much as a serious protest from within the ecclesiastical camp' [IEG, 27].

From the emerging pattern to which we have referred above, we should expect JATR to do three things. Firstly to claim that modern man need not be alienated from this doctrine; secondly to blame theology for misrepresenting it; and thirdly to attempt to clarify what the biblical basis of the doctrine really is, confirming that it is not alien to the experience of modern man. If we describe this movement as a theological circle, we shall find that JATR can enter it at any point. Each point is covered, but it is not necessary to treat them in any particular order. In this case he begins with contemporary experience. And herein lies the paradox, that the very experience which makes the doctrine incredible in its theological form, that very experience is not at all alien to the biblical faith, properly understood. JATR was writing in the years immediately following the Second World War, in a period in which Europe had been all but destroyed by National Socialism advancing from Germany. The conflict had spread throughout the world before fascism was finally overpowered. And yet the very lines along which that conflict was ended became the frontiers of another, a Cold War. The modern world, which in the West at least has seen a decline in institutional religion, has been dominated by the rise of two great ideologies, communism and fascism, Marxism and National Socialism. They cannot be understood simply as irreligious systems, for in many fundamental respects they have replaced religion for their followers. They have offered new values and social structures, but more important for our purposes here, they have created new mythologies. Each has in its own way provided an understanding of past history, which includes an account of the origins of evil. Each has offered a means of redemption and the promise of a new future. These ideologies have given millions new meaning and purpose for life, a faith that history is moving towards its consummation in which their hopes will be fulfilled and their sufferings in the present rewarded.

This then is JATR's starting-point, and herein lies the paradox. The New Testament is dominated by a highly eschatological faith. The modern world is dominated by eschatological faiths. Why then is modern man alienated from Christian faith? Surely his susceptibility towards teleological faiths, even including their own mythologies, should mean that he is *more* not *less* capable of hearing and accepting the gospel. It must be that Christian theology is not properly presenting the eschatological dimension of Christian faith.

JATR therefore turns to examine how biblical eschatology has been distorted till in its present form it is both incredible and unacceptable to a generation which is otherwise well-equipped to understand and espouse it. The actual exposition of New Testament eschatology, and in particular the eschatology of Jesus himself, would later be published in *Jesus and His Coming*, which we examined in some detail in Part One above. There we saw that according to JATR the influence of apocalyptic thinking led to a formulation of eschatology which tended, 'if not to destroy it, at any rate to bring it into disrepute' [IEG, 52]. He repeats his discussion of *chronos* and *kairos*, set out in his dissertation. *Chronos* describes time in an objective and impersonal way, it is 'momentary rather than momentous' [IEG, 57]. The ultimate is therefore no longer the moment of highest importance, but

71

simply the last moment. In terms of *kairos* the coming of Christ is *the* eschatological event, everything is given meaning and purpose with respect to it. But in terms of *chronos* the ultimate must be not the coming, but a second coming, in the last moment. Although *kairos*, God's time, is historic, it must be described mythologically. The last things, understood chronologically, are assumed to be historical, but 'the Christian has no more knowledge of or interest in the final state of this planet than he has of its first' [IEG, 80–1]. When eschatology is understood objectively theology sets itself up as a deductive science with privileged information. For JATR theology must be inductive, arising from experience of God. In this we see the perspective of his dissertation influencing his position. Eschatology must not be approached impersonally, it must express how things are now if God is the God revealed in Christ. He quotes E. Lampert with approval: 'Few realize that, in point of fact, *eschatology is not the teaching about the last things after everything else but rather the teaching about the relation of all things to the 'last things' or, as it were, about the lastness of all things*' [IEG, 134].

When theology presents eschatology objectively and impersonally, it makes it not only incredible to modern man but completely irrelevant to his life now. The eschatological perspective, properly understood, refers to the way in which the present is related to the historic Christ event, not chronologically, but teleologically. *Tetelestai*, 'It is finished' (John 19.30); in Christ the purpose of God is at last revealed. Eschatology is therefore placed at the centre of Christian faith and not at the chronological end. The issues traditionally associated with it are now discussed, including human freedom, divine judgement, the omnipotence of love, universalism, death, the resurrection of the body, heaven and hell. These have already been discussed within the dissertation. They are dealt with in the context of the I-Thou relationship with God and not with reference, objectively or impersonally, to supposed events lying in the inconceivably distant future.

Along these lines JATR brings together the three elements of his theological method. He expounds the biblical faith, criticizes traditional theology, and indicates how this faith is open to modern man. Ironically, of the three faiths with which we started, Christian faith is now the only one which has clarified its relationship to history. The two ideological faiths still confuse the mythological and the historic: it is they rather than religion which should be incredible to modern man.

In the End God was published while JATR was teaching at Wells

Theological College. He had been appointed to lecture in New Testament and ethics, in addition to his work as chaplain. He was soon to move to Cambridge, to be Dean of Clare College, where he would establish his reputation as a New Testament scholar. Because of these commitments he did not have the opportunity of pursuing his original theological concerns, and it was not until 1963, after his consecration as Bishop of Woolwich, that he took them up again. Looking back a few years later he could see a clear continuity:

> So *Honest to God* was born. The underlying concern had not changed. It was still to give expression to the form of the personal at the level of the universe as a whole, to the overwhelming conviction of the ultimate reality of the 'Thou' at the heart of all things. [EIG, 22–3]

While this is perfectly clear to anyone who has read his dissertation, it was far from clear to those who first encountered JATR's work in *Honest to God*. In consequence, as already indicated, many misread it, misunderstood it, assumed that they knew in advance what he was advocating, questioned his competence to deal with the issues, or took the patronizing view that he was only rehashing what others had written. At the end of our discussion of the dissertation JATR looked forward to reinterpreting Christian doctrine from the perspective of personalist philosophy. Now he felt the need to attempt a reinterpretation within his new pastoral and evangelical situation. But for most readers it was necessarily like being offered the answer to a mathematical problem without access to the careful and even laborious calculations on which it was based, like being shown a recommended route without any indication of how this road had been selected from the various alternatives. Although to readers of *Honest to God* it may have seemed a new venture for the bishop, JATR saw it as a time to take stock of where he had reached: '. . . I returned to the doctrine of God some fifteen years later and tried to gather up what in the interval had been collecting under the surface. . .' [EIG, 22].

Neither the author nor the publisher of *Honest to God* could have anticipated that the book would sell over a million copies or be translated into seventeen languages. Nor would it have been possible to write the book any differently if this response could have been anticipated. What should have been changed? It obviously communicated its message admirably. It must have had a predominantly lay readership, untrained in theology and unfamiliar with theological terms or references. For some reason this was not an obstacle, and readers intuitively knew that this was written for them, in their situations, even if at times the argument got away from them. As in so many matters, the fact that the right *questions* were asked may have been more important than the tentative answers suggested.

If in his New Testament studies the missionary element – what we have been referring to as the broadly evangelical concern – is almost entirely absent, it becomes here both the starting-point and the guiding consideration. It is possible, indeed normal, to treat theological subjects historically, to establish what was believed at some formative period in the life of the early Church. Any revision of them would then be according to canons of criticism internal to theology. JATR's dissertation could, as we have seen, be taken as an example of this approach. The question, And what does this doctrine mean for us today? is by comparison motivated by a concern for religious edification. It is not regarded as a very academic question: it belongs within homiletics rather than dogmatics, in the pulpit rather than the library. In addition to the homiletical question, for the edification of those already within the Church, there is the evangelical concern for those outwith it. Traditionally these two statements of the faith were described as dogmatic and apologetic. The *apologia* was a statement of the faith which accommodated it in some respects to the thought-forms, culture or religious assumptions of the potential converts. But once within the Church converts would be expected to come to hold the faith in its normative dogmatic form. For this reason many theologians regard the question, What does it mean today? as less serious and worthy of their academic efforts. Their answer is that it means exactly the same today as it meant in the fourth century or in the first century. The fear is of course that if the dogmatic form is compromised by any modern apologetic tendency, the continuity will be lost and so will the faith.

JATR begins *Honest to God* by acknowledging the sincerity of these theologians and churchmen, 'who see the best, and indeed the only, defence of doctrine to lie in the firm reiteration, in fresh and intelligent contemporary language, of "the faith once delivered to the saints" ' [HTG, 7]. But even at that time it was perfectly clear that the best of such restatements were failing to convince the contemporary generation. Failing to convince: indeed, failing to make any sense. The message was not being rejected: it was not capable of being understood. Quite apart from what *should* be the case, even at a statistical level more of the same would lead to disaster. JATR as a bishop in London therefore found himself in a missionary situation in which the message was incomprehensible. People were not rejecting the gospel: they could not make a responsible choice about it in the form in which it was being presented. If this had been true of the worst, wildest, most inhumane and reprobate sections of society, then perhaps it would have been possible to see in their indifference somehow a confirmation of the hard words of Jesus about sheep and goats. More distressing was the fact that it was not the worst but the best of that generation who could not choose for or against religion.

JATR makes several preliminary points. The first is, as we have already noted, that the fault does not lie with those outside the Church. We saw in his first book, *In the End God . . .* that he assumes that the gospel is for everyone to hear, that properly understood they will be able to see the similarity between their own experiences and the situation of the early Church: 'For while they imagine they have rejected the Gospel, they have in fact largely been put off by a particular way of thinking about the world which quite legitimately they find incredible' [HTG, 8]. He therefore begins with the assumption that contemporary people basically know what is real and unreal, and on this basis they are perfectly justified in their rejection of a great deal of religion. The second point follows from this, that the fault lies not with the modern world, but with theology. The new element in the current situation is that dogmatic theology no longer provides a secure base. Certain things which are known and taken for granted in the modern world are incompatible with the old dogmatic theology. In such cirumstances modern people cannot and *should not* accept what they are being asked to believe. The current situation therefore cannot be met by apologetics if that means some minor cosmetic adjustments to the manner in which traditional dogmatic theology is expressed. JATR sees that a much more comprehensive approach is required if the Church is not to have 'lost out to all but a tiny religious remnant. A much more radical recasting, I would judge, is demanded, in the process of which the most fundamental categories of our theology – of God, of the supernatural, and of religion itself – must go into the melting' [HTG, 7]. A third point is that if the old distinction between dogmatics and apologetics is questionable, so is the line dividing those who are inside and those who are outside: 'Moreover, the line to which I am referring runs right through the middle of myself, although as time goes on I find there is less and less of me left, as it were, to the right of it' [HTG, 8]. Christians are also inhabitants of the modern world, and many assumptions embedded in dogmatic theology are as alien to them as to their non-Christian contemporaries. What is required is not a watering down of the faith to enable them still to count themselves as Christians. As Christians they now see that in quite fundamental respects dogmatic theology is a misrepresentation of the gospel. It may not have misrepresented it when it was first formulated, within its own time and cultural place, but it misrepresents, distorts and sells short the faith in this time and cultural place. There is a fourth, more ominous point to be made at the outset. Many of those who are comfortable with the old formulations, who were described at the beginning as attempting to defend the faith by a 'firm reiteration' of the tradition, will regard this new attempt at reinterpretation as a betrayal. They will take an entirely negative view of the work to which these new missionaries feel called. But more than that will be the bitterness of the accusations made by those who still affirm the traditional categories against those who do not: 'What dismays me is the vehemence – and at bottom the insecurity – of those who feel that the Faith can only be defended by branding as enemies within the camp those who do not' [HTG, 9]. If JATR knew this to be the case before the book was published, he could hardly have been prepared for the forms in which it was later to manifest itself. Yet, for all that, there is a final point, both prophetic and courageous: 'What I have tried to say, in a tentative and exploratory way, may seem to be radical, and doubtless to many heretical. The one thing of which I am fairly sure is that, in retrospect, it will be seen to have erred in not being nearly radical enough' [HTG, 10]. What matter how far along the road he progressed: much more difficult was the attempt to convince theologians and church leaders that the present road was the wrong road, leading to disaster and unworthy of the custodians of the faith that once was given. What must have given JATR heart in this difficult and thankless task was, by comparison, the enthusiasm and gratitude with which the book was received by ordinary people, both outside and inside the Church.

Since this is to be a book about God, or the doctrine of God, we might have expected it to begin with a popular account of the main themes of JATR's dissertation, *Thou Who Art*. But in spite of his own perception of the work in retrospect, as already quoted above, no hint of this is given in the opening chapters. Consequently it is not at all clear to the reader what JATR's own position is. He begins by outlining alternative ways in which God's relationship to the world has been conceived. His own personalist approach is not brought forward, and in consequence it is all too easy to think his conception of the problem superficial or merely impressionistic. In the Bible God is spoken of as being 'up there'. The three-storey universe is presupposed, with heaven above the earth and hell beneath. JATR claims that this picture was taken literally. There may however be an element of anachronism here. To take something literally it is probably necessary to have reached a level of consciousness in which alterna-

tives are presented. However this may be, it does not affect the point
that the three-storey universe provided the world-view within which
the biblical writers functioned. Paul and John speak of Christ coming
and going, and the ascension account in Acts presupposes the
structure, however literally *it* is to be taken. Because of certain
developments in relatively modern times, it is no longer possible to
share this ancient world-view. However, an alternative way of
thinking has been developed which has enabled a fundamental change
in perspective to take place with remarkably little disturbance: 'For in
place of a God who is literally or physically "up there" we have
accepted, as part of our mental furniture, a God who is spiritually or
metaphysically "out there" ' [HTG, 13].

We now come to the fundamental premise of *Honest to God*: 'But
the signs are that we are reaching the point at which the whole
conception of a God "out there", which has served us so well since the
collapse of the three-decker universe, is itself becoming more of a
hindrance than a help' [HTG, 15–16]. It is because of this assertion
that the hostility, abuse and name-calling began. And it need not. It
seems quite obvious to many who are still comfortable with the
traditional terminology that to deny that this terminology can any
longer be used is to deny the existence of God. At this point I wish to
intervene, with some comments on what JATR might have been
expected to do, which could well have avoided the confusion and
alarm caused by this early premise. The other side of the coin is that if
JATR had begun differently his argument might have had a more
positive effect on those whose minds were immediately closed against
anything which was to follow, regardless of its merits.

For those familiar with JATR's dissertation it is surprising that he
does not make use of its basic position at the outset of *Honest to God*:
He speaks of a transition from one conceptual framework to another,
characterized by the substitution of the picture of God 'out there' for
that of God 'up there'. What we should have expected as this point was
for him to indicate the basis of this new framework. No doubt he
would have said that theology transferred from the highly mythological biblical world-view to the highly metaphysical world-view
based largely on Aristotelian ontology. The fact that he does not so
identify the basis of 'out there' thinking has unfortunate consequences. Religious people have tended to find developments in the
modern world disturbing, and to interpret them very often as
irreligious. The most famous example is the nineteenth-century
controversy over evolution, but the whole movement referred to as
secularization is another. JATR is now claiming that 'out there'

thinking is now becoming a 'hindrance'. Many readers – and more who heard only second-hand accounts of the book – must have taken this to mean that the modern world was now attempting to undermine the very foundations of the faith, the doctrine of God. Dogmatic theologians might see in this the realization of their worst fears, namely, that the substance of the faith was being sold out to accommodate it to the thought-forms acceptable to the modern age. This interpretation could have been avoided. I am not setting out here what I should have done, but rather what JATR might well have done, given his own position as already worked out in his dissertation.

It will be recalled that *Thou Who Art* presents a sustained critique of traditional theology based on classical Greek ontology. As already indicated, questions such as, 'And what does it mean for us today?' or, 'How are we to communicate with modern man?' play no part in this academic work. JATR argues that, (a) the classical ontology is wrong, misrepresenting human experience, (b) traditional theology is wrong, misrepresenting the biblical understanding of God, and (c) personalist philosophy offers a more promising basis for the reinterpretation of the doctrine of God, which is different from anything in the ancient world, but which is more faithful to the fundamental tenets of biblical religion. With these points in mind his opening analysis in *Honest to God* could have been presented quite differently in important respects. An alternative to 'out there' thinking has to be found, not because atheists or secular fellow-travellers do not like it, but because it misrepresents God as revealed in Jesus Christ. This way of thinking has to go regardless of how the modern world-view has developed. In this respect Christians have nothing to fear from yet another change in secular thinking. If JATR had taken this line then he could have appealed to all Christians to join in this attempt to find a more faithful way of speaking about God and thinking about his relationship to the world, natural and social. The necessity for change would not then have been based on the vague cultural observation that people cannot think in this way any more – when clearly many if not most Christians still did think in this way – but rather on the clear and telling arguments of his dissertation, that this kind of theology must go.

Even if his arguments, or a simplified version of them, had been included in *Honest to God*, few of his readers would have felt equipped to join in the enterprise. JATR himself had anticipated that the transition would engage several generations. But at least they might have approved of the project and wished it well. As it was many took fright and opposed any call for change. If truth be told, for them 'up there' and 'out there' thinking came to about the same thing. It must be reckoned a grave mistake on the part of JATR that he did not sufficiently distinguish for his readers between the ancient mythology and the ancient ontology. The former could be preserved and understood through demythologizing; the latter had been overtaken by the modern world-view and shown to be mistaken and wrong. According to JATR's own premises there is nothing wrong with 'up there' thinking, so long as it is not taken literally: he can deal with that later. But 'out there' thinking is based not on a three-decker universe but on a metaphysical system which JATR now regards as wrong, which cannot be rehabilitated. Because he did not make clear the basis of each way of thinking, those who did not think there was any real difference between them assumed that in rejecting one he was rejecting both. To reject a way of speaking about God and the world shared by the biblical writers and Jesus himself deserves more careful presentation than JATR gave it at this point. However that may be, JATR's highly abrasive start, without the analysis which we have suggested, must have alienated many who resented the category into which he relegated them: 'Have we seriously faced the possibility that to abandon such an idol may in the future be the only way of making Christianity meaningful, except to a few remaining equivalents of flat-earthers. . . ?' [HTG, 17].

Honest to God was read with more enthusiasm by those outside the Church who could function with neither 'up there' nor 'out there', and also by Christians who realized at least intuitively that 'out there' thinking was somehow incompatible with their experience more generally. Thus the book became a source of division, or at least a line on which previous division hardened. This was doubly tragic, since it was no part of JATR's intention, and also because it prevented many able and committed Christians from participating in a long-term project which required to be undertaken then as now.

In retrospect JATR claimed that *Honest to God* was a continuation of the concerns first set out in his dissertation. It certainly should have been, and it would have been a rather diffferent book if it had been. But for what it is worth I am inclined to think that this is a view which JATR came to later, tidying things up with hindsight, as we all do. If he had begun the book on the basis of his dissertation the intellectual originality and religious integrity of *Thou Who Art* would have struck the reader from the outset. Instead, after fifteen years he seemed to forget that he was a philosopher and theologian of proven capability – 'For I am not writing this book as a professional theologian: indeed this is not my own academic field' [HTG, 26]. Yet the doctrine of God was precisely his original academic field. Instead, he begins with a vague and unsubstantiated observation about the way people think today, and then immediately goes on to declare his dependence on several contemporary theologians: 'I am struggling to think other people's thoughts after them. I cannot claim to have understood all I am trying to transmit' [HTG, 21]. Yet his own position in his dissertation was the place from which to begin. None of the theologians he was to use extensively had made anything like his critique of the whole tradition of Western metaphysical theology. Could he understand their thought? Personally I found passages in *Thou Who Art* more demanding than anything I have read in Tillich, Bonhoeffer or Bultmann. But for many the effect of his modest disclaimer was to aggravate the situation. They suspected he was beginning by selling out to secular humanists; now apparently he was slavishly following various (incompatible) fashions in German theology. He was later to describe *Honest to God* as his least original book. It could have been his most original if he had in fact, and not simply in hindsight, continued the work he had already begun in *Thou Who Art*.

After these critical comments, we can return to the main argument of *Honest to God* itself. JATR explicitly mentions the three theologians whom he has found important in his present reflections, but before he begins to deal with them it is possible to detect elements of what I should describe as his own position, not yet overlaid. Philosophers and most theologians who dialogue with them, take it for granted that God is a being 'out there' and that arguments for his existence can be evaluated, and his non-existence can be discussed. And yet this is a quite artificial way of proceeding:

> Rather, we must start the other way round. God, is by definition, ultimate reality. And one cannot argue whether ultimate reality *exists*. One can only ask what ultimate reality is like – whether, for instance, in the last analysis what lies at the heart of things and governs their working is to be described in personal or impersonal categories. [HTG, 29]

In passing we might admit to some amusement at this reverse play which JATR runs on the philosophers, many of whom adopt a rather superior attitude towards religion. Such philosophers like straw positions even when they themselves are drawn into the assumptions of a previous world-view: 'Is it necessary for the Biblical faith to be expressed in terms of this world-view, which in its way is as primitive philosophically as the Genesis stories are primitive scientifically?' [HTG, 33]. The transcendence of God must be affirmed, but is it necessary to express this in terms of a supernatural frame of reference? But as we have already noted, JATR in declaring an end to traditional theism omits to criticize the non-biblical ontology upon which it is based. After all, the deity so much discussed by philosophy of religion is not the biblical God, but the conception of God which JATR rejected in his dissertation. We have argued earlier that he does not sufficiently distinguish, in his own terms, between the 'up there' biblical tradition and the 'out there' metaphysical tradition. It is in fact the latter which on his own premises presents the greater problems: 'If Christianity is to survive, let alone to recapture "secular" man, there is no time to lose in detaching it from this scheme of thought. . .' [HTG, 43]. The fundamental objection to the conception of God 'out there' is that it does not describe the Christian experience of God, nor the biblical understanding of God's relationship to the world. How then is this relationship to be described if not on the model of tradition theism, of a Being over against the world? In turning for assistance to Tillich's concept of God as the 'ground of being' or the depths of existence, JATR seems to be simply exchanging one set of spatial metaphors for another. But of course Tillich in calling God 'Being itself' specifically rejected the idea that God is *a* being, even the greatest of all beings. What is said about God is not said about a being, but rather about reality. JATR, who in his dissertation was severely critical of Feuerbach, can at least on this occasion find something suggestive in his thought. Feuerbach claimed that 'To predicate personality of God . . . is nothing else than to declare personality as the absolute essence' [HTG, 49]. That, if it could be affirmed from experience, would be a tremendous act of faith, perhaps even more significant than declaring oneself on the existence of a being over against the world. In these terms

> Belief in God is the trust, the well-nigh incredible trust, that to give ourselves to the uttermost in love is not to be confounded but to be 'accepted', that Love is the ground of our being, to which ultimately we 'come home'.
>
> If this is true, then theological statements are not a description of 'the highest Being' but an analysis of the depths of personal relationships – or, rather, an analysis of the depths of *all* experience 'interpreted by love'. [HTG, 49]

If this is a general, phenomenological account of religion, it has its more specifically Christian form, 'that the final definition of this reality, from which "nothing can separate us", since it is the very ground of our being, is "the love of God in Christ Jesus our Lord" ' [HTG, 49–50].

JATR is fulsome in his praise of the great German–American theologian: 'This, I believe, is Tillich's great contribution to theology

– the reinterpretation of transcendence in a way which preserves its reality while detaching it from the projection of supranaturalism' [HTG, 56]. I believe that it was unfortunate that JATR allowed his exposition of Tillich to guide and to some extent to take over from his own understanding of the problem and his view of the most hopeful course to follow towards its solution. Although Tillich's position was in some respects suggestive and fruitful for JATR, it arose from very different premises. We have seen the influence which Buber's personalist philosophy exerted on the young JATR, and we began the discussion of this part of *Honest to God* with a quotation which ended with the emphasis on the ultimate as personal. Tillich, by his own account, came from a very different direction. He was an ontologist whose work was deeply influenced by Parmenides, Plato and Plotinus in the ancient world, Schelling in the modern. It is unfortunate that JATR gave the impression that he was really only repeating Tillich's critique of theism and supranaturalism. Thereby he omitted what he could have said, which Tillich never said.

This is not intended as a criticism of the work of Tillich, simply that JATR has something to say on his own account which is not found in Tillich and is in danger therefore of being omitted. A similar point might be made concerning JATR's use of Bonhoeffer. The prison writings of Bonhoeffer by their nature are fragmentary and programmatic. They are suggestive, and indeed they have suggested lines of development to different theologians which are mutually incompatible. But the impression is given that in Christology JATR simply produces an interpretation of the most famous of these enigmatic sayings. A case in point is the title chosen for chapter 4, 'The Man for Others'. But on closer inspection this is far from being the case. For JATR the starting-point for a new Christology is the rejection of supranaturalism and traditional theism. If God is no longer to be thought of as 'out there', as a being inhabiting another sphere of reality, then the traditional christological model no longer works. Christ cannot be a supranatural being who 'comes to' this world from 'out there'. If God and man are two unconnected beings then the God-man of traditional theology is never more than a divine visitant. The Chalcedonian doctrine of the two natures is no more than a statement of the problem. In fact JATR could have found support at this point in some very explicit criticisms which Tillich makes of this theology. JATR makes reference here to the Christmas story, but since he omitted earlier to give any continuing significance to the 'up there' mythological as opposed to the 'out there' metaphysical he is not well placed to make the following distinction. He probably wishes to say that the traditional theology (based on Greek metaphysics) is now untenable and meaningless, but that the biblical stories still retain their religious value. They can be demythologized to yield their spiritual teaching in a way that metaphysical theology cannot be. This approach owes something to Bultmann, whose work is referred to less often than that of Tillich and Bonhoeffer, but even so, the fundamental position is still that of *Thou Who Art*.

In passing we might call attention to the very ambiguous position given to Bultmann in *Honest to God*. At the outset he is listed as one of the big three, and yet he is hardly mentioned throughout the text, certainly not to the extent of the other two. Yet the distinction between the biblical world-view and the biblical message probably comes from Bultmann. Ironically, as we have noted, JATR docs not make use of this idea as much as he should, for example in distinguishing between 'up there', which is capable of reinterpretation, and 'out there', which is not. In this way, although Bultmann is said to be influential, and then largely ignored, he is in fact the only one of the three whose contribution is actually greater than JATR acknowledges. The irony here is heightened by the fact that Bultmann wrote an extremely perceptive review of *Honest to God*. He defended it against those German theologians who thought – as indeed JATR himself implied – that there was nothing new in it for them. It was Bultmann himself who saw that there was more to JATR's position than a mosaic of German theology. Specifically he noted that JATR was not arguing against speaking of God as a person, 'for the deepest level of reality is personal in character; it is love' [HTGD, 137].

Returning to our earlier point, neither does JATR's treatment of the christological doctrine of *kenosis* derive from Bonhoeffer. I wish to quote a long passage from this chapter dealing with the subject. Standing under the chapter heading as it does it might be assumed to be dependent on Bonhoeffer, but anyone familiar with JATR's early work will recognize that it comes entirely from the dissertation:

> It is in Jesus, and Jesus alone, that there is nothing of self to be seen, but solely the ultimate, unconditional love of God. It is as he emptied himself utterly of himself that he became the carrier of 'the name which is above every name', the revealer of the Father's glory – for that name and that glory is simply Love. The 'kenotic' theory of Christology based on this conception of self-emptying is, I am persuaded, the only one that offers much hope of relating at all satisfactorily the divine and the human in Christ. [HTG, 74]

This comes directly from JATR's personalist philosophy, owes nothing to Bonhoeffer and in fact strikes out in a quite different and positive direction. The rest of the quotation comes almost directly from JATR's dissertation:

> Yet the fatal weakness of this theory as it is stated in supranaturalist terms is that it represents Christ as stripping himself precisely of those attributes of transcendence which make him the revelation of God. The underlying assumption is that it is his omnipotence, his omniscience, and all that makes him 'superhuman', that must be shed in order for him to become truly man. On the contrary, it is as he empties himself not of his Godhead but of himself, of any desire to focus attention on himself, of any craving to be 'on an equality with God', that he reveals God. For it is in making himself nothing, in his utter self-surrender to others in love, that he discloses and lays bare the Ground of man's being as Love. [HTG, 74–5]

This personalist philosophy and in particular the critique of objective and impersonal divine attributes comes directly from *Thou Who Art* and the rejection of the classical theology based on Greek assumptions about the deity.

Having laid out his own personalist position, in which God is experienced as Thou 'in, with, and under' relationships with other thous, JATR can take up some points from Bonhoeffer, for example that Christ is 'the beyond in our midst'. But these points illustrate JATR's position, which has been carefully developed elsewhere in more detail than Bonhoeffer was in a position to do. Even Bonhoeffer's sayings about a non-religious understanding of Christianity were not new to JATR, who a few pages earlier quoted the words of John Macmurray: 'the great contribution of the Hebrew to religion was that he did away with it' [HTG, 61]. The right relationship to God depends on nothing religious, and indeed religion can be a barrier to it. Although JATR appreciated the work of Bonhoeffer we should not fall into the trap of assuming that his own work was in any sense simply an exposition of the prison writings.

The implications of all this run on into liturgy and ethics, but these are subjects to which we shall turn in Part Three. Re-reading *Honest to God* after a generation it is difficult to see why it caused such a stir. It is very easy to concentrate on the familiar passages from Tillich's *The Shaking of the Foundations*, Bonhoeffer's *Letters and Papers From Prison* and Bultmann's essay 'New Testament and Mythology'. But to do so is to miss JATR's own position. This is to a large extent his own fault, partly because he explicitly claims to be but a pedestrian follower of the great men, and partly because for some reason he omits so much of his own position developed in his doctoral dissertation. Yet what is quite clear is that his own position is more radical and fundamental than any of the other three. But because he purports to be representing their views rather than producing his own, his challenge to theology was never understood, let alone taken up. He did not conceive of it as simply his task, as if he alone could construct the new theology, but he did in subsequent books attempt to pursue the matter, partly by way of clarification and defence, partly breaking yet new ground. In everything he followed his theological motto: 'All I can do is to try to be honest – honest to God and about God – and to follow the argument wherever it leads' [HTG, 28].

8 The Divine Field

Included at the end of the posthumous collection of his papers, Where Three Ways Meet, is the complete bibliography of JATR's published works, a list which JATR himself kept up to date. It is interesting to compare bibliography with biography, what he published during the successive periods of his career. It begins in 1945, the year in which he completed *Thou Who Art*, and is followed by a few New Testament studies until 1950, when he published his first book, *In the End, God* . . . which we have already examined. From then until 1954 he produced articles on a variety of subjects, biblical, liturgical, doctrinal and ethical. It is not at all clear at this stage in which direction his work was to develop. In retrospect JATR seems to suggest that his mind was still occupied with the main themes of his dissertation, and that his transition to New Testament studies arose not through turning away from these matters, but precisely out of the attempt to clarify them further. He traces the movement, beginning from the dissertation: 'Personality is essentially a corporate, social phenomenon. Indeed, it was because of this emphasis that I was drawn into New Testament study through the insights of St Paul on "the body" (the nearest equivalent Biblical concept to our "personality") . . .' [EIG, 24]. However, once back at Cambridge and closely associated with C.F.D. Moule, biblical studies suddenly takes over. From 1955 till the publication of *Honest to God* in 1963 he published almost exclusively in the New Testament field. It was presumably for this reason that he claimed that by that time theology was not his academic field. But with the publication of *Honest to God* the position was entirely reversed, and for the next ten years JATR published virtually nothing at all in the New Testament area. His books and articles in that decade indicate how he had to respond, both positively and negatively, to the new situation into which he was catapulted. All his available time was spent in explaining what he had meant and defending himself against misrepresentation, innocent and wilful. But above all his publications in that period trace his attempts to continue with the quest which he had first set for himself and now found others expecting him to pursue either with them or on their behalf, namely the 'exploration into God'.

Many of these pieces were written for readers who had little contact with the Church. The fact that they were commissioned by the secular press would seem to be evidence of two things. The first is that JATR had raised issues which were important to a large number of people. The second is that these same people could not identify with the issues when dealt with in the traditional religious context. Both points support basic premises of JATR's position. We should therefore not be dismissive of these popular articles. Although not couched in the language of his dissertation, the treatment of these basic issues stems from his own distinctive theological position. They are not 'popular' in the sense of communicating in street language the old traditional theology, which theology it will be recalled JATR had criticized and largely rejected in its classical form. *But That I Can't Believe* was published in 1967 (and reprinted twice within the year). The first half of the book gathers together articles published in the *Sunday Mirror, TV Times, The Sun,* and *Tit-Bits* a salutary reminder that these mass media institutions are perfectly willing to treat their readership seriously if experts for their part can address people where they live.

The article which gives the book its title deals with the theological literalism which seems to require belief in the wrong aspects of religion. This is illustrated by the virgin birth and the resurrection. Do you believe in these things, Yes or No? 'For the answer I want to give is that I believe profoundly in what these doctrines are concerned to say but that the traditional ways of stating them so often put the crunch at quite the wrong place' [BTICB, 12]. In Part One we considered JATR's position on the New Testament evidence for these events, but we should be clear that now he is dealing with them from the perspective on religious faith. The truth of what happened is not at all the same as the truth of what is therein asserted: 'In the past men had not worried very much to ask what *kind* of truth they were asserting [BTICB, 14]. In another article JATR takes comfort from the positive outcome of a controversial book of the nineteenth century, *Essays and Reviews*: 'To-day we can see that, so far from selling the pass, they made it possible for intelligent people to accept the findings of modern science and still to believe in the Bible' [BTICB, 20]. Will that be the final evaluation of *Honest to God*? In the context of discussing Christmas, JATR interprets the Advent in ways which remind us that a serious academic position underpins his popular presentation: 'We are not just being battered around in an alien universe. The personal purpose behind it comes through to us in Jesus . . . [BTICB, 29]. Of the miracles, another topic which modern people find quite incredible, we see the same personalist context, which departs from the old metaphysical framework: 'They are remarkable not because in some arbitrary supernatural way they "break the laws of nature", but because "this is what love can do" when the creative and transforming presence of God is really given free rein' [BTICB, 31]. Life after death is also tackled, not from speculation about things of which we have no experience, but from those of which we have. 'From such a love neither cancer nor the H-bomb can separate . . . For the rest, with so many of my generation, I am prepared to be agnostic. I just can't imagine an after-life, and it doesn't help much to try' [BTICB, 46]. 'But nothing turns on what happens after death. For, whatever happens, we already know a reality we cannot escape from which nothing can separate' [BTICB, 46].

The articles forming the second part of the book were originally addressed to people more closely related to the Church, but who wish to keep the faith without having to be dishonest about what is credible to them today. The question, Do we need a God? enables JATR to take up the matter of human projection and also the concept of God as *a* being: 'I am convinced that this projection of God as a Being in another realm has equally succeeded in making him marginal to vast numbers of people to-day' [BTICB, 61]. He can also deal with the I-Thou and I-It relations. We are on familiar ground; the question is not does God exist, but what is our deepest experience of life? 'It comes with the same sense of inescapable, compelling objectivity – of something profoundly disturbing yet profoundly gracious, ultimate yet intimate' [BTICB, 63]. The ascension is dealt with not as a movement in space or a moment in time, but as the recognition by the early Church of 'Christ's ascendency, of his claim to control the entire universe. That's why the Ascension has been called the most political of all Christian doctrines' [BTICB, 79]. Discussions of the Holy Spirit, the Trinity, angels and the ministry are all set within JATR's new theological context.

The book ends on an up-beat. JATR takes comfort from a review of *Honest to God* which concluded with these words: 'The book is fundamentally not an essay in unorthodox theology, but a venture in evangelism' [BTICB, 122]. Well said, but as we have seen, those addressed are not in a remote country, but form a growing majority in this land: 'To-day it is not the heathen who are remote but the word "God" itself' [BTICB, 123]. He closes with the now-familiar claim. 'The difference between "I-Thou" and "I-It" is meaningful to a generation for whom the classical distinctions between time and eternity, God and the world, are almost meaningless. And this I

believe is an important way into theology – that is, to the understanding of ultimate reality as personal' [BTICB, 126].

These articles reflect the heady days of the period immediately
following the publication of *Honest to God*, a frenetic period which
must have alarmed as many as it excited. To his critics JATR seemed
to be sweeping things away for the hell of it (old-style theological
language). But to those who understand his fundamental position his
radicalism is the freedom – and the responsibility – of the Christian to
discover God in new ways: 'The centre for the Christian is firm: the
edges and the ends are gloriously and liberatingly open' [BTICB,
127].

These popular pieces were intended to communicate the essential
position of *Honest to God* to a wider audience: they do not extend the
argument substantially. However, in 1966 JATR delivered the
Raymond Fred West memorial lectures at Stanford University,
California. This provided him with the occasion to expand on the
subject, beyond the frontiers of his earlier book. The time was
opportune and JATR recalled the lines from Christopher Fry: 'Affairs
are now soul size. The enterprise is exploration into God.' The
following year an expanded form of the lectures appeared, entitled
Exploration into God.

Understandably JATR begins with a partial explanation of the fuss
created by his earlier book, attributing it to a 'failure of communication . . . more at the level of presupposition than of proposition'
[EIG, 14]. But, as we have seen, this may well have been presupposition on JATR's part, for he did not take time to establish his
own position, from *Thou Who Art*, at the outset. His criticism of
theism was therefore taken to mean, not surprisingly, that he was an
atheist. On this occasion he is more careful to begin with a positive
statement of his position. He can associate himself with the experience
of Pascal: 'Thou wouldst not be seeking me if thou hadst not found
me.' This is the paradox, since finding normally *ends* a quest: 'It is one
of those things of which one can simply say that it is so, reality is like
that: it is prevenient, life is response – and hence responsibility – to
something that encounters one, as it seems, with the claim of a 'Thou'.
This is the mystery that lies at its heart' [EIG, 16].

We might speculate that if *Honest to God* had begun like this its sales
might have been measured in hundreds rather than hundreds of
thousands. It is a very interesting personal confession of faith, but so
far as seekers are concerned it is about as helpful as the observation by
Rudolf Otto at the outset of his classic analysis of the experience of the
holy. Otto advised that if anyone had not had this experience, there

was no point in reading his book any further! And what if your experience of 'reality' is not that of being addressed by a Thou? 'It is one of those things of which one can simply say that it is so, reality is like that . . .' But how do you begin the quest if reality is not like that? *Exploration into God* is a much more defensive book, perhaps understandably so given the misrepresentations which had circulated about *Honest to God* and the frequent personal attacks on the religious integrity of its author. But by taking the more comfortable route of establishing his own religious position at the outset JATR must have closed the door to many who could no more affirm that reality is Thou than they could affirm the existence of the God of traditional theism.

This careful start is followed by a brief intellectual biography up to 1963, with references to his early studies of Kant, his discovery of 'Martin Buber's dull-brown paperback *I and Thou*', the influence of Kierkegaard and the writing of his PhD dissertation. By this route he traces his rejection of traditional theism and the successors of Boethius. We have already questioned whether sufficient use was made of all this in the actual writing of *Honest to God*, but it probably served its purpose on this occasion of warding off premature accusations of irreligion or atheism.

Exploration in any field – and this includes exploration into God – takes place either where there is no map, or at the very least where the existing maps are regarded as flawed and distorting. Where there is no proper map, 'Here be monsters'. Ignorance has not prevented maps from being filled in in detail, creating enduring myths in the process. Where there is an existing map, the attempt to project the three dimensions of reality onto the flat page of knowledge necessarily distorts. Exploration into God will be met by myths and projections, all held dear by many people and not recognized for what they are. To expose the myths and question the projections must not be seen as dismissing the field, but on the contrary as an invitation to all to contribute to the exploration.

> Similarly, the conception of God as *a* Being, a Person – like ourselves but supremely above or beyond ourselves – will, I believe, come to be seen as a human projection. (Most people already recognize this in the case of the Devil.) It is a way of making real and vivid to the imagination, by personification, the conviction that reality at its deepest is to be interpreted not simply at the level of its impersonal, mathematical regularities but in categories like love and trust, freedom, responsibility and purpose. The real question of God is not the *existence* of a Being whom we visualize as embodying these in his Person. It is whether this conviction about the ultimate nature and meaning of things is true. [EIG, 36]

90

The fear is always that something will be lost, that the result will be unreal. But JATR argues that this is the effect of the existing theological map: 'In fact, the projection may actually diminish the reality rather than express it' [EIG, 37]. And further, 'to represent the spiritual reality (in its transcendent aspect) as a Being in another realm is to make it unreal and remote for vast numbers of people today' [EIG, 37]. This is a gentle reminder of a point made in the dissertation but omitted from *Honest to God*, that the existing map is not all right, even for those who have used it all their lives. It is a 'hindrance' to a better knowledge of God.

The concern for the outsider, however, is still prominent. 'My concern has been positive – removing that which removes God' [EIG, 43]. He is claiming that the basis of religion is not the knowledge of the existence of a supernatural Being, but the experience of reality as fundamentally like a Thou. The most obvious way to picture this, to represent it on a map, is to speak of a divine Being. That is better than impersonal deism, but today it has its limitations: 'Personifying the reality of God in human experience as the existence of a supranatural Being, so far from strengthening and sustaining the reality, has the effect in this age of evacuating it of power' [EIG, 46].

It is in this context that JATR discusses the slogan, 'the death of God'. To digress, for a moment, we might note that in the following year, 1968, JATR published a new edition of his first book, *In the End, God. . .* It was originally about eschatology, but of course the phrase now had resonances with that more ominous slogan, 'the death of God'. JATR struggles manfully to make some connection in a new introduction between the 'end of *God*' and the '*end* of God'. However, he was intrigued to find that in the original book, written in 1950, he had attributed the lack of interest of modern man in an after-life to 'the fact that for the mass of his generation "God is dead"' [IEG, 31]. JATR himself never found the phrase useful in any positive sense. It was used in the 1960s in a variety of ways, but insofar as JATR feels he has to respond to it, he gives it yet another meaning:

> It is registering the fact that for millions today the living God has been replaced, not by atheism in the sense of a positive denial of God, nor by agnosticism in the nineteenth century sense, but precisely by a dead God. The reality of God has simply gone dead on contemporary man in a way that has never quite happened before. [EIG, 51]

The slogan has probably constrained JATR here, for we should have expected him to make a rather different point. In his terms many people today cannot conceive of a supranatural being, or rather, although they can just about imagine one in the crudest terms, they can neither believe he exists, nor do they particularly care whether he does or not. But this is not described simply as atheism, because the reality which that God was supposed to personify still exists. And at least on JATR's view many people recognize and respond to reality as personal, but could not do this through a supranatural being. Therefore, in a somewhat Nietzschean sense, the death of the old God is a liberating experience, except that for JATR it is the liberation to concentrate on the mystery that reality is personal. A change in consciousness seems to have taken place which has resulted in a situation in which the language of traditional theism no longer describes our deepest perceptions.

If we can no longer begin with the map, the projection represented by traditional theism, what is the reality as it appears today without this projection? There have been various moves attempted by those influenced by linguistic philosophy. They have inquired about the cash value of statements about God. Do they express fundamental convictions, are they primarily emotive in nature or do they give expression to our intentions to act in certain ways? They are no doubt all of these, but JATR is concerned to avoid all forms of humanist reduction. They express these things, but they cannot simply be equated with them. They are not theological statements simply because they express secular attitudes in terms of language about God. Theological statements refer back behind our commitments, emotions, actions, to the grounds for such things. Anglicans are not normally given to holding Luther up as an example, but the claim, 'Here I stand: I can do no other' illustrates the point: 'Luther certainly, if he uttered these words [the knee-jerk reaction of the biblical critic!], believed himself to be up against something to which his unqualifiable reaction was the *response*. It said something to him of "how things are" and *therefore* of how things must be for him' [EIG, 65]. Religious statements cannot be translated without remainder into the categories previously suggested, for this reduction omits an experience which is recognized to be more than a mood. It is 'the consciousness of being encountered, seized, held by a prevenient reality, undeniable in its objectivity, which seeks one out in grace and demand and under the constraint of which a man finds himself judged and accepted for what he truly is' [EIG, 66].

We might make the same observation, as in the case of JATR's treatment of the slogan 'the death of God'. It would seem as if he is too easily lead into the terms of the ongoing discussion with linguistic philosophy. This philosophy, at least in its empiricist form, begins from the starting-point of traditional theism. If God exists, he exists as a supranatural being with all the attributes identified by Greek philosophy. But empiricist philosophers cannot accept that there are grounds for believing in such a being. They therefore assume that theological statements, *if* they are to have any meaning, must refer to the private existence of the individual making or subscribing to them. We might have expected JATR to begin his critique of those influenced by this approach by rejecting both premises, that is, rejecting that theological statements refer to a supranatural being, and rejecting the concept of the private existence of the individual (Cartesian model). Theological statements do refer to God, but not the God of traditional theism, and they do not arise in private existence, but in the I-Thou relationship. We noted earlier that JATR could refer to a form of philosophy as primitive. We might have expected him to repeat this observation with respect to a school of philosophy which is not only pleased to relate itself to Hume, but in important respects shows itself to be still contemporary with that great Scottish leader of the Enlightenment.

This discussion draws to a conclusion:

> God-language does not describe a Thing-in-Itself or even a Person-in-Himself. And yet it does more than register our commitments. It points to an ultimate relatedness in the very structure of our being from which we cannot get away. It is a way of keeping guard over the irreducible, ineffable mystery at the heart of all experience. Traditionally, theology – our map of this mystery – has depicted God at the *frontier* of human existence. But this has come to mean for most people today something at the periphery of their experience or beyond it. [EIG, 72]

If God is not 'up there', or 'out there' or at the far frontier of our exploration, where are we to seek him? Perhaps we must look in the only place left.

In this metaphor of map-making, 'theography' as JATR terms it, the transcendence of God over man has been represented traditionally as distance. Although God is also immanent, he is separate from and stands over against his creation. Yet this way of thinking is under attack from many quarters, by theologians who in other matters are far from agreement. While there is no sympathy for monism, as if the whole of reality was of a piece, yet there is a growing rejection of dualism, certainly in its supernaturalist form. It is a movement to seek, discover and express the transcendent, in, with and under the immanent. But more than that, there is 'a strong insistence that we can say *nothing* of God *apart* from these relationships' [EIG, 80]. Not monism or dualism, not pantheism or theism. A third way is required by contemporary experience, and JATR chooses to call it 'panen-theism': 'Theism rejected the depersonalization of God in deism but retained its projection. Can we reject the depersonalization of God in pantheism but retain its projection? Can we, in fact, depersonify but not depersonalize?' [EIG, 87].

Pantheism is nothing but God, or nothing but the world; theism is God *and* the world. But neither has been able to establish a proper relationship between God and the world. The image of the potter is biblical, it presents God as purposive, but it is an impersonal metaphor. For panentheism JATR suggests the metaphor of 'the divine field', as a physicist might refer to a magnetic field: 'Somehow we must find a projection which enables us to represent the divine initiative as in the processes of nature rather than as acting on them from without, as exercised through the events of secular history rather than in some sacred super-history' [EIG, 105]. The difficulty is well illustrated in the traditional treatment of the problem of evil. It is reduced to the dilemma of an omnipotent, omniscient being, who is good, causing or permitting human suffering. It will be recalled that JATR spent a good deal of time in his dissertation contesting this scenario, but for some reason he does not refer to these objections here. He goes directly to the point that evil is whatever threatens or weakens our response to the divine Thou. But if nothing can separate us from the love of God, then – and the following claim must be understood precisely in this context – 'God is *in* the cancer as he is in the sunset, and is to be met and responded to in each' [EIG, 109].

In this exploration into God, not far off in another realm, JATR quotes the words of the late Dag Hammarskjöld: 'The longest journey is the journey inwards' [EIG, 111]. He concludes that 'in the last analysis the way of exploration into God is the way of prayer' [EIG, 111]. We shall take up the subject of spirituality in Part Three, but of course worship is greatly influenced by theology and the images and metaphors approved in a particular religious tradition. For example, a good deal of prayer would seem to be the communication of information about local matters to a supernatural being who exists in another realm. 'Lord we pray for the victims of the rail crash which, as Thou knowest Lord, took place yesterday morning.' If prayer has gone dead for many Christians a cause or at least an important contributory factor must be the conception of God as remote from and by definition not directly involved in or moved by the particular details of our lives. Within that understanding of God, prayer is not a way of penetrating the deepest levels of reality, but precisely of avoiding them. It can encourage us to avoid commitments to other thous, under the pretext of an obligation to seek the divine Thou. It leads back again into the metaphysical dilemma of the problem of evil and of 'unanswered' prayer. Although JATR declares himself to be 'the least mystical of persons' he finds in the writings of many mystics a spirituality which rejects the old dualistic relationship with God pictured within theism: 'The language of the mystics is that of "transcendence *within* immanence"' [EIG, 118].

It is certainly in the context of prayer that most people would find it very difficult to give up the image of theism, of God as a person. It is an image we find in the Bible, though the Bible warns against all images of God, all objectifying tendencies. 'But to talk of God as *though* he were an invisible Father seated in heaven presented no difficulty – let alone stumbling-block – when the whole universe was peopled with invisible personal beings in a quite naive way' [EIG, 135]. But in a world in which such beings are no longer thought to exist, insisting that God still be conceived of in this way makes belief impossible for many and causes problems even for those who continue with the image. The problem is how to continue to affirm the reality which not only exists, but which pre-dated the theistic mode of thought, to affirm the reality as personal without feeling constrained to use one severely restricted way of conceiving of it? It was originally the great contribution of theism to insist on the personal at the heart of reality. And naturally the highest understanding of the personal was used as the model, human personality. The objection now is not so much that this is anthropomorphic, conceiving of God in terms of man, but rather that in the meantime (and it is a *very* long time) our understanding of man has changed. At this point JATR brings forward an observation by Alan Watts: 'To go deeper and deeper into oneself is also to go farther and farther out into the universe, until, as the physicist well knows, we reach the domain where three-dimensional, sensory images are no longer valid' [EIG, 143]. JATR goes on to draw his own conclusion: 'And the whole of reality, too, must ultimately be seen in terms, not of a God, a monarchical Being supreme among individual entities, but of a divine "field" in which the finite "Thous" are constituted what they are in the freedom of a wholly personalizing love' [EIG, 144].

9 The Humanity of Christ

It was JATR's hope as he finished his dissertation that a thorough revision of Christian doctrine would be initiated on the basis of the new personalist philosopy, ensuring that it benefited from recent insights of contemporary thought, but above all making it more faithful to the Bible. His own contribution was to begin with the doctrine of the Trinity, which he included in the dissertation, but as we have seen his next attempt to tackle the doctrine of God was delayed till 1963 and the publication of *Honest to God*. The obvious sequel was to be on Christology, on the person of Christ. But such was the response to *Honest to God* that it was another ten years before his major work on Christology appeared. *The Human Face of God* was based on the Hulsean Lectures for 1970, delivered at Cambridge. We have previously argued that JATR's work should be seen in continuity with the position developed in his dissertation. This is true also of *The Human Face of God*. Works on Christology tend to focus on certain controversies in the early history of the Church, and writers feel that they must be careful to keep their theological balance as they proceed along the tight-rope. It is very easy to become so absorbed in this exercise as to lose sight of the true subject. Although JATR was well equipped to deal with the controversies, and in the course of the book they are given their due place, the work was motivated by something other than guarding the door against error: 'It is more concerned to be an honest trail of exploration than a balanced construction carefully compacted against all heresies' [HFG, xi].

Exploration into God, and now exploration into Christ. He does not make so much of the metaphor in this case, but if we are not to become bogged down in the controversies of the past it is necessary to anticipate the route he is likely to take. The exploration into God ended with a criticism of the human as the image of God, not because there is any more appropriate one available, but rather because the image of the human which is in fact used has long since been overtaken by the cumulative discoveries of the modern age. We should now expect JATR some years later to carry forward this critical point. The ancient controversies over Christology concerning the relationship of God and man in the God-man presupposed an understanding of God which JATR has criticized. They also presupposed an understanding of man which he may also reject. Consequently the work on Christology will not be simply a review of the past, but a questioning of whether the terms of these controversies should be accepted any longer. Once again the radicalism of his position will be not in providing an answer to an inherited question, but an examination of the way in which the question is raised. As in other theological matters we should anticipate that an axis will be formed between the best understanding of man available in the modern world and the teaching of the Bible on this subject.

In a purely historical study of Christology it would be enough to establish what patristic writers said on the subject. But a theological treatment must also attend to the question of Bonhoeffer of 'who Christ really is, for us today' [HFG, 13]. This, of course, is not an invitation to modernize Jesus, to make him one of us: 'The aim of a contemporary Christology is not to sweeten the pill but to hinder hindrances, to remove obstacles in order that the real "offence", of Christ and him crucified, can be exposed rather than overlaid' [HFG, 14]. The offence should not be the insistence that people today say exactly what was said two thousand years ago, or believe exactly what was believed, in the way in which it was believed: 'To *mean* what the New Testament writers or the Fathers *intended* to say of Jesus' humanity or divinity we may well have to say different things' [HFG, 16–17]. To insist that the same things be said may be a pointless exercise, but it could be worse than that if the net result was to make it impossible for people today to find in Christ the truth about God and about themselves: 'Our *first* preoccupation cannot be to ask, Are we saying the same thing? It must be, Are we saying our own thing? Are we really attending to *our* authentic questions? If not, the answers may have orthodoxy but they will not have integrity' [HFG, 17]. In order to discover the truth and to affirm it, it may be necessary to withdraw from the traditional categories of the patristic writers, and even from the categories of the New Testament itself. Certain developments in the modern world have made traditional categories problematic.

The first concerns the modern view of myth. For example, an account of an event in the ancient world often includes features which now appear to us not as elements in a sequence but rather as evaluations of it. What appeared then as a description of an event we now understand to be an interpretation of its significance. The mythical element is originally of subjective origin, but is stated in such a way that it becomes objectified. While this distinction posed no problems for those who accepted the mythological world-view, it raises a stumbling-block for people in the modern world. It seems to them that they are not being asked to share the faith of the early Church, affirming the subjective evaluation of the historical events, but rather are being required to believe that certain 'objective' features of the events, which are of course quite incredible in the modern world, actually occurred. The requirement has nothing to do with faith, and indeed is a distraction from it. JATR will later discuss the virgin birth at some length, but we might use it as an example here. The story of the virgin birth is about Jesus rather than Mary; it is an affirmation about the significance of Jesus. It is theology, not gynaecology. To ask people to believe that a virgin birth took place is to require them to believe something in the face of everything they know about the world. But worse, it has nothing to do with challenging them to affirm the faith of the early Church. And most damaging of all, it is objectifying the religious uniqueness of Jesus, transforming it into a physiological uniqueness. This physiological uniqueness is simply odd, but is not inherently religious. This gives a preliminary indication of why it is that to affirm the faith of the early Church it may be necessary to sit loose to the categories which they used: 'The self-authenticating objectivity of certain supernatural events or acts of God which for our fathers explained the course of nature and history has been irrecoverably shattered' [HFG, 21].

If myth has become problematic, so also has metaphysics: 'What myth is to the imagination, metaphysics is to the intellect' [HFG, 21]. All societies live within metaphysical systems, but JATR has in mind the classical ontology which he criticized and rejected in his dissertation. Although there is a structural similarity between ancient idealism and the biblical world-view, there is as we have seen a profound difference between metaphysics and mythology. Although biblical mythology has to be reinterpreted in order to allow faith to arise, the metaphysical system which provided the intellectual context for patristic theology cannot, and must be rejected:

> Above all, confidence has gone in the type of supranaturalistic ontology to which Christian theology in its classical presentations has been attached. According to this, what is 'really real' (*to on*) is located in another realm, above, beyond or behind phenomena (the latter belonging to the world of appearance rather than reality). [HFG, 22]

According to theology based on this metaphysical system Jesus is the Son of God because he came from that 'other' realm and returned to it. Now although this is superficially like the mythological picture, it is fundamentally different. In this case the person addressed in the modern world is not being asked to affirm the faith of the early Church concerning the significance of Jesus. Instead he is being asked to accept Platonic dualism, the division of reality into this world and another completely separate realm. But this is not a matter of faith and has nothing to do with Christian faith. But worst of all, this presentation reverses the whole historical process. On this view Jesus is affirmed to be religiously significant not because of Christian experience, but rather he is significant because he has come to this world from another realm. In the mythological the subjective affirmation of faith is transformed into the supposed objective elements in historical events. But in this metaphysical presentation it is the other realm which is real, and events in this world are but appearances. Not surprisingly this way of thinking is inherently docetic, undermining the humanity of Jesus in every affirmation of his divinity.

The third category which has become problematic today is that of the absolute. Behind JATR's presentation stand other aspects of his original criticism of the classical tradition, as found in *Thou Who Art*. The absoluteness of Christ can be affirmed within an ontology which has no positive place for change or development. As an academic exercise it is possible to define and defend his absoluteness in these terms. But it may well be that this defence has the unfortunate consequence of severing contact with the modern world, in which change and development are regarded as real and positive: 'To go on saying the same thing in the old terms is to be in danger of rendering Christ invulnerable but meaningless – unquestionably the answer because he corresponds to no questions' [HFG, 24]. If our picture of the world is constantly developing, if our experience is inexorably changing then absolute faith in Christ will not be expressed by making him part of an absolute system of the past. A corollary to this is the question of how Christ makes sense of the modern world. In idealist metaphysics the world is in order as it is, except that we are aware of the appearances only and do not perceive the inner reality. JATR might have illustrated this point from Hegel's aphorism in the Preface to his *Philosophy of Right*, that, 'What is real is rational, what is rational is real.' But Christ must not be taken to legitimize an absolute system. We must not eliminate the prophetic criticism of evil. JATR quotes William Temple at this point: 'We must still claim that Christianity enables us to "make sense" of the world, not meaning that we can show that it *is* sense, but with a more literal and radical meaning of making into sense what, till it is transformed, is largely nonsense.' [HFG, 26–7].

The fourth of the categories which now make the traditional

approach to Christology problematic is the modern understanding of history. This has produced the running debate concerning the relationship of the historical Jesus to the Christ of faith. The rise of historical consciousness has led to a separation of these two figures. It has been possible for theologians throughout the centuries to make the most fantastic claims about the Christ of faith, but in so far as Christianity is rooted also in history then what is known of Jesus of Nazareth must act as some kind of constraint and criterion about what can be affirmed by Christian faith. We saw in Part One that JATR is in fact more conservative than most critical scholars on the question of what we know of the historical Jesus. But that is a matter of position on a spectrum. It does not affect the general point that 'the old securities in history on which Christology was based may indeed have been undermined beyond repair . . .' [HFG, 31]. As in the discussion of mythology, we have now to recognize that the picture of the historical Jesus at many points in the Gospels may be influenced by the openly declared intention of the writers to present Jesus as the Christ, the Son of God. Thus what at first sight appear to be statements of historical fact may be basically affirmations of apostolic faith.

Our understanding of the world and of ourselves has substantially changed with the development of what is called the modern world. But this need not cut us off from the traditions of the Fathers, or the faith of the Bible. The thought forms of each are different and the question is how to affirm the same faith but in relation to our own experience. JATR is fond of referring to a classification by Cornelius van Peursen, that man has moved in the ways in which he has sought to represent reality from a mythological way of thinking to an ontological, and is moving from an ontological to a functional. In the last century it was thought necessary to defend mythological language against questions raised by the contemporary sciences. That project is now seen to be quite mistaken, not simply as an intellectual exercise, but more importantly as a way of defending and promoting the Christian faith:

> Similarly today, to speak of Jesus in the ontological categories of divine consubstantiality or 'impersonal' humanity may appear to be defending the faith against those who would sell it short. But we must have the courage to ask our own questions in terms of what is most real for us, and not be put off by the presumption, for instance, that what is sometimes rather sneeringly called a 'degree Christology' is somehow lower-class or less respectable than one which asserts that Jesus was different *in kind* from all other men. [HFG, 34–5]

We should therefore view JATR's project on Christology dynamic-ally, as a contemporary exploration of the way to life and not statically as the antiquarian restoration of an uninhabitable memorial.

Reformulating the doctrine of Christology today and for today may require beginning at a different point from traditional works on the subject. Nothing distinguishes the two approaches more than the place of the humanity of Christ. Whatever more the early Church wished to say about Jesus, however they sought to express his significance, he is recommended to us a man, as a human being. Peter's speech on the day of Pentecost represent what JATR can call 'a very primitive, not to say simplistic, Christology' [HFG, 37]. 'Men of Israel, listen to me: I speak of Jesus of Nazareth, a man singled out by God and made known to you through miracles, portents, and signs, which God worked among you through him, as you well know' (Acts 2.2, NEB). While in the New Testament Jesus is remembered as a man, it was not long before a process began which was to compromise his humanity: 'As soon as Jesus Christ was, or could be, represented as a pre-existent being who had come down from heaven, then the genuineness of his humanity while he was on earth was open to question' [HFG, 37]. The confession of faith of the significance of Jesus was translated into terms of the classical metaphysics already discussed: Christ the God is substance, Jesus the man is accident. When Jesus is called man, but not *a* man his humanity is com-promised:

> The orthodox doctrine of Christ's 'impersonal humanity' (of *anhypostasia* or *enhypostasia*), according to which the individual personality of the man Jesus was applied by, or included in, the *hypostasis* or substance of the second person of the Trinity, so that what was human was the *nature* this superhuman person assumed, strikes us as threatening the very core of his manhood. [HFG, 39]

What distinguishes a Christology for today is not just that it must begin with an assurance that Jesus was not simply man, but a man, but also that he was so in what is regarded as constitutive of being a man. This will as a matter of course include his culture and environment, but today it must also include genetics: 'No one can just *become* a man out of the blue: a genuine man (as opposed to a replica) can only come out of the process, not into it' [HFG, 43]. But is this modern view at odds with the biblical? JATR in his New Testament studies draws attention to the Gospel of Matthew as a new book of Genesis; further, as he point out: 'It is not for nothing that the New Testament begins with "a table of the descent of Jesus Christ"' [HFG, 45; Matt. 1.1]. Jesus is not presented as a being who appeared suddenly without any real connections with others. Nor is he simply standing within a religious or cultural tradition. He is of the *seed* of Abraham, by fruitful intercourse over many generations.

It is at this point, however, that the ambiguity enters Christology. Does Matthew recount this long genealogy to show that Jesus was the fruit of this genetic line, or to show that he was not? What is to be made of the fact that Joseph is not the father? While Matthew notes the malicious rumours put about by the Jews to the effect that the disciples stole the body of Jesus (Matt. 28.11–15), in the case of the parentage of Jesus he uses questions about the legitimacy of Jesus to make an important theological point. Matthew's genealogy unexpectedly includes reference to four women, Tamar, Rahab, Ruth and Bathsheba, who have in common the dubiety of their sexual relations. The fifth woman is Mary. 'He does not simply deny the irregularity as pure fabrication. Evidently he could not. On the contrary, he implicitly acknowledges it, and from the evidence of the past sets out to show that it is entirely compatible with it all being of God and with Jesus being the Christ' [HFG, 61–2]. The life of Jesus, like his teaching, illustrates the point that 'the scandal of the divine love is revealed as an affront to all legal righteousness . . .' [HFG, 66].

I have included this point, although it has already been referred to in the New Testament studies in Part One, not so much for its scholarship but out of interest in the psychological reaction it causes. There are historical grounds for thinking that Jesus might have been illegitimate. But for many this is entirely unacceptable – regardless of the historical evidence. Whatever Matthew intended he certainly had no wish to cast doubts on the fact that Jesus was a man. The virgin birth is not intended to compromise his humanity either. As we have already noted, it is a mythological way of affirming that, no matter his origins, Jesus was of God and is the Christ. The compromise to the humanity comes not from Matthew, but from later traditions influenced by Greek metaphysics which had a very different view of what it was to be a man. According to that view sexuality is dehumanizing. It could not have been by this process that Jesus came into the world – nor could he have been a sexual being. According to Matthew Joseph did not have intercourse with Mary 'until she had borne a son . . .' (Matt. 1.25). The existence of Jesus' brothers is attested in Mark 3.31; John 2.12; Acts 1.14; 1 Corinthians 9.5 and Galatians 1.19, yet JATR draws attention to the outburst by Thomas Aquinas on the point: 'Without any hesitation we must abhor the error of Helvidius, who dared to assert that Christ's Mother, after his birth, was carnally known by Joseph, and bore other children' [HFG, 47]. The historical facts are in conflict with the metaphysical principles underlying Aquinas' position. In such a case, so much the worse for the facts. On this view Jesus could take impersonal humanity from his mother, and receive the life principle from God the Father. But this depends on accepting the biological theories of Aristotle, now completely disproved by genetics. We now know that Jesus would inherit genetically from his mother's side, but if the classical tradition is to be maintained, then he must have been given elements in his own personal genetic code which did not come from an earthly father's side, but functioned as if they did. Of this complex form of docetism, JATR makes the following comparison:

> By the time we reach this point we are bound to ask whether anything different is being asserted than was asserted by the defenders of conservative orthodoxy in the last century when they said that God created rocks with fossils in them to look as though evolution were true. The appearances may have been saved, but the position was fundamentally untenable. [HFG, 51]

This metaphysical position is profoundly different from the mythological position of the Gospels. The myth of the virgin birth was not intended to distinguish Jesus physiologically from other men or to cut him off from his genetic line. But in its metaphysical context the virgin birth does just that. And that is precisely what it is intended to do, since the presuppositions of Greek philosophy required it. JATR distinguishes between the usage of two Greek words meaning 'new'; *neos* meaning novelty, and *kainos* meaning renewal. The 'new man', the 'new creation' and the 'new Jerusalem' do not require that God begins again with totally different material, but that he renews and remakes. For Paul it is only as Christ shares our common flesh that he can save (Rom. 8.3).

As already indicated, the classical view includes anti-sexual premises about what it means to be human. We have noted that these assumptions have led to a psychological resistance to admit that there is some evidence that Jesus may have been illegitimate, that Mary was not a moral example in such matters. This extends to a reluctance even to consider Jesus' own sexuality. There is little evidence: the importance of raising the matter is to indicate how deeply the classical assumptions must run to make us feel that such discussions are offensive. JATR mentions the furore which greeted Hugh Montefiore's raising of the question whether Jesus might have had homosexual tendencies. He also quotes from a Council of Churches' Conference on Family Life, in Canada in 1966, which raised the following question: 'When the woman wiped Jesus's feet with her hair, she performed a highly sexual action. Did Jesus at that moment experience an erection?' [HFG, 64]. There is no answer to the question, but its importance concerns our understanding of the humanity of Jesus. In the normal course of events we should regard sexuality as a basic mode of human existence, and also as a basic ingredient in the capacity to relate to other people. To deny out of hand any sexuality to Jesus would be to dehumanize him. He would not, on our understanding of such matters today, be more human but less, not more capable of relating to others but less. The Gospels give us no grounds for compromising the humanity of Jesus. The faith of the early Church declares that he was more than a man, not less.

An outsider might be surprised at the twists and turns of this discussion, but more surprised that it should have to take place at all and at such length. Christianity is distinguished from other religions not least by its claim that the Saviour was a historical person. How strange that the basis of this claim should be undermined not by the enemies of the faith but by its upholders. But as we noted at the outset, the point of contention for a modern Christology concerns our understanding of what it is to be a human being. Given JATR's personalist philosophy we might have expected him to make more of this point. His criticism of traditional christological formulations based on Greek metaphysics might have led on to some indication of how a modern restatement of the doctrine would make use of a more contemporary philosophy. In several academic disciplines use is made of the concept that individuals are born incomplete, not simply biologically, but in specifically human terms, for example consciousness and self-understanding. If we say that an individual is not born a man but becomes a man, this is a rejection of the same essentialist metaphysics identified by JATR. It is also part of the personalist movement to which Buber belonged. An individual only becomes himself or herself through socialization. We might have expected JATR to add such a point: Jesus to be fully human must have formed close relationships. He does however refer to Pasolini's film *The Gospel According to St Matthew*, which although made by a communist presents Christ in a way which was widely accepted by Christians. In it Christ comes as a visitor to a family. He changes their lives, but he forms no relationships and is not himself touched by those he affects.

By comparison, a modern Christology must begin with an understanding of the uniqueness of Christ which is based on the fact that he is normal – the norm for man – not that he is abnormal, not even a man. Even in this, however, history is constrained by piety. The norm for man in a biblical context would mean his complete obedience to the will of God. We are not speaking here of an individual such as Plato, handsome, socially at ease, skilled in all the arts and knowledgeable in all the sciences of his day. Indeed it may be that we cannot usefully describe Jesus as perfect in any sense, so much is this approach influenced by classical or Renaissance rather than biblical assumptions – 'Why do you call me good?' (Mark 10.18). We should not too lightly attribute a perfection to Jesus which deprives him of that real struggle with evil which is referred to in the temptations, Gethsemane and the Epistle to the Hebrews. As Barth pointed out, when Luke tells us that Jesus 'increased' in wisdom and stature (Luke 2.52), the verb used is *prokoptein*, which means 'to extend by blows, as a smith stretches metal by hammers' [HFG, 80]. When Jesus is described as being made perfect, it is by living through very human experiences and becoming a different person because of them. To say otherwise is to dehumanize him.

Although the humanity of Jesus is constantly attested in the Gospels and specifically affirmed elsewhere in the New Testament, the perspective was to change radically as theology came under Hellenistic influences. Although the various patristic schools were divided on fundamental issues, they shared basic metaphysical assumptions. They approached the christological issue not from the humanity of Jesus but from their understanding of divinity:

> The Alexandrians, who were working with a basically Platonic view of God, were prepared to see the line between God and man blurred by divinization. The Antiochenes, with a more Jewish and in some cases more Aristotelian cast of mind, saw God so transcendently 'other' that he could not effectively become one with man, though they had to our mind a profounder and more moral understanding of what full personal union would mean – on which indeed they wished to insist as strongly as anyone else.
>
> This doctrine of two separate 'natures', each with its own inalienable properties, was regarded as essential if Jesus was to be *both* Son of God *and* Son of Man. [HFG, 110]

A modern restatement of Christology should begin with the humanity of Jesus and proceed by such claims as that 'God has made him both Lord and Christ, this Jesus whom you crucified' (Acts 2.36) and that 'God was in Christ' (2 Cor. 5.19). The early Church made two different kinds of statements about Jesus. On the one hand were historical (very recent in their case) statements about the man Jesus, 'whom you crucified'. On the other hand were statements of faith, 'God was in Christ'. These latter statements inevitably employed mythological thought-forms and expressions. The two kinds of language meet because the man is also the Son of Man, but the early Christians were able to express the highest faith in Jesus Christ without compromising his humanity. The patristic schools to which we have just referred attempted to express these two realities on the basis of classical metaphysics. Most of the ink spilt in the past over the christological controversies has in effect accepted these metaphysical premises and sought to determine which school solved the problem consistently in these terms. We might simply decide today that since we do not share this metaphysical view we shall simply set that period aside. JATR's criticism, however, has not been that these controversies are now to be regarded as harmless but irrelevant. The premises of that period lead to claims which are incompatible with the biblical presentation of Jesus and compromise his humanity. They are to be rejected not because dated, but because wrong:

> If we wish, as assuredly the New Testament does, to go on to say that Jesus' words and works are not simply those of any man faithful and open to God but the self-expression of God acting in him and through him, this is still not because there were some things he could not say or do as a man, and which therefore required of him a second nature, but because what he said and did must also be seen as 'bespeaking' God as well as man.
>
> In other words, the formula we presuppose is not of one superhuman person with two natures, divine and human, but of one human person of whom we must use two languages, man-language and God-language. [HFG, 113]

As already indicated, these two forms of language can overlap. Indeed that is precisely the point, that this man is the Son of Man, God is in Christ. There is no supernatural without the natural. We have two stories, not two storeys: 'The supernatural is not a parallel and superior causal sequence, but an interpretation or unveiling (*revelatio*), in terms of myth or a "second" story, of the same process studied by science and history' [HFG, 117]. The historical is the historic, as we observed earlier in the discussion of *kairos*. Thus whoever was the human father of Jesus, the mythological narrative about the virgin birth was not intended to destroy or falsify Jesus' history. To confess faith that Jesus is of God it is not necessary to deny that historically his birth was normal. But since we today do not think in mythological categories, we must be careful to avoid taking such mythological narratives literally, making quasi-objective events which destroy history and compromise humanity. Similarly terms such as 'sinless', 'unique', or 'perfect' are confessions of faith, and belong to the God-language. As man-language they commit believers to historical claims which simply cannot in the nature of things be substantiated. A more contentious example is resurrection, a subject already treated in Part One. We saw then that we simply do not have the evidence to say what happened to the body of Jesus. There is no attempt in the New Testament to describe the resurrection as a historical event. Resurrection is the mythological name for this historical reality, the God-language statement to interpret and understand it. To describe that reality (in man-language), JATR quotes Gordon Kaufman: 'The finite objective historical reality correlative to faith was not in fact the reawakened Jesus of Nazareth but *the new community of love and forgiveness*, recreated and recognized under the impact of the resurrection appearances' [HFG, 131].

But if the New Testament writers do not compromise the humanity of Jesus in their claims about his historic significance, there is one further area in which the true humanity of Jesus is threatened, namely the concept of pre-existence. If his pre-existence is affirmed, as it is in several New Testament writings, notably in Hebrews, surely this means that Jesus could not be human in any normal sense? Pre-existence and humanity seem incompatible, especially if pre-existence is understood to refer to a divine being in heaven who enters into history, taking human form. That was certainly its meaning in patristic theology, where 'pre-existence meant the prior existence in heaven of an individual *hypostasis* or *persona* who was in the fullness of time to become the subject of the human nature taken from the virgin Mary' [HFG, 148]. It is tempting to say that this process represents a shift from the mythological to the ontological which occurred as the theological initiative moved from the context of Judaism to that of Hellenism. But as JATR points out, the shift had already begun to take place in the development between prophetic and apocalyptic Judaism (a distinction already made in Part One with reference to eschatology). On one side of the divide figures such as the Son of Man and the Messiah refer to Israel or to the actions of God; on the other they come to be defined as existent or pre-existent beings with a life of their own. It is JATR's contention that the references to incarnation and pre-existence in the New Testament belong to this former tradition, and do not involve the hypostatization of an individual heavenly person.

Thus in Jesus the pre-existent Word of God is embodied. This does not imply that a pre-existent being entered the world through him, rather that he is sufficiently faithful to be its incarnation. He is the Son of God because he embodies the divine will and character. It is not a supernatural being who is sent, but a human being who is called to be

Son. As Christ he is the expression or agent of the purpose which God established before the creation. But in none of these roles is it intended that he was not a man, as other men are.

> *Qua* Son, indeed, he is not *of* this world and does not have his origin in space or time, where anyone can know or locate it. And yet, as we have seen, as the man from Nazareth he is born and bred completely within the local human situation, with a parentage that is open to anyone's inspection – or insinuation. [HFG, 154]

The author of the Epistle to the Hebrews can even combine apparent pre-existence with adoptionism in this understanding: 'Thou hast loved righteousness and hated lawlessness; therefore God, thy God, has anointed thee [*echrisen* 'made Christ'] with the oil of gladness beyond thy comrades' (Heb. 1.9). Earlier, in rejecting the essentialist view which sees man born with his nature complete, we referred to a man becoming who he is through coping with the experiences of life – 'Although he was a Son, he learned obedience through what he suffered; and being made perfect he became the source of eternal salvation to all who obey him . . .' (Heb. 5.8–9).

Turning to Pauline literature, Philippians 2.5–11 is usually taken as the *locus classicus* of pre-existence, of the supernatural heavenly Redeemer visiting earth in the form of a human being: who, 'though he was in the form of God, did not count equality with God a thing to be grasped, but emptied himself, taking the form of a servant, being born in the likeness of men'. But JATR does not accept this interpretation:

> Jesus was not, I believe, for Paul, as he became for later dogmatics, a divine being veiled in flesh or one who stripped himself of supernatural attributes to become human; he was a man who by total surrender of his own gain or glory was able to reveal or 'unveil' the glory of God as utterly gracious, self-giving love. [HFG, 166]

We have claimed on several occasions that it would have been helpful if JATR had made clearer his own position, as developed in his dissertation. This in fact lies behind the interpretation of the Philippians hymn. It goes back to the doctrine of God, not as understood within the Greek metaphysical context, with divine attributes which attach to his being, but as revealed in one who would give up not a divine self, in this sense, but rather the goals of the self and the glory of man. From time to time JATR seems to become so absorbed in the christological debates and the key passages for interpretation as to forget to place the subject in the setting which he has already created by his reconstruction of the doctrine of God.

Not suprisingly JATR leaves to the end the prologue of the fourth Gospel, the incarnation of the Logos. But we saw in Part One that John is probably the most important single New Testament source for JATR and therefore, as we should expect, his presentation of the position in this Gospel corresponds exactly to his general understanding of the question of pre-existence. We are being presented throughout this Gospel with two languages, two stories, one superimposed on the other. Although Jesus was born into this world, he cannot be understood in terms of this world. But for the writer the two realities, though completely different, are so closely related in Jesus that to be in the presence of one is to be in the presence of the other. The tragedy is that some who see, fail to see.

JATR therefore rejects the 'two natures' approach to Christology, and pre-existence too, when it involves the hypostatization which belongs to that position:

> The sole question is whether this is the only or indeed the original understanding of what incarnation means. I believe that the word can just as truly and just as biblically (in fact more truly and more biblically) be applied to another way of understanding it. This is: that one who was totally and utterly a man – and had never been anything other than a man or more than a man – so completely embodied what was from the beginning the meaning and purpose of God's self-expression (whether conceived in terms of his Spirit, his Wisdom, his Word, or the intimately personal relationship of Sonship) that it could be said, and had to be said, of that man, 'He was God's man', or 'God was in Christ', or even that he *was* 'God for us'. [HFG, 179]

JATR is making a bold claim here. There are mythological ways of speaking about the incarnation, and, as we have seen, the point of this mode is to make abstract ideas or value judgements objective. There are also ontological ways of describing the incarnation, which in their own terms are equally substantial. Following van Peursen's analysis JATR is proposing to investigate a third way of speaking about incarnation, namely the functional. The problem, of course, is that this way of representing incarnation looks reductionist, as if it is saying much less than the other two. God and man are brought together in this case through *verbs* rather than through personification or objectification. In this way of speaking the incarnation means that Jesus

> stands in the place of God, speaking and acting for him. The issue is not where he comes from or what he is made of. He is not a divine or semi-divine being who comes from the other side. He is a human figure raised up from among his brothers to be the instrument of God's decisive work

and to stand in a relationship to him to which no other man is called. [HFG, 184]

This seems to say less, but it is JATR's claim that it actually says more, or at least that it is closer to the meaning of the biblical confession of faith. The appearance of objectivity in the other ways of speaking, especially the ontological, may be no more than a misleading and distorting impression. The functional language may be more appropriate in speaking of the God who acts, to thelematology rather than ontology. Sonship might better describe a functional relationship rather than ontological status. Certainly sonship in this context can be better understood in the modern world. In its ontological context we are being faced with assertions which belong to metaphysical speculation rather than human experience. Yet it is as Son that Jesus is called at the baptism, not because of some special physiological constitution, but, in Zahrnt's words, 'because he alone allows God really to be his Father' [HFG, 191].

The early Church remembered Jesus as one who stood in the place of God, whose teaching begins (rather than ends) with 'Amen', who overrules and revises the law of God. JATR quotes Bornkamm's summary of the synoptics with approval, 'To make the reality of God present: this is the essential mystery of Jesus' [HFG, 194]. This is the highest claim that can be made, and yet the Church translated it first into mythological language and then into that of ontology: 'But this, though it appears to us to be higher doctrine, is in fact only translation – translation into terms which enabled men to "place" the mystery of Christ where they located what to them was most real' [HFG, 195]. It has been JATR's argument throughout that while first mythology and then ontology made the mystery of Christ real for previous ages, they make it entirely unreal today. The challenge today is to make the mystery real without diminishing it in any way.

The dilemma is that from our perspective today the other two ways of speaking seem inherently docetic, based on supranaturalist projections. Jesus can never be truly human within these schemes. But viewed from their perspectives, to begin with a Jesus who is human, *fully* human, seems inherently adoptionist. Yet adoptionism may well be a position which can only be chosen within the mythological or ontological schemes. If we proceed within a modern functional context it would be anachronistic to attach labels which make sense only within those positions which have been specifically set aside. The metaphysical presuppositions of patristic theology meant the divine initiative could only break in upon the world from outside, it could not come to expression 'in the fullness of time': 'One of the effects of the supranaturalist projection, which locates God outside the process and over against it, has been to confirm the impression that nothing that does not come into it from without can really express his initiative' [HFG, 201–2]. Given our understanding of human existence and the natural world, adoptionism is ruled out for us just as surely as the two-nature doctrine.

The way forward for Christology therefore depends on the more general understanding of theology, starting with the doctrine of God and his relationship with the world, human and natural. For JATR that means a Christology which is based on panentheism. When God is not thought of as external to the world then incarnation need not be understood as an invasion from outside the process. The world is therefore not inherently alien to God, and incarnation can express a mystery which 'could be embodied in a man born and bred and evolved from within it, a product of it rather than an invader of it' [HFG, 203]. JATR, having already rejected the ontological interpretation of the Logos in the fourth Gospel, can now propose another: 'The Word is seen, as in the Johannine prologue, as moulding the process from the beginning, drawing it onwards and upwards like light, immanent in it yet constantly transcending it, rather than as something transcendent that *became* immanent' [HFG, 203].

As a graduate student I wrote my master's dissertation on the comparison of the work of Rudolf Bultmann and John Knox. Bultmann in the neo-orthodox tradition presents Jesus as the Word, but Knox, influenced by the Chicago school of process thought, presents Jesus as an event. In this way he makes a final break with the ontological tradition, which locates the uniqueness of Christ in the metaphysical understanding of his Person. It is significant, therefore, that JATR concludes this discussion with a quotation from Knox:

> The 'divinity' was not half of his nature or a second nature, but was that purpose and activity of God which made the event which happened around him, but also in him and through him, the saving event it was. The divinity of Jesus was the deed of God. The uniqueness of Jesus was the absolute uniqueness of what God did in him. [HFG, 211]

The 'Christ-event' is of course much more than Jesus. In a real, though demythologized and de-ontologized sense, we can speak of the pre-existence, resurrection and consummation of Christ. Incarnation is not now a mythological or metaphysical concept to describe an intrusion into history at a particular moment. But it presupposes a-theism, the denial that God is a being existing over against the world. In Christ God is now continuously incarnate; this is how we

111

experience him. At this point JATR might have returned briefly to his original thesis, that we now experience the Thou in the thous. 'He who receives you receives me, and he who receives me receives him who sent me' (Matt. 10.40). The ultimate mystery of the world is at last personal: 'The Christ is God with a human face' [HFG, 229].

10 The Inclusive Christ

At one stage JATR had to argue that a modern understanding of Christology is not reductionist. It does not say less than traditional formulations, but indeed says more. Incarnation is not now to be viewed as a 'moment' in history, but the way in which we now encounter God in the midst of the life of the world. Christ is the final revelation in the sense of *kairos*, not *chronos*. There is no revelation more ultimate, but there are many things yet to be revealed. Precisely because the incarnation is the outcome of the purposes of God from the beginning, for the whole world – as was seen by the author of the Gospel of John – salvation in Christ cannot be restricted to those who are adherents of the Christian religion. It must be possible to conceive of Christ encountering those of other traditions. JATR distinguishes between the 'inclusive' finality of Christ and the 'exclusive' finality, the latter being characteristic of religious imperialism. This is a pressing question in a pluralistic world. JATR does not explain why it is pressing, but there may be here another source of unreality for modern man. It is unlikely that all truth resides only in one tradition, and that no truth is to be found in all others. Alternatively, it is unlikely that the other world religions are going to wither away, and indeed multi-faith ecumenism is comfortably based on the assumption that no one religion is going to gain the allegiance of the population of the world. But whereas this might be accepted reluctantly by some who wish it were otherwise, JATR is attempting to extend his understanding of Christology to provide a theological basis for believing that it not only is so, but should be so.

Many Christians who participate in multi-faith dialogues, at all levels, do so in order to maintain 'good relations', but are entirely vague about the basis on which they meet. But can they still affirm the uniqueness of Christ? JATR is perfectly clear on the finality and uniqueness of Christ, and draws an interesting parallel with the situation in the early Church. Was it necessary to become a Jew into order to become a Christian? For Paul the question is whether it is necessary that all come under the law in order to receive the promise. The answer was to be No, that salvation is to be found in Christ apart from the law:

But this is very different from saying that Christianity as a religion is the

113

only true path to salvation. That is to turn Christ into a new and exclusive law. It is to say that everyone has first to become a Christian, as the Judaizers whom Paul fought said that everyone had first to become a Jew. [HFG, 227]

JATR affirms his faith that, at its deepest level, reality is personal and that Christ is the human face of God. That is why he is a Christian and cannot be anything other. But he is grappling here with something which may well be entailed in the faith, though at first sight it seems to threaten it. Only those who acknowledge this final and ultimate place of Christ are Christian, yet JATR is searching for a way of saying that this truth about reality could be confirmed within other religious traditions. This would seem to require that those who belong to these other faiths must have Christ proclaimed to them, but not necessarily in the terms of traditional Christian theology. Indeed JATR has been so critical of the traditional forms that we should expect him to warn people away from approaching Christ by this route. And so he comes to a conclusion which, far from weakening faith in Christ, extends its implications: 'The finality or universality of Christ is not to be identified with the finality or universality of the Christian religion. In fact it would be nearer the truth to say that Christ is the "end" of Christianity as he is of Judaism – and that both positively and negatively' [HFG, 229]. We might say that on this view, if man is not made for the sabbath, neither is Christ made for the Church.

The preparation and delivery of the Hulsean Lectures took place in what JATR recognized to be a predominantly Christian context, and we should no doubt see the point at which they finished as the end of one journey of exploration rather than the starting-point of another. However, in 1976 he received an invitation to deliver the Teape Lectures in India. Since they had to lie within the broad field of relations between Hinduism and Christianity, in accepting he was committed to further travels and more specific explorations. The haven reached at the end of the Hulseans proved to be but the base camp for the Teape Lectures.

The preparation for these lectures was very different from that for the Hulseans. JATR openly admitted that world religions, and in this case Hinduism, was not his academic field, but steeped himself in the literature during the time available. He found this a corrective to the all too common myopia of Western scholarship, but more positively he sought to gain a new perspective from the encounter. We focus on a subject when we make use of both eyes. The lectures were published with the title *Truth is Two-Eyed*, and in them JATR pursued the questions already raised concerning the inclusive, the exclusive and the unique.

We noted in an earlier chapter that the questions about God raised by JATR were not simply associated with one 'side' or another: the debate was in a real sense also taking place within each person. JATR now begins with the recognition that although certain positions are identified as Eastern or Western, they are also poles within each of us. It is for this reason that we respond to the best of a tradition even when it is in all other respects foreign to us. We might illustrate this in passing by noting that when Thomas Merton eventually was able to make his journey to the East, he described it as coming home to a place where he had never been. JATR does not introduce himself as a monk or mystic, but he does identify his starting-point – now familiar to us – as personalism, the appreciation of the centrality of the I-Thou relation, the affirmation of reality as personal, and faith in the decisiveness of the one who could address God as *Abba*. He has already distanced himself from the classical Western tradition and from its modern Cartesian extension. He is therefore able to hear another account of reality. *Tat tvam asi*, 'That art thou', is not the same as I-Thou, but it does contain a similar corrective: 'The emphasis is on union rather than communion, on the overcoming of separation and individuation' [TTE, 10]. As we have already learnt, for JATR the personal is not the isolated individual, nor does God exist as a being over against us.

But JATR is not going to settle for an uncritical syncretism. He finds in Hinduism, and more so in Buddhism, 'a static monism, in which not merely are dualities overcome, but differences are submerged in an acosmic pantheism which denies the values of personal and individual identity' [TTE, 20]. JATR is therefore critical of the monism of the East, as he is of the dualism of the West. He rejects pantheism as much as theism. He therefore proposes a relational or 'field' view of reality which he finds more adequate to the modern Western scientific understanding of man and the world, but at the same time strangely resonant with the Eastern mystical tradition. In offering this third way, which is in any case the position which JATR developed in his earlier explorations, it is difficult to avoid the conclusion that it is not that he is learning from his encounter with the East, but rather that he is personally acting as an honest broker between East and West in an area in which both are deficient:

There is a distinctiveness, a dimension of transcendence, which demands

115

God-language, just as there is a distinctiveness about fields of particles that constitute human and not merely inorganic or organic being: they are the expression of a purposiveness and freedom which finally transcends and accounts for them. [TTE, 26]

There is however an area in which JATR does genuinely enter into dialogue, and that concerns God and evil. He conceives of the subject more widely than the problem of evil, certainly as it has been treated within the Western classical tradition. It has to do with what Jung calls 'the shadow'. In Jewish Hasidic mysticism Satan is the other side of God, and is also holy. In Hinduism Shiva is both creator and destroyer. But in Christianity the dark side has been detached, personified and projected on to the Devil. Christ and Anti-christ. God and his alter ego. In ancient Judaism the projection of evil is on to the scapegoat. In the modern world it can be on to social or racial groups. If God in this tradition is 'out there' and 'up there', the devil is 'out there' and 'down there'. Christ becomes completely dissociated from evil, and thereby less than human. JATR finds in Hinduism a different approach, 'not of rejection and repulsion but of acceptance and resignation' [TTE, 32]. The two are represented as Krishna god of joy and life, and Kali the dark mother of suffering and death. In one tradition the dark side is repulsed and defeated, but not by love. In the other it is accepted for what it is, but not lived through positively or integrated. 'By contrast the great strength of the panentheistic position is that it makes God the person, yes, the loving, ground of *all* being, of the impersonal and evil as well as of the moral, of volcanoes and tape-worms and cancer as much as of everything else' [TTE, 35]. Although JATR seems to be drawing aspects of the two traditions together to form an eclectic position, it will be recalled that this was a position he had already reached in his reinterpretation of the doctrine of God, long before reaching the dialogue with other religions. God is not apart from evil, or outside of it, but within it, and in Christ transforming it 'through wood and nails'.

JATR goes on to deal with two further issues, the historical and the material. In one tradition God creates the material world and sets in train a purposive history. Reality is not simply what is, but what by the will of God it will become. For the other tradition history has no such significance. Its symbol is a wheel rather than a road. Salvation does not come in the fullness of time, but in release from time. In JATR's terminology there is *chronos* but no *kairos*. Although these two positions can be overdrawn, yet the fundamental difference in attitude obviously affects the place of Christ, especially the status of the historical Jesus. But at a time when some Hindus are developing their understanding of the historical, it could be pointed out that on JATR's view Christianity has compromised the historical through its uncritical acceptance of classical ontology. At the same time the Eastern emphasis might challenge a Western tendency towards literalism, which fails to distinguish between the historical account of the life of Jesus and its mythological interpretation. As JATR never tires of pointing out, for John it is all too easy to see the historical without perceiving the historic. On this view the historical events themselves are not unique or exceptional, they do not disrupt the historical flow. The corollary is that there is no reason why other events, in someone else's history, should not become revelatory of the universal Logos.

On the other issue, the material world, JATR begins by recalling the famous claim of William Temple that Christianity is 'the most avowedly materialist of all the great religions' [TTE, 68]. The doctrine of creation distinguishes the Jewish-Christian tradition from the Hindu-Buddhist. It is world-affirming, in which the material is neither divinized nor considered illusory, unreal or evil. It is not necessary to turn away from it to find God, but it is in it that he is to be found and obeyed. 'And man is called to share in the divine creativity, in this freedom over nature out of which he comes. Yet it is a dominion tied to responsibility for it, summed up in the relationship of stewardship' [TTE, 69]. Man is made in the image of God the Creator. The spiritual is to be sought through the material and the political. God is to be found in the establishment of justice rather than in the sacrifice of the temple. This materialist view is re-enforced in the New Testament with the doctrine of incarnation, the enfleshment of the Word. Consequently nothing material can be called common or unclean (Acts 11.8–9).

The other tradition seeks attachment to the inner spiritual centre and consequently detachment from the outer material world, the life which if not evil is at least less real. The renunciation of the cravings of the world, the stripping away of the layers which obscure the real self and prevent union with reality. JATR sees this tradition as predominantly concerned with rising above suffering and evil, rather than wrestling with them, and he notes the distinction made by Hermann Hesse 'between the Buddhist ideal of invulnerability and the vulnerability of love to being touched and tied by relationships' [TTE, 75]. There are of course exceptions, including Gandhi and *satyagraha*, the transforming power of truth, the highly political self-immolation of the Vietnamese monks, and the reading of the Vedanta as a 'social gospel', but JATR still maintains there is a profound difference between the two traditions.

It is not difficult to see Western materialism as the outcome and distortion of certain biblical motifs, but on the other side there is a benign neglect, which seems indifferent towards human suffering and fatalistic about its occurrence. JATR notes the emphasis in Hinduism on self-harmony rather than the love of the neighbour, while in Buddhism suffering is approached by identification rather than by social transformation. He is suspicious of the authoritarianism of the one-sided master-pupil relationship in spiritual instruction. In contrast to previous discussions JATR does not seem to reach a position which draws from both sides. He earlier noted that it is probably no coincidence that it is in a culture profoundly influenced by the biblical doctrine of creation that natural science, secular-ization, capitalism and democracy arose. Perhaps he could have followed up some of his earlier thoughts from Bonhoeffer in this context. After all Christianity, or at least the Church, has been deeply opposed to most of these developments at one time or another. As with his previous discussions, JATR might have been able to argue that the third and integrating way lies not in Christianity when it opposes the autonomy of the world, not in Hinduism when it despises that autonomy, but in following the higher way of love, which does not seek God apart from the world but finds him in the neighbour.

But finally JATR turns to the central question of the uniqueness of Christ. He has already made it clear that for him this uniqueness is not because Jesus is an abnormal man with an abnormal history. To the contrary, he is unique because he is the norm, and his history reveals what all life should be, sonship. And if this is 'the true light that enlightens every man' (John 1.9) what is revealed is the uniqueness of the universal. The uniqueness of Christ is inclusive, available to all, not exclusive, available only to those who think they control it. Ironically, we might say that the situation recalls several of the parables of Jesus, in which those who thought themselves close to God are rejected because they have not shared their light with the 'lost' for whom God has a special concern. JATR notes the danger: 'The significance of the "once", of the decisive expression within history of the all-illuminating Christ, so easily gets transformed into a closed corpus of revelation, a deposit "once and for all delivered to the saints", denying other revelation and even its own open-endedness' [TTE, 103]. The inclusive Christ is denied when appearing with either 'the unacceptable face of Catholic triumphalism or of Protestant particularism' [TTE, 104].

It is in the new situation of pluralism – pluralism within one country as much as throughout one world – that the claim for the uniqueness of Christ has to be defended. Wherever Christianity is the only or dominant religion, the assertion is simply made. But there is an additional problem. JATR has argued that in the modern world, where functional ways of thinking have replaced mythological or ontological ways, the uniqueness of Christ can no longer be asserted on the grounds that he belonged to a supernatural realm. This is to state the matter the wrong way round. Such language does not describe a matter of fact, but provides us with a statement of faith. The basis of any claim for uniqueness must be on what he did or still does. JATR quotes J. A. van Leeuwen with approval: 'The uniqueness of Christ can only be established via his humanity . . . The divinity must be perceptible *in* his humanity itself' [TTE, 122]. As we saw in the previous section, we should not seek to assert uniqueness based on abnormality, nor total claims for the historical Jesus which cannot be defended by evidence.

Throughout JATR's entire theological corpus we have seen him questioning presuppositions, not least those embedded in traditional terminology. Perhaps the term 'uniqueness' belongs within the classical ontological scheme, and should not be defended, at least in its own terms. In keeping with the more functional approach JATR is impressed by the suggestion of Chaon-Seng Song that we should speak rather of 'the decisiveness' of Christ. Although in the end it is a question of faith, an affirmation that it is in Christ rather than in Krishna that the mystery is most truly disclosed, yet there is some scope for dialogue. In the modern world we expect knowledge and experience to increase, not simply to duplicate the past. Any affirmation of uniqueness, or preferably decisiveness, must come to terms with experiences which have not previously been central to the understanding of the Christ. The shadow has already been discussed. The place of the feminine is another. This underlines the fact that the decisiveness cannot simply refer to a moment in history, which took place within specific cultural, geographical and historical limitations. JATR ends this discussion with a quotation from V. Chakkarai: 'To believe that God is best defined by Christ is not to believe that God is confined to Christ' [TTE, 129].

It is very easy to see the whole area of the relationship of Christianity to other world religions as a specialist question to be addressed by those involved in comparative religion rather than by theologians. This may be an attitude readily adopted by those who live within an enclave still predominantly Christian or at least without a sizable immigrant population. But JATR has attempted to integrate the issue in such a way that it constitutes the basis for the next advance in theological thinking. Christian theologians have to come to terms with the implications of the question for a proper understanding of the universal Christ. It is not simply a matter of community relations but of the things of God which have yet to be revealed. JATR returned to the theme in October 1982, when he was Visiting Professor in the Department of Religious Studies at McMaster University, Hamilton, Ontario. On the annual Divinity Day, he delivered a lecture entitled 'What Future for a Unique Christ?' He reaffirmed the position developed in the Teape Lectures and ended with a call to treat the matter with urgency:

> No other task, I believe, is more urgent for the church today than to learn how to restate its conviction of the centrality of Christ both in relation to other faiths and in relation to insights of modern psychology without on the one hand being imperialistic and triumphalist (which, let us face it, we were when in the period of Christendom we had it to ourselves) or lapsing into a helpless syncretism, in which all religions and all insights are as good as each other or can be regarded ultimately as saying the same thing (which they are not). [WTWM, 12]

Although JATR came to regard himself as primarily a New Testament scholar, his textual studies were pursued in order to provide a proper biblical basis for his theology. He never saw theology as excavation within a closed site, but rather as exploration of an ever-increasing field. But if we are to pursue this metaphor we must say that the positions he reached were never discarded or forgotten. They were the foundations of the next phase of his journey. In the Preface to his dissertation he claimed that 'the systematic elaboration and application of these ideas in connection with the philosophical concept of the personality of God and His relation to the world is a need which we feel has hitherto hardly been met' [TWA, iii]. In a real sense his entire theological pilgrimage of exploration was to bring him back to the place from which he first began, except that he now understood the mystery of God and the world – the whole, modern world – at a profoundly deeper level.

PART THREE

Social Exploration

Introduction

In Part One we followed the dialectic of radical/conservative in JATR's biblical studies. In Part Two the dialectic was between the biblical faith and the modern world. His position was not a reiteration of the biblical, largely mythological faith, but neither was it an uncritical acceptance of the perspectives of modern man. Now in Part Three we go on to consider his social concerns.

This might seem an obvious and unobjectionable sequence to follow, but elsewhere it has proved frustrating and unprofitable. We are all familiar with a course of lectures in theology which are at the outset attractive and even compelling because they promise to address one of the great issues of modern times. The lectures begin with what theology has to contribute to the contemporary debate. Well, no, in fact they begin with what the Bible says on the subject. Some unsuspecting texts from the Old Testament are examined in detail, followed by their counterparts in the New Testament. And now for our real subject. No, because it would be as well to have before us what patristic sources have said, and that involves a good deal of explanation of terminology. Suspicions begin to arise as the next stopping point is either the Medieval or the Reformation documents. Frequently, by the time the nineteenth century has been culled for references, the course runs out of time.

Alternatively the course might be a modular one, in which a different scholar appears at each session to cover one of the periods already mentioned. In this way the participants can be assured that, short of a flu epidemic or icing up of the points on the mainline, someone will appear at the end to show how this long historical introduction contributes to the contemporary debate. But of course this is not what happens either. One of two experts comes on at the end. The first is a theologian who is perfectly at home in the ancient world, and is comfortable with the reaffirmation today of what has been said before. In other words the traditional position cannot be applied. Everything else in society is moving rapidly like galaxies hurtling away from their earlier relative position. There is no possibility that the traditional position will apply. But sometimes a very different figure is wheeled out to end the course. He knows little of theology, but he is a graduate in one of the social sciences. As a

Christian layman he is therefore able to say something illuminating about the contemporary issue. It is not theology, but he is able to introduce a gospel saying or a patristic aphorism in a suggestive but enigmatic way, to give his secular analysis a religious dimension.

Such performances take place every winter in universities, seminaries and parish halls up and down the country. They bear witness to the fact that people feel intuitively that Christianity should have something to say about contemporary issues. The evidence is not just that theology is not applied to the issues, but rather that this kind of theology *cannot* be applied to them. The fault lies not in the issues or our grasp of them, but rather in the character of the theology itself.

Traditional theology cannot be applied to contemporary social issues, not because it is not contemporary, but because it is not social. Of course it is not contemporary: it was developed in a world which has long been superseded in every field of human knowledge and experience. It could not be contemporary, but that is as nothing compared with the fact that it is not social. And this is the strength of JATR's position, because it is inherently social. His theology does not have to be stretched and distorted to make it reach the social world: it is based on a social view of reality, the I-Thou and the I-thous. Therefore we say that in this Part we 'go on' to his social concerns, not that we 'turn to' these concerns. They constitute part of the exploration of God, Christ and the eschatological unity of mankind. It is not necessary to break off from theology vainly and pretentiously to attempt to solve the problem of the world through perspectives which simply do not connect with the issues. JATR's theology is inherently social and therefore is already there in the contemporary scene. It does not have to be brought in nervously across a spidery bridge, which is thrown desperately from another age and constructed of good intentions.

We have dealt with JATR's work throughout as dialectical. In this Part we shall be considering moral questions, but also liturgy and evangelism. If the last two (and perhaps even the first) do not initially seem to be social issues, the dialectic is that the social theology reconceives them in social terms. They are seen to become social, properly understood.

11 The Higher Way

If we begin by considering JATR's treatment of moral issues, we see that this is a particular case of the general position which we have just described. British theology has been characterized by historical studies, mainly biblical and patristic, with philosophy of religion also well represented. Unlike American theology it has not given a prominent place to ethics. When this distinction is noted some attempt is often made to attribute it to national characteristics: old Europe rooted in its own past, young America with a more pragmatic attitude. However this may be, there is a tendency in both cases to treat ethics as a separate department, applied or practical theology.

I believe that in JATR's case a much more integrated approach must be adopted. For him ethics is not an appendage to his biblical or doctrinal work. He presents us not simply with Christian ethics, but with a *moral* theology. In this respect there are two important elements in his position. The first is that because his theology is personalist, his theology is itself inherently moral. We have already seen examples of this. Philosophy of religion, if it is dealing with the Christian religion, with the God and Father of Jesus Christ, cannot presuppose divine omnipotence, which would be depersonalizing and coercive. The theological position is itself moral. Ethical issues are not dragged in as an after-thought. The second element concerns God's relationship to the world. If he is not 'up there' or 'out there', then our relationship to the Thou is established in our relationships with the thous. There is no supernatural or neutral 'space' in which we can relate to God, free from the tedious and distracting claims of our fellows. We are given not one but two commandments.

> You shall love the Lord your God with all your heart, and with all your soul, and with all your mind. This is the great and first commandment. And a second is like it, You shall love your neighbour as yourself. On these two commandments depend all the law and the prophets. (Matt. 22.37–40)

But if there is no space between the two, then *all* theology is moral theology, and there is no theology that is not moral theology. Or if there is, we should treat it with great suspicion.

In many theological works we should therefore say that it is time to 'turn' to ethics, as if we were turning aside, leaving behind the serious and central concerns of theology. But in the case of JATR there is a dialectic which will not accept this dichotomy. It is in the fulfilment of the second commandment that the first commandment is addressed. Except that it is only because of the first commandment that the second commandment can be entertained. It is not that we have a theological system which can somehow be stretched to 'apply' to everyday life. Rather theology is already a moral theology. To do theology we must seek God where he has said he will be found: '"With what shall I come before the Lord, and bow myself before God on high?" . . . He has showed you, O man, what is good; and what does the Lord require of you but to do justice, and to love kindness, and to walk humbly with your God?' (Mic. 6.6,8)

Much theology is done without reference to guiding ethical considerations, and it must be said that very often what passes for moral theology is simply what the average decent middle-class person believes to be right, legitimized by dragging Jesus in or invoking God's name. If theology is inescapably moral, then for Christians morals are inherently theological. If what we have said up till now fairly represents JATR's thinking, any substantial change in theology should have a corresponding effect on moral theology. And a fundamental reinterpretation of the doctrine of God should have immediate consequences for moral values and decisions. It is therefore not surprising that one of the later chapters in *Honest to God* should be on ethics.

In Part Two we dealt with mythological and ontological ways of speaking about God. They also appear in connection with ethics. Thus in mythological terms God's will is given to men on tablets of stone, delivered to Moses on Mount Sinai. When this is translated into ontological terms, it becomes a natural law, which God has established, immutable and objective. God is either 'up there' or 'out there', delivering positive law. But since JATR has been attempting to revise our view of God, the foundations of morality are also affected: 'For assertions about God are in the last analysis assertions about Love – about the ultimate ground and meaning of personal relationships' [HTG, 105]. Just as belief has become problematic in the modern world when directed 'up there' or 'out there', so morality has become problematic when it is based on a law given from another realm. Such heteronomy having lost its authority lacks conviction: 'It cannot answer the question "*Why* is this wrong?" in terms of the intrinsic realities of the situation itself' [HTG, 113]. Nor will autonomy do in its Kantian form, which in fact is dependent upon a religious context which can no longer be presupposed.

Instead, JATR chooses the 'theonomous' foundation, as proposed by Paul Tillich:

> What does Tillich mean by this word 'theonomy'? It corresponds with his concern to push 'beyond supranaturalism and naturalism' to a third position, in which the transcendent is nothing external or 'out there' but is encountered in, with and under the *Thou* of all finite relationships as their ultimate depth and ground and meaning. In ethics this means accepting as the basis of moral judgements the actual concrete relationship in all its particularity, refusing to subordinate it to any universal norm or to treat it merely as a case, but yet, in the depth of that unique relationship, meeting and responding to the claims of the sacred, the holy and the absolutely unconditional. [HTG, 114]

Moral judgements, decisions and actions are therefore not based on an unchanging, obective law which increasingly to people today seems quite arbitrary and clearly related to the cultural circumstances of its first formulation. Nor does it collapse into the sheer relativism of truly automonous morality. It is based on the experience of reality as personal, and is therefore coherent with relations with persons. Theonomous ethics can therefore be accepted not only by religious but by non-religious people: 'The claim of the Christ may come to others, as indeed it often comes to the Christian, incognito: but since it is the claim of home, of the personal ground of our very being, it does not come as anything foreign' [HTG, 115].

On this view, even where there is disagreement over moral decisions or guidelines, the issues can at least be discussed meaningfully. Christian moral judgements can be advocated in a secular culture without recourse to claims about their supernatural origins. Nor can the words of Jesus be taken simply as binding commandments or expressions of natural law. They were spoken in specific situations, and they indicate what is required of such a person or persons to enter the Kingdom of God: 'This insistence on the parabolic character of the ethical saying of Jesus should deliver us from the danger of taking them either as literal injunctions for any situation or as universal principles for every situation' [HTG, 111]. Although in the Sermon on the Mount, Matthew, for his own purposes, presents Jesus in parallel to Moses on Sinai, the contrast could not be greater between the imposition of a set of binding laws, and the insistence that evil lies beyond the definition of the law, in the heart, in the glance and the thought. Is it wrong to break the sabbath?

Nor if it is out of love of God, and the neighbour. The sabbath law is good, but it was made for man.

Such moral teaching is as threatening as it is liberating. In taking away the constraints of the law it places on individuals the great burden of responsibility. In refusing to allow men to hide behind the law, it opens itself to the charge of antinomianism. In insisting that moral judgements must concern the heart and not just the hand, the thought and not just the deed, it condemns men beyond the law. And yet in basing morality on the higher consideration of love, it seems to open the door, in a world of sin and hypocrisy, to self-indulgence and permissiveness. This charge was to be made against JATR's position in *Honest to God*, and as a misrepresentation of his arguments he found it most hurtful. But then it was first made against Jesus when he advocated a higher morality than the law. But there is no doubt that in attempting to lay the foundations for a new understanding of morality based on the new understanding of God, JATR makes some unguarded statements which out of context proved to be offensive.

JATR was certainly not arguing for an end to moral standards, conventions of behaviour or even rules for living. But for these to be *moral* they must be accepted theonomously, not heteronomously, and certainly not out of fear or social coercion. As we saw in an earlier quotation, an action is not wrong because it is judged so on the basis of an external, objective law. It is wrong because in this particular case it is unloving or depersonalizing. Now that is in fact a much higher standard by which to judge our actions, but in a world of sin and hypocrisy some mechanism has to be joined to it to make sure that people face their real motives, and the actual consequences of their actions. But in concentrating the attack on the traditional bases of morality, mythological and ontological, but above all objective and universal, JATR seemed on occasion to pay less attention to the second element. In consequence he can say that 'nothing can of itself always be labelled as "wrong"' [HTG, 118]. Now unfortunately, a generaton later, there is growing evidence of the widespread sexual abuse of very young children. Surely this must be wrong, in *every* case. The answer is Yes, and indeed such is the disgust and anger roused in every decent person by such socially unacceptable actions that there is nothing to discuss. The only point to be made is that the actions are wrong because they are perpetrated without any human love. They depersonalize, they reduce individual children to objects, things, each is treated as an It. That is why it is wrong, and not because it breaks a specific obective moral law. This is perhaps a point which it is not necessary to make in a case where there is complete agreement throughout society. But it is an important practical point precisely on issues where there is no such consensus.

In the 1960s there were urgent questions about many issues, including premarital sexual relations, and divorce. But the fact that questions were being raised indicated firstly that the old moral basis had broken down, and that secondly, and notwithstanding the reputation of the times, people did actually want some moral context for their lives. But it had to be a moral basis which they understood and to which they could subscribe with conviction. It is in this context that the contentious claim was made, and in context it is perfectly clear what it means:

> For nothing can of itself always be labelled as 'wrong'. One cannot, for instance, start from the position 'sex relations before marriage' or 'divorce' are wrong or sinful in themselves. They may be in 99 cases or even 100 cases out of 100, but they are not intrinsically so, for the only intrinsic evil is lack of love. [HTG, 118]

What might well surprise those who came across the opening sentence only out of context, is the conservatism of JATR on these matters. The passage as it continues shows that JATR was well aware of the two sides, the moral basis and what we referred to earlier as the social mechanism to deal with human sin and hypocrisy: 'Continence and indissolubility may be the guiding norms of love's response; they may, and should, be hedged about by the laws and conventions of society, for these are the dykes of love in a wayward and loveless world' [HTG, 118]. Indeed far from being the high priest or episcopal advocate of permissiveness, JATR draws up very demanding moral requirements indeed: 'Chastity is the expression of charity – of caring, enough. And this is the criterion for every form of behaviour, inside marriage or out of it, in sexual ethics or in any other field. For *nothing else* makes a thing right or wrong' [HTG, 119].

The chapter is entitled 'The New Morality' and situational ethics are widely assumed to be more lax than older standards. But as we have seen, for JATR this is far from being the case. Hitherto it was possible to live within the moral law and yet to fail to live by love. Who ever spoke at that time of a woman being raped by her husband? But as indicated, the new basis for morality, while it is not heteronomous, is not autonomous in the sense of deriving simply from the individual. It has its own objectivity, and not only for the Christian. JATR first came to prominence in the debate about moral issues when, in October 1960, he appeared for the defence in the prosecution of Penguin Books arising from the publication of *Lady Chatterley's*

Lover. In Lawrence JATR found confirmation that even those who are not identifiably religious in an institutional way, may still recognize that the new basis for morality comes from what JATR has already called 'the sacred' within. He quotes D. H. Lawrence at this point: 'And then – when you find your own manhood – your womanhood . . . – then you know it is not your own, to do as you like with. You don't have it of your own will. It comes from – from the middle – from the God. Beyond me, at the middle, is the God' [HTG, 120].

The response to *Honest to God* was overwhelming. The new understanding of God brought immediate reactions, both critical and congratulatory. But the chapter on morality produced even more empassioned reactions. Seven months after its first publication JATR went to Liverpool to fulfil an engagement entered into two years previously. But by this time the announcement that he was to give three lectures on ethics led to a public threat to picket the Cathedral. The lectures were published as *Christian Morals Today*, and in the Preface JATR recalls such scenes as part of 'the passions and follies of 1963'. In *Honest to God* the chapter on the subject was entitled 'The New Morality', but it was set in quotation marks, since it came not from JATR but from the Pope, or at least the Supreme Sacred Congregation of the Holy Office. But in spite of the stringent moral standards which he advocated in *Honest to God* JATR was identified with the phrase, and with the permissiveness and licentiousness it was assumed to condone and encourage. The abusiveness of the reaction JATR took to be symptomatic of deeper problems: 'For so much inability to "hear" what the other side is saying comes from unexamined presuppositions that go very deep, and they are reinforced psychologically by insecurities and fears which make us unreceptive and aggressive when on the defensive' [CMT, 9].

Not surprisingly, we can see a parallel here with issues raised in the theological discussions of Part Two. Just as the mythological and ontological forms of Christology look absolute and objective compared with the new Christology, so the 'old' morality looks to be committed to absolute and objective standards compared to the relativism of the 'new'. In both examples, however, the issue is not between absolute and relativie, but wherein lies the absolute. Is the old morality only deceptively objective? Is the moral law any more 'out there' than the God of traditional metaphysics?

As with theology, it is a question of perspective or starting-point. On one view there are objective commandments, a body of moral teaching which remains unchanging in a changing world. By casuistry the universal laws are applied to particular situations. On the other view we start from the demands of love. JATR does not mean by this that there should be no 'net' below society, no dykes or guidelines around it. Far from it; the demands of love in a sinful world require such supports in order that society and human relations can exist. But just as Christ does not supply a legal system within which to live, a form of government or an economic order, so neither does Christ supply an ethical code. In the relativities of human life there are the constant and absolute demands of God's rule of righteous love. This rule is not to be identified with rules. Obedience will require different things in different circumstances. This puts a heavy responsibility on to each age.

At the point where these two views of morality meet the older view sees absolute standards being eroded, and dykes torn down. In the perspective of the new, the same fundamental absolute is being maintained, but expressed in different ways, and in some cases through the defence of different standards of behaviour. The dykes are not destroyed but rebuilt in more strategic places, closer to where people now live. Much of what goes into making an ethical decision is not itself ethical, deriving from new knowledge from the natural and social sciences. The demands of love require that these factors be fully taken into account. Recognition of the fact that we live now in a process of constant change was to become an important element in JATR's thinking at this time. In a period when many people found this frightening and threatening, he displayed a pastoral concern in pointing with assurance to that which is constant and unchanging, the love of God. Our response, if it is to be constant and appropriate, cannot be through the reliance on laws and codes, useful though they can be at a secondary level.

This is but another form of the criticism of the classical tradition. There is a tendency to see God in the unchanging and to associate change with human experience: 'We identify him instinctively with what is permanent and see ourselves commissioned to stand for the changeless in a welter of chaos not of his making. But that is a Greek assumption, not a Biblical' [CMT, 18]. When it is said, perhaps too easily, that God is the God of history, entailed in it is the recognition that God is found in the movement and change, the living and the lively.

It is not difficult to see why JATR's work should produce two very different responses. There was hostility and rejection from those who saw it as the unravelling of the safety net, the dismantling of the framework of civilization. But there was a much more positive reaction from those who saw in it the possibility of being more morally responsible. If they were irked by existing moral laws and conventions it was not because they wished to be less moral, but because intuitively they felt this approach to be an obstacle to being moral.

The negatve reaction might be thought more surprising, since JATR's position is very Pauline. It is similar to Paul's teaching on the relationship of law and love. Love in the New Testament is the fulfilment of law in the Old: 'The Christian can never say that he is beyond or outside the sphere of law. He needs it for himself, he needs it for his children, and he certainly cannot dispense with it for his society' [CMT, 21]. It is the tutor and not the master. It is the first mile, love the second. But the second mile changes the basis of the first. Christ is the end of the law, the *telos*, the new foundation and inner meaning of it. JATR therefore did not regard his position as new at all. It was certainly not new in the sense of being brought about by a puerile capitulation to the demands of the worst elements of the modern age.

In giving the law its place, or rather *a* place, though not the place it had in orthodox Judaism, Paul could not fairly be charged with antinomianism or permissiveness. And JATR stands in this tradition. In fact there are better grounds for the charge of antinomianism levelled against Jesus. His typical teaching is addressed to individuals in their specific circumstances, facing them with 'the total demand of love, *as though no other claims existed*' [CMT, 27]. It gives a glimpse of the absolute demands of love compared with the requirements of the law. But it could hardly be the basis of an ongoing life in a family or society: 'Regarded as a code of conduct, prescribing what one should do in any situation, the Sermon on the Mount is quite impracticable. It tears the individual loose from any horizontal nexus' [CMT, 27]. Many of the most difficult decisions we have to make arise because of legitimate and competing claims upon us. We cannot take even the words of Jesus from specific situations and transform them into new absolute laws. It is not that they cannot be useful as rules, as guidelines, but that to adopt this whole procedure is to revert to a previous metaphysical model which as we have seen is incompatible with the God of love who is encountered in the convolutions of history.

Not surprisingly we can see the outworking here of the implications of JATR's Christology. Christ is not a supernatural being from another realm, bringing a changeless law from an unchanging sphere. He is the Christ because in his life and teaching men experience the absolute demands of the God of love. This is the basis of the authority with which he speaks. We can see here also the justification of JATR's previous claim that theology should be inductive rather than deductive. The teaching of Jesus arises from particular circumstances, from discerning the demands of love which may be surprisingly different from the requirements of the law. And this JATR takes to be another reason why the 'new' position, which is not at all new, has such a strong appeal to many in the modern world: 'For I believe that an ethic will have authority for most of our generation only if it is empirical and starts firmly from the data of actual personal relationships as they now are' [CMT, 37].

The greater danger to the moral life of the nation lies not in the new morality, which earns its own authority, but from an old morality which is unable to take into account the fruits of new knowledge and experience. The danger is that when its pretentions to absoluteness are discredited a moral vacuum is left. Alternatively there may remain for social, psychological or political reasons a series of rules more honoured in the breach than in the observance.

Although the lectures were delivered in Liverpool Cathedral, to a predominantly Christian audience, they seem to reflect JATR's concern for those outside the Church. He probably had in mind those who are still interested in the Church, who though critical and even alienated believe that it has a potential. These are people with whom it is possible to make common cause in influencing a society which is not necessarily going to become more committed to institutional religion. To that extent JATR considered in retrospect that he had perhaps been too one-sided in his presentation. The following year he attempted to correct this imbalance, in a lecture given at Hartford Seminary and Cornell University. When the Liverpool lectures were republished along with other writings from the period, this American lecture was added to them [CFPS, 43–51].

It sometimes seems impossible to say anything positive or appreciative about the modern world without being accused by some Christians of approving of everything which characterizes it. Even Bonhoeffer is dismissed as someone who did not take sufficient account of evil in man – and he was in the hands of the Gestapo! Happily JATR did not endure such experiences, but he was more sensitive than most to the inhumanity and degradation which characterized an increasingly affluent and materialistic society. He wrote about morality precisely because he saw the crisis, and he wrote as he did because with the breakdown of the old morality the challenge and opportunity arose of a new morality. In fact, although he takes over the phrase 'the new morality', what he is proposing is not in fact morality with a new content, so much as a new basis for being moral. Or, since he is constantly critical of the classical perspective, he is advocating a recovery of the foundations of morality clearly set out in the New Testament. He is far from approving what had become common practice. But he urges Christians to accept the facts of the present situation. If morality is now not going to be based on a static body of laws, neither is there any possibility of a return to a previous age when such a structure could be imposed and maintained by fear if not conviction. How then does the Christian affirmation of the absolute demands of love become the basis for a new morality in an age in which the old morality, whether we like it or not, no longer commands respect or compliance? In the next chapter we can examine how JATR sought to explore the interface of the Christian affirmation of love and the great moral issues of the day.

12 Morality Old and New

In his Liverpool lectures JATR had dealt mainly with the new basis of morality, rather than any possible new context. Naturally he illustrated the new position by reference to such matters as marriage and divorce, but they include no extended treatment of particular issues. In 1960 he published a collection of lectures and articles he had issued during the 1950s, entitled *On Being the Church in the World*, and we shall refer to some of its discussions in due course. In 1970 he repeated the process, by gathering lectures and articles from the 1960s under the title *Christian Freedom in a Permissive Society*. The titles and the contents of these collections indicate the substantial differences between the two decades, both for the Church and for society at large. As we shall see, the former collection reflected a period in which progressive thinkers were asking about the social nature of Christianity. This was an important matter, because of the Church's central place in the life of the nation. However, by the time the second collection was complete the situation had markedly changed. Society was going its own way, taking responsibility for its own values and priorities. Although the former agenda was still considered relevant by many Christians, JATR read the situation differently. The question was whether the Church was to be a ghetto community, increasingly cut off from the mainline society, and if not, what could Christians contribute to the newly emerging society, the first society for more than a millennium which was substantially free of religious control. If the Church is a servant, then like servants it must live in someone else's house. What could Christians contribute in a land which was, in a cultural sense, no longer theirs?

As noted in the previous section, when JATR came to publish the Liverpool lectures as *Christian Morals Today* he wished to add a corrective. This was to be 'Starting from the Other End', the lecture given in America. But in it he went on to discuss precisely the issue of the Christian contribution to a society not of its own making. This went beyond the subect of the Liverpool lectures, but in any case what JATR said at this point was so contentious that he was advised against including the material in *Christian Morals Today* in case everything else was ignored.

The example he took was premarital sexual relations. This has been a central topic in Christian morals, and that fact has its own significance. JATR agreed with Colin MacInnes, that one of the biggest barriers between the Church and the world is 'the almost indecent obsession that the churches have with sex' [CFPS, 45]. He chose this issue, however, because it is a good example of a subject on which the Church begins, not where society actually is, but with its own position, 'which it regards as absolute and unalterable, in a way that it has long ceased to do in fields like those of economics or war' [CFPS, 46]. This is an example of the old and new moralities. The old 'Thou shalt not' is simply being brushed aside, and there is nothing left. Christians can either repeat the old formula, which when it is ignored condemns society to an unrestrained and dehumanizing permissiveness, or they can attempt to bring forward a moral position which can be understood and even accepted in the modern age. Nothing would be easier than to take this to mean settling for whatever society will now accept. But in the light of the very careful position set out above, nothing could be further from the truth. As we have already seen, the demands of theonomous ethics, the demands of absolute love, are likely to be higher than the mere requirements of the law. And if in any society these demands prove unacceptable, so be it, but at least people can appreciate the basis of the demand. It does not strike them as simply arbitrary or stemming from assumptions which they cannot share.

In fact such assumptions are quite clear to us in even the most cursory review of changing attitudes towards marriage. The polygamy of the earlier sections of the Old Testament is not condemned by the prophets later, nor is it deprecated by the historical writers with hindsight. The change would seem to have taken place for social rather than religious reasons. Yet Western Christianity has made it an absolute sticking point in its missions to the under-developed Third World. Marriage in the Old Testament looks more like a contract concerning property, and adultery is condemned in the same terms as the theft of another man's possessions. Following Paul, the Preface to the 1662 Marriage service of the Book of Common Prayer presents matrimony as 'ordained for a remedy against sin, and to avoid fornication; that such persons as have not the gift of continency might marry' [CFPS, 47]. As JATR points out, today these would be thought very poor grounds indeed on which to embark on marriage.

As pointed out earlier, the natural and social sciences have brought great changes to our understanding of the world and human society. But in this matter the medical sciences have introduced developments which have completely altered the basis on which people relate to each other. For the first time in human history sexual intercourse need not lead to conception. This medical development has the most profound social and psychological repercussions. Sexuality is one way, perhaps the most fundamental way, in which human beings relate to each other. Medical advances could well allow it to become precisely that, without its other associations. As JATR concludes, 'with the fears of conception and infection lifted, the stigma of detection, which induces furtiveness, insecurity and guilt, and condemns the possibility of deep, free, and therefore truly loving relationships outside a certain area of society's approval, are likely to disappear rapidly' [CFPS, 48]. It is not surprising that JATR was advised that if this kind of argument was included with the Liverpool lectures they and the position carefully set out would be brushed aside in the general condemnation.

It is important to remember here that JATR is not offering an episcopal seal of approval to all casual sexual liaisons. He is asking what differences medical advances make to human relations. Now he is able to point to the positive possibilities: the negative ones we know of already. In former times, viewed obectively, sex within marriage was good, sex outside of marriage was bad. The former brought the blessings of children, the latter brought the punishment of children, not to mention various diseases. But the circumstances themselves have now been entirely changed. Also, the capacity of objective laws to determine moral value is being questioned: 'Morality could increasingly come to be judged by the inherent quality of the relationship, by its maturity, freedom and responsibility, rather than (as so often at present) by its degree of sexuality' [CFPS, 49]. In the social history provided by literature we can see very clearly that sexual relations within marriage have as often as not been the occasions of I-It rather than I-Thou relations. Under the influence of religious and social stereotypes the idea that a wife might be able to express her deep love for her husband through her sexuality – as opposed to making herself available to him – would have been a disgusting and degrading thought. In the new situation marriage is not the moral indicator that it was. Those who have paid no attention to the actual argument might nevertheless be surprised at the way in which JATR finally speaks of the moral requirements of marriage:

> Within this situation, marriage will continue to mean the life-long and exclusive commitment of two persons to each other with all they have and are, and acceptance of the responsibility for children. It will preclude

> other relations, whether sexual or not, which threaten the precedence of that total mutual commitment. [CFPS, 49]

In the mid-1960s JATR was also drawn into the debate about abortion, and, although the situation described was overtaken by the Abortion Act of 1968, his treatment of the subject further illustrates the difference between the old and new approaches to moral issues. Everyone regrets that abortions take place, and at a moral level this is perhaps true even of those who make money from performing the operations. It is not in itself a positive or creative thing. By this time we recognize the pattern of the discussion. On the older approach to morality, abortion is therefore defined as intrinsically wrong. The newer approach will begin from the other end, asking about the human context in which it occurs. In patristic times, following Aristotle, it was believed that the rational soul was not present in the foetus till it was forty days old (or eighty in the case of a female). This view has been superseded in the Catholic Church by 'immediate animation', the view that from the moment of union of the cells a human person has come into being with absolute right to life. JATR considers that this stems from a Greek, rather than a biblical, assumption that the individual possesses an immoral soul. It leads to the anomalous position that a miscarriage, occurring naturally, is not regarded as a death, and even in the case of a foetus spontaneously aborted no funeral service takes place.

In approaching the matter JATR rejects the view that we can begin by identifying actions which are inherently wrong. (We noted in the last chapter that we can still say that on moral grounds a certain kind of action will in every specific instance be judged to be wrong.) His starting-point relates to our previous subject. It should now be possible by modern contraception to avoid all unwanted (as distinct from all unplanned) pregnancies. Contraception could of course be another issue to illustrate the different starting-points, since once again on the old approach to morality an action would be intrinsically wrong, regardless of the human situation in which it occurred. But 'should a mechanical – or a human – failure compel enforced parenthood?' [CFPS, 57]. JATR adopts a position which was to anticipate the subsequent legislation, and illustrates his approach to moral matters:

> In the last resort, the right to decide must rest not with a doctor or a judge, or any third party, but with the mother herself. This is in no way to prejudge the moral issue. She still has the responsibility for choice – supported by all the pastoral concern and clinical advice that can be made available to her. [CFPS, 57]

This is an indication of the burden of moral responsibility. It is a consequence of human freedom, but unless it is central, human actions will not be moral even when legal.

Once again, the careful statement which he makes could easily be distorted. He is against what is now called 'abortion on demand', abortion when it is taken out of the context of moral responsibility and seriousness. And of course he is very much aware of the opportunities which exist for abuse and exploitation. As in previous discussion JATR does not deny the need for good laws; the question concerns the place of legislation:

> Hitherto, and equally under any new legislation we may get, the place of the law had been to *make* the decision: it is ultimately the judge who decides with or without the consultation of doctors. I believe, rather, that the place of law is to *safeguard* the decision, to enhance and protect the freedom to decide, which must lie ultimately, if it is to be a moral decision, with the woman herself. [CFPS, 64]

Legislation has since taken place, though the debate is far from over. JATR's contribution is still relevant, since it is clear that the division is between two ways of approaching moral decisions: 'The tragedy is that most moralists are by instinct prohibitionists, and they tend to think that those who are anti-prohibitionist are enemies of morality' [CFPS, 67].

Before we leave this subject, we might note the reaction of JATR to the encyclical of Paul VI, *Humanae Vitae*. He sees it as a classic example of the old morality, employing as it does, 'a concept of authority which is as alien to the New Testament as it is an anachronism to the second half of the twentieth century. The imposed, heteronomous authority of *Roma locuta est, causa finita est* (Rome has spoken, the issue is settled)' [CFPS, 114]. He clearly considers the claim to papal infallibility as the outworking of the older view of morality, that it is possible to proceed by identifying specific actions as always immoral. The fact that many Roman Catholics ignored the instruction indicated not that it did not suit them, but that they had transferred to another understanding of how moral issues are approached: 'Few will now bother to ask whether the Pope is infallible. The credibility gap is too great. They are much more concerned with whether the pill is infallible' [CFPS, 115]. Paul (the apostle, that is) could say that the Gentiles 'show that what the law requires is written on their hearts' (Rom. 2.15), but he refers this to their consciences. He is not speaking of an objective law from which they can become alienated and which then carries no conviction.

We have noted throughout that JATR's understanding of morality flows from his work on the doctrine of God. At this point he applies an earlier argument which we met in his Christology:

> The trouble is that the traditional concept of natural law has yet to catch up with the understanding of personality in the modern world. What is 'natural' is defined in sub-personal, biological categories rather than in terms of what makes for deep, free, mature, responsible personal relationships. So far from exceeding the morality of the secular humanists, the Catholic theology of natural law falls far short of it. [CFPS, 229]

The purpose of this book is to present the main works of JATR in such a way as to bring out their coherence and originality. As I have already made clear, where I have criticized him it has not been because he has failed to say what I should have said were I tackling these issues, but rather because on occasion he has not been true to his own position. I believe that such a criticism has to be made of his treatment of several moral issues. As we have just seen, his approach to the questions of sexuality and marriage, abortion, and contraception are very closely related to his biblical studies and also to his theological works, but this is not true of his discussions of other matters. This can be illustrated in a chapter on 'A Christian Response to the Arms Race', first published in 1982 and included in the posthumous collection, *Where Three Ways Meet*. He begins by noting the typical condemnation of war by ecclesiastical bodies, and claims that nuclear war cannot fulfil the traditional requirement of proportionality of response: 'And there would be unanimous agreement among moral theologians that unrestricted nuclear warfare could never be justified under the doctrine of the "just war"' [WTWM, 78]. He is not a pacifist, but supports the idea of a peace tax campaign. He also has some salutary words on the split between unilateralists and multi-lateralists which has weakened their common cause, offering along the way what are called ominously 'a few fraternal home-truths about how unilateralists look to the other side' [WTWM, 80]. He goes on to question why Britain should want to have a first-strike capability, and in what circumstances it could be used. With reference to the work of the Max Planck Institute in Germany he advocates reliance on light, precision-guided missiles using heat-homing and laser-beam technologies which would make the invasion of Europe too high a price. One of the greatest problems to be overcome is public lethargy before this numbing issue, and this requires 'a massive campaign of conscientization to bring people to the point of saying, "This is no way to live"' [WTWM, 87].

What JATR writes to this point is interesting and discussable, and it is to his credit that as a concerned citizen – and grandparent – he feels the responsibility of getting involved. But it is difficult to argue with his summing up, 'Most of what I have been saying so far could have been said by anyone, Christian or non-Christian' [WTWM, 88]. He goes on in the final paragraphs to distinguish between peace-keepers and peacemakers, and to refer to one of his favourite passages, from the second-century *Epistle to Diognetus* on Christian detachment and concern, as citizens and as strangers.

There is a difference between scholars who know the authorities, and prophets who speak with authority. The former can introduce the arguments and texts of the past which might be relevant in addressing a contemporary problem. The latter have a distinctive perspective from which they view the complex issue. They cut to the heart of the matter because they do not share the assumptions and pre-suppositions which act as a log-jam to the rest of us. In the first two parts of this book we have been setting out JATR's position, which falls on the prophetic side, and which as we have seen enables him to approach issues from a new perspective. This is true of the moral issues so far discussed. But it is entirely absent from his treatment of the arms race. Someone who had read nothing of his other works would be completely unaware of the fundamental criticisms which he has made of the doctrine of God, Christology, impersonalist ontology and objective morality. Our criticism is not that he has said what anyone else could say (if they had taken the time to become as well-informed), but that he has said it instead of what he might have said from his own distinctive perspective. Prophets should not contribute to interminable debates, they should blow the whistle on them.

Later in 1982 JATR delivered the first annual McAndrew Lecture at Christ's Church Cathedral, Ontario. It was on 'The Church's Most Urgent Priority in Today's World', addressing the issue of war and specifically nuclear war. Once again, although church statements are regularly made about the unacceptability of war as a means of settling international disputes, there was an almost deafening silence from the Churches that summer as British and Argentinian troops fought bitterly for the control of the Falkland Islands. JATR did not consider himself prophetic when he publicly pointed to this anomaly, but the response he received convinced him that ordinary people throughout the country could not believe what was being done in their name at this stage of the twentieth century. In a general context JATR's point is that certain social ills in the course of time come to be regarded as unacceptable: slavery, capital punishment, racism, sexual discrimination. In his previous treatment of the subject he called for 'a massive campaign of conscientization'. It would seem now as if he sees evidence, in the public reaction, that like these other social ills, war is now being regarded as unacceptable. In the real world some defensive capability has to be maintained – and he has already indicated what this might be – but could it be that people will come to find all arguments for nuclear warfare unacceptable? The most urgent priority of the Church is to bring about this general awareness about nuclear warfare and avert the possibility of the total destruction of life on earth.

Up to this point, once again, what has been said is not distinctive. But at least on this occasion it occurs to JATR that there has been very little 'hard and searching theological thinking' on the subject [WTWM, 103], certainly compared with the other issues previously mentioned, notably racism and sexism. And he goes on to examine the New Testament references to peacemaking. In the Beatitudes Jesus teaches, 'Blessed are the peacemakers, for they shall be called sons of God' (Matt. 5.9). In the only other use of the word in the New Testament, Paul speaks of what God has achieved through his Son, 'making peace by the blood of his cross' (Col. 1.20). As peacemakers the sons of God follow the Son. In urging the Church to address this issue JATR is not advocating a narrowing down to a single issue. This is part of the full gospel which the Church has to proclaim, and the costly way along which Christians themselves are committed to travel. He ends with a call reportedly from Raymond Pannikar, that 'what we need is not a Vatican III – a Jerusalem II is far more urgent' [WTWM, 122]. Up till now JATR has said little which arises from his own distinctive position, but at this point he develops the theme with which we ended Part Two:

> The first Council of Jerusalem recorded in Acts 15 marked the break-out of the gospel from the shell of Judaism. The second . . . must see its break-out from the shell of Christianity as one religion among many. The preaching of peace, to them that are far off and to them that are nigh, and the abolition of war from all the earth, could be the one issue big enough, and urgent enough, not merely to requicken the church and its unity, but to take it out of itself to become the instrument of that universal vision glimpsed by the prophet, without which the people perish, where 'The wolf shall dwell with the lamb . . . and a little child shall lead them . . . They shall not hurt or destroy in all my holy mountain; for the earth shall be full of the knowledge of the Lord as the waters cover the sea' (Isa. 11.6–9). Amen. So be it, Lord, beginning with me. [WTWM, 105]

13 Liturgy as Social Action

The preceding quotation ends with an illustration of the connection between morals and meditation, struggle and spirituality, life and liturgy. But it is an inherent connection. As we noted at the beginning of this Part, liturgy is included here not for convenience, not because it cannot be credibly fitted in anywhere else, but for theological reasons. When reality is personal, when there is no neutral gap between the world of God and the world of men, then there is no sacred space in which we encounter God by turning away from our neighbours. JATR often refers to the writings of George Macleod, the founder of the Iona Community. One of his favourite texts is the warning of Joseph (unrecognized) to his brothers should they seek him again, 'You shall not see my face, unless your brother is with you,' (Gen. 43.3). Lord Macleod saw here a truth for ecumenism, including the unity of the Eucharist. In Part Two we saw that for JATR we encounter the Thou in the thous: life and liturgy belong together – and both are social realities. –

It is not unique to Anglicanism, but it is a feature of academic life in England that some individual scholars move to and fro between university and ecclesiastical appointments. It was true of JATR's own family, notably his uncle Armitage Robinson, and of course of the man he so greatly admired both as a churchman and scholar, J. B. Lightfoot, the subject of his Durham Cathedral Lecture, 1981. The coincidence of vocations was characteristic also of JATR himself. At Wells Theological College he was both chaplain and lecturer in New Testament, while at Cambridge in the 1950s he was Dean of Clare College, and establishing his reputation in the field of New Testament. Just after his move to Woolwich, JATR published an account of his work at the College, entitled *Liturgy Coming to Life*.

JATR admits that as a theological student he had never been interested in liturgiology. (Indeed written thus, the term is depressingly onomatopoetic.) The subject, or at least his image of it, seemed quite remote from a concern for the gospel and its relevance for the modern world:

> And those of my contemporaries who were most enthusiastic about it only confirmed my worst suspicions. For they seemed to be indulging in a purely antiquarian pastime of the narrowest ecclesiastical interest, from

which they emerged from time to time to pontificate on what was 'correct' in the public address of the Almighty. [LCL, 9]

But as a curate in Bristol he had been introduced to a Parish Communion which was 'the centre and power-house of everything that was done in the week, both within the life of the Christian congregation and in the world outside' [LCL, 10]. As Dean of Clare College he was responsible for worship in the life of the community, and sought to establish there what he had found in the parish, the integral connection between evangelism and liturgy: 'It is in the Holy Communion supremely that the Gospel is shown forth: liturgy is the heart of evangelism' [LCL, 1]. This was the goal towards which he strove, not the point from which he started, for most of those coming to the College brought a tradition of individualistic piety quite unrelated to evangelism or indeed to the life of the world. Two objectives were clear. Liturgical reform was not to be undertaken for its own sake, but to make real the connection of liturgy and life. And the changes had to be worked through by the community, rather than imposed by one man.

Experiment, growing together, was possible in an ecumenical context because of the special position accorded to such college chapels, in which any full communicant member of any Christian denomination could be admitted to the Communion. The importance of this legal point at that time is but one example of how significantly things have changed in the intervening thirty years, at least in some respects. Yet some developments regarded then as a breakthrough now seem positively derisory:

> For a time, too, we were able *to use a Presbyterian minister* in residence as a research student to assist with the administration of the chalice, regarding it as a legitimate extension within such an ecumenical community *to allow to a non-Anglican minister what in principle any layman can do* and which is now being widely permitted to lay-readers. [LCL, 17; italics added]

We began this chapter with a theological grounding of the relationship between liturgy and life. We should expect JATR's distinctive theological position to provide a fresh perspective from which to reassess and reinterpret all the interconnected issues of liturgy, spirituality, baptism, ecumenism, ordination, inter-communion. But already he is lapsing into traditional terminology and apparently sharing many of the assumptions surrounding the issues. We have noted this tendency when dealing with moral questions. Before proceeding to examine how far this is the case with regard to the liturgy, we can illustrate the point from JATR's treatment of some of these other matters.

In the last quotation JATR was able to find an ordained minister of a non-Anglican Church was able to perform a function which an Anglican layman could perform. We might begin, therefore, by examining JATR's thoughts on priesthood, ministry and inter-communion, to see whether they provide a new perspective on these issues or whether they simply reflect the assumptions of his tradition.

In 1957 JATR gave an address to the Rochester Diocesan Clergy School entitled 'The Priesthood of the Church', later reprinted in *On Being the Church in the World*. In it he notes the astonishing speed at which early Christianity set aside the whole priestly tradition of Judaism. Even in the Epistle to the Hebrews priesthood belongs to Christ and not to the Church: 'As is well known, nowhere in the New Testament or in the early period of the Church is the word *hiereus*, priest, used of the Christian ministry, though all the other offices – bishop, presbyter and deacon – were evidently adapted from Jewish models' [OBCW, 89]. Even when Old Testament passages concerning priesthood are applied to the Church, towards the end of the New Testament period, the references in 1 Peter and the Apocalypse concern the whole of the people of Israel and not a professional class. However this was to describe the Church, priestly language is never applied to the Eucharist: 'But nowhere in the New Testament is the Eucharist called a *thusia* or sacrifice, nor is its meaning drawn out in priestly categories' [OBCW, 96]. Towards the end of the address JATR came to the following, balanced conclusion:

> But this ordained ministry, which is priestly because the whole ministry of the Church is priestly, is in the strict sense representative, not vicarious. The priesthood does in the name of the Body what, essentially, the whole Body is doing: it is not doing for the rest of its members what only it can do – except in so far as by ordination the Church as a whole deliberately reserves certain of its functions to certain authorized persons. [OBCW, 98]

But although JATR is struggling here to see a connection between the ordained priest and the eucharistic theology of the early Church, it is quite unrealistic to ignore the fact that the intervening theology of the Church is entirely at odds with his revision. The organization of the early Church did not flow from Old Testament models, but from the example of the Empire which Christians were committed to win for Christ. And to do this the new faith had to be established as a religion within the Hellenistic culture of that Empire, with the recognizable features of religion, including rites and officials. This is perhaps the most important period in the life and development of the Church after the apostolic era, and yet it is one of the least researched. The formation of a Christian priesthood derives from this period, and what the early Church thought about Jewish priesthood was not a primary criterion in the process. We should in the normal course of things have expected JATR to take this historical-critical line, and yet instead he adopts the conventional attitude of ecclesiastical fundamentalism, expecting to find a connection between the New Testament understanding of priesthood and the practice of the Church of England in the twentieth century. Surely this is a subject which is ripe for the typical criticism which he mounted so consistently in Part Two. For example, should we not have expected him to declare priesthood when linked to holiness to be a mythological way of representing the qualitative distinction between the human I and the divine Thou? His second line of criticism has been against the ontology of the classical tradition. And what could have suited his approach better than to expose and dissociate himself from the Aristotelian foundations of the traditional view of the male, celibate priesthood?

Therefore, although JATR begins with a critical biblical appraisal of the evidence, he does not carry through his own typical method to deal with the mythological and the ontological. He ends the address by reference to the ministry of healing, taking as an outstanding example the weekly healing service, with laying on of hands, as practised by the Iona Community:

> Nothing was said, apart from simple words of Scripture. But one sensed there the priesthood of the Church being exercised very palpably, both in word and in deed. We went away knowing that we had seen and felt the healing community. How often do we see that in our churches?' [OBCW, 101]

While it is gratifying that JATR should have had this experience, the theology and the liturgy of the Iona Community are entirely opposed to the concept of priestly ministry. Should the experience not lead to a proper reinterpretation of priesthood and its surrounding mythology and ontology?

Connected with priesthood, we might consider intercommunion as a second example of an issue on which JATR's characteristic critical approach is missing. As we have seen, it was a matter of practical importance in his days at Clare College that all Christians were welcome to the Anglican communion service. But that is not intercommunion. In the following decade, with the great increase in ecumenical contacts at all levels, this was to become an urgent and distressing problem. In 1962 JATR dealt with it in 'The Church of England and Intercommunion', included in the collection for the 1960s, *Christian Freedom in a Permissive Society*. Needless to say he is concerned on the one hand that Christians should be free to do in new circumstances what is right, without being necessarily bound by practices appropriate to former circumstances. And on the other hand he wants to avoid irresponsibility which does not properly preserve the heart of Christian faith and experience. He begins from the New Testament, relating these two concerns to Paul's teaching, 'For any one who eats and drinks without discerning the body eats and drinks judgment upon himself' (Cor. 11.29). We cannot take liberties with the Eucharist. But on the other hand JATR brought forward a text which was always decisive in his understanding of this matter, 'Because there is one bread, we who are many are one body . . .' (1 Cor. 10.17). There has been a tendency to concentrate on the first position: intercommunion should not take place indiscriminately in disregard of real divisions. This means that the Churches, in practice the ordained ministers, have to negotiate and find a way of over-coming the divisions. And what is the source of the divisions? Ordination! Those who are the embodiment of the problem are to be entrusted with its solution! (I should say that the exclamation marks are mine, not JATR's.) The other position quoted begins at a very different point. Christians are already one not because of anything they have done, and perhaps in spite of anything they do, but because there is one Christ. Intercommunion is not the fruit of negotiation, but the gift of God. 'Intercommunion is then the great sacrament of justification by faith, the pledge of our new being in Christ, and all that is required for it is the trust that grace indeed does meet through each of our sacraments however defective' [CFPS, 180].

But why are they 'defective'? Presumably because they violate the first position, the Eucharist is celebrated while the great Church is divided. But it also has to do with the 'validity' of ministries: 'The Free Churches do not possess, and do not claim to possess, ministries which Anglicans can acknowledge as valid according to the criteria required by the preface to the Ordinal (namely, episcopal ordination and consecration)' [CFPS, 179]. Yet nowhere does JATR subject this claim to his own distinctive critical survey, the criteria of the biblical, the mythological and the ontological. Is man made for the sabbath? Is the Church made for the historic episcopacy? And what of Christian freedom from the institutions of men when new circumstances pose new responsibilities? Is there not a precise parallel here with earlier discussions about morality: is mechanical succession not simply another example of impersonal objectification comparable to the concept of natural law?

I propose to digress for a moment on this subject, and the reader may wish to proceed directly to the next paragraph. Some people in the USA seem to assume that being neurotic is as American as apple pie. One young comedian claims that he woke up to discover that during the night thieves had broken into his home and stolen everything, but replaced it with an exact replica. Although the Church of Scotland is the established Church in Scotland, just as the Church of England is in its country, JATR is quite capable of treating it as a Free Church [CFPS, 178]. There seems to be an assumption among many Anglicans that during one night in December 1560 all Christians in Scotland were stolen overnight, and replaced with exact replicas. Except that the replicas were immigrants from Presbyterianland, far across the sea. In fact the Catholic Church in Scotland used its Christian freedom to reform itself. The people were not stolen and replaced. The continuity lies in the people of God, and not in the ordained ministers. Correspondence with Rome during the previous decade expressed fears that a reformation was inevitable unless the ministry was substantially improved: it had failed the people. At the Reformation the new ministry was created, on what were understood at that time to be biblical models. The ministry was made for the Church. What was this if not the responsible exercise of Christian freedom in new circumstances? But there is no reference whatsoever by JATR to the mythological and ontological assumptions which underlie traditional conceptions of ministry. Why is difference a source of division?

Although we should expect JATR's views on the subject to become more progressive with changing ecumenical circumstances, his more enlightened position in fact came much earlier, in an article published in 1957, while he was still at Clare College. It was entitled 'Intercommunion and Concelebration' and was republished in *On Being the Church in the World*. On the resistance to breaking bread together prior to a mutually recognized ministry JATR makes the following point:

> This is to give the ordained ministry of the Church an absolute significance and veto over the rest of the life of the Church that theologically it cannot possess: it is to subordinate the Church to the ministry, and not the ministry to the Church, which is the only true order. [OBCW, 119]

We should conclude that on many of the issues closely associated with liturgy JATR simply continued with inherited positions and assumptions. There was great scope for the application of his own distinctive critical perspective, but no such work was undertaken. He therefore did not contribute as he might have to making a breakthrough in these areas. But returning to the subject of liturgy itself, we can see the application being made at least in some respects.

In 1958 JATR delivered the Reinicker Lectures at Episcopal Theological Seminary, Alexandria, Virginia, on the subject of 'Matter, Power and Liturgy', subsequently published in *On Being the Church in the World*. They reflected his experience at Clare College, and the emphasis, as can be seen from the title, is on presenting Christian faith in relation to the fundamental realities of life. Even the word 'liturgy', which has now become a specifically ecclesiastical term, entirely separate from the secular world, derives originally from the realm of municipal affairs and local politics:

> In ancient Greece a citizen might be called upon to discharge his responsibility to the community, such as we should pay in rates or income tax, by making himself responsible for some piece of public works, like repairing the local dockyard or equipping so many men for the militia. This was called his *leitourgia*; and the word is derived from *laos*, people, and *ergon*, work. From this it came, in due course, to be applied to *the* Christian social action, *the ergon* of the *Laos* or people of God. [OBCW, 72–3]

But even as the word liturgy was being applied to the religious service, it did not lose its original meaning. Paul can use it when referring to the collection made to relieve the economic conditions of the Jerusalem church, an action which gives him special pleasure, 'for the rendering of this service not only supplies the wants of the saints but also overflows in many thanksgivings to God' (2 Cor. 9.12). (JATR might have pointed out the fact, surely significant for his argument, that in this matter, which is apparently welfare work, Paul not only uses the word *leitourgia* from which we derive liturgy, but *eucharistia*, here translated as 'thanksgiving', from which we derive Eucharist.) It is therefore entirely fitting that the liturgy is the corporate action performed by the followers of Christ: 'For it is here that the religion of the Word made flesh receives its crucial, continuing and most distinctive expression' [OBCW, 73]. And ironically, those who are concerned primarily with liturgy and liturgical reform very often break this connection, alienating the sacrament from everyday life.

Liturgy, then, is originally Christian social action. In the command of Jesus to his followers, 'Do this . . .', the verb is in the plural. JATR was much impressed by the point made by Dom Gregory Dix in *The Shape of the Liturgy*, that the pattern is not determined by words, but by the four-fold *actions* of Jesus at the Last Supper. He took, blessed, broke and shared the bread. But it is not a memorial of the Last Supper, rather a memorial of the death and resurrection, till Christ comes. JATR can use traditional terms, but the context makes them vibrant:

> The Eucharist is *the* Christian action, the heart of all Christian action in the world, because it mediates and makes present, in all its efficacy and power, the great saving act of God in Christ once and for all wrought out on Calvary. For all Christian action in this world is really nothing else than the finished work of Christ becoming operative through his body, the Church. [LCL, 22]

JATR thus combines the traditional interpretation of the death of Christ with the immediacy of Christian response:

> This is the point where all Christian action begins, where we are united with his act, and where what he had done *for* us is renewed *within* us for transmission to the world. This is the crucible of the new creation, in which God's world is continually being fashioned out of the old, as ordinary men and women are renewed and sent out as the carriers of Christ's risen life. [LCL, 22]

Liturgical reform does not arise out of antiquarian interest in early rites, nor the self-indulgence of romantic revival, but out of the necessity of understanding the Eucharist as 'the heart and hub of social action, the point where this world is taken and consecrated, broken and restored for God and his kingdom, and where the Church itself is renewed as the agent of the Christian revolution . . .' [LCL, 22].

The twin obstacles to reform are the almost universal tendency to destroy the corporateness of the action, and a false view of the holiness. With regard to corporateness, JATR sees common expressions as symptomatic of underlying attitudes: 'saying' or 'hearing' Mass, 'going to' Communion, 'making my Communion'. But the individualism of the piety is to be found along the entire Catholic-Protestant spectrum:

> The presbyter or bishop was never called 'the celebrant' in the primitive church, but 'the president'. And in that distinction there is a world of a difference. It is the difference between the two worlds of the early Church and the medieval Church, between the conception of the Eucharist as a celebration of the whole Body of Christ and that conception of the Eucharist as something done *by* the priest *for* the people. [LCL, 26–7]

In practical terms, JATR countered the clericalization of the liturgy by assigning to members of the congregation those parts which did not essentially belong to the priest. He introduced the westward position of the president, and the people round the table. Although these things have since become common, they were not done for sociological reasons, to create a sense of togetherness. They were based on theological grounds which are now familiar to us from Part Two. The eastward position not only made the liturgy into a spectacle to be observed, it expressed the doctrine of a God who is 'out there' to whom individuals relate in their personal devotions. The liturgy is not only the receiving of the body of Christ, but the sharing of his body. And beyond that, it is for the building up of the Body of Christ, the Church, in order to do his work in the world. JATR quotes with approval Cullmann's answer to the question about the specifically Christian aim of gathering for worship: 'The occasions serve for the "building up" of the community as the *Body of Christ*, the spiritual body of the risen Lord' [LCL, 34]. Based on the individualistic view of the Eucharist a candidate for Confirmation might ask, How often should I go? On the corporate view this is an incredible question, 'as if the disciples had asked *that* night in which he was betrayed, "Need I be there?" There was one only who could think of leaving that evening, and when he went out it was night indeed' [LCL, 61].

Liturgical reform has therefore to overcome the obstacle of individualistic piety, which distorts and conceals both the nature and purpose of the Eucharist. The liturgy is an occasion of celebration and thanksgiving, but is threatened by the imposition of a false sense of holiness. JATR's theological position is even more clearly seen as the basis of his attempts to dismantle this barrier. When God is 'out there', when the Eucharist is an occasion for the individual's communion with God, then there is a sharp line drawn between the holy and the profane. The holy is that which is specifically religious, peculiar, belonging within the sanctuary. The profane is literally that which is *pro fanum*, outside the temple, which belongs to the world of common things. While this may have been true for ancient Judaism, it has nothing to do with Christianity, the religion of the Word become flesh.

It might have been appropriate for JATR at this point to relate the issue to his Christology, and we shall attempt to indicate the connection which could have been established. There is an obvious parallel in what is happening in liturgy with docetism in doctrine. In Christology the danger is that Christ is not really a man, does not take upon himself real flesh, does not share our life completely. The same reluctance to find God present in the material world leads to a refusal to meet him in the most fundamental element of the common life – a loaf of bread. The docetism of doctrine is extended into a docetism of liturgy:

If the Eucharist is the most political thing to which the Church sets its hand, it is even more obviously the most material thing for which it comes together. At the very centre stand bread and wine – matter and the sharing of matter. These, one would think, were inescapable, and yet they have been so spirited away in performance of it, and so removed psychologically from any other kind of bread, wine or matter, that the Holy Communion has become in most of our minds the service with the least contact with the stuff and muck of this world, and certainly with such unholy concerns as politics and economics, business or finance. [LCL, 37–8]

Once launched into this attack, JATR sees current practice in all the Churches as a caricature of what the liturgy so obviously should be. Instead of the original elements, clearly described, we have

wafers in place of ordinary bread, or bread pressed and diced into some unrecognizable form, wine supplied by ecclesiastical purveyors that no one in their senses would ever drink for pleasure, served up in ecclesiastical cruets by altar-boys in fancy dress. The whole thing reeks of a conception of holiness that is almost the complete opposite of everything for which Christianity stands . . . [OBCW, 82]

In passing we might observe that with regard to the elements of the common life, some lives are more common than others. 'For our own College Communion at Cambridge we insisted upon an ordinary loaf baked in the College kitchens and some claret from the College cellars . . .' [OBCW, 82].

In the former understanding the taking up of the common means the desecration of the holy, but the incarnation means the sanctification of the common: 'But we shall never break through the thought-barrier between the Eucharist and the secular world, and so liberate the powers of the Eucharist into the secular world, until we have first removed the barrier *in church*' [LCL, 39]. Ordinary bread and wine, together with money, are brought forward in the Offertory by lay people. These elements announce that Christ is to be met not in the fruits of the natural world, but in the products of manufacture. They therefore challenge Christians about the common life, about economics, commerce, politics. If they are shared in the liturgy of the table, what of the liturgy in the world? What of the division of the world by race, gender, economics and social class? 'What we do with matter here has tremendous implications for what we do with matter everywhere' [LCL, 43]. It is here that the words of Paul sound their warning to those who join in the liturgy without discerning the implications of receiving the body of Christ. A false understanding of what is holy can mean that we seek God apart from where he has promised to be found. JATR returned to this issue in *Honest to God*, with a quotation from his colleague, now biographer, Eric James: 'The great danger is that liturgy creates a world of things over against the secular, instead of a vision of the sacredness of the secular' [HTG, 90].

We have questioned whether JATR's understanding of such matters as priesthood, ministry and intercommunion was based on his own distinctive theological position, but there is no doubt that his understanding of liturgy can be directly linked to his doctrine of God and his Christology. He could have explored the link further, as we have suggested in the parallel with docetism. It is perhaps surprising that he did not specifically deal with transubstantiation, which from his perspective would have been a good example of classical ontology and objectification. Before leaving this area there is one further subject to be raised, prayer.

When JATR was exploring liturgical reform in the 1960s there was a tendency to retain the King James Version of the Bible, but to adopt contemporary language for prayers. JATR was convinced that this was exactly the wrong way round. He advocated using the most modern translations of the Bible, but using the most traditional language for prayer. He does not anywhere attempt to justify this retention of the archaic forms, and I think that we have to recognize that despite his reputation there were areas in which he was perfectly comfortable with traditional forms. It may be that in our discussion of priesthood, ministry and intercommunion we uncovered such areas. But I have always thought that prayer was something of a test case for JATR's theology, and indeed for anyone who proposes a substantial revision of the doctrine of God.

The problem is obvious enough. Prayer as normally understood, and practised, presupposes precisely the understanding of God which JATR rejects, that is God 'up there', or 'out there', but quite definitely a supernatural being existing quite independently of the human world, though capable of intervening in its workings. It is possible to refine this model through a thousand qualifications, but in the end is prayer still a distinctive form of activity? It used to be said, latterly by those who preferred double-time to churchgoing. 'To work is to pray.' But this merely leads us to clarify what kind of work Christians might undertake and to what ends. It might be claimed that 'Prayer is reflecting with compassion on the world'. And this tells us something about how we should use our time and resources responsibly in caring for those in need. But if the model is not reasonably accurate in some residual sense prayer seems to be nothing additional to other forms of human activity, merely an adverb appended to them.

JATR saw the problem clearly and addressed himself to it in *Honest to God*, in a chapter entitled 'Worldly Holiness'. In the light of his critique of traditional theism, prayer cannot be a turning away from the world towards God. We can only find God as we turn towards the world, especially perceiving the Thou in the thous. God is not remote from the world, not unmoved by human life. This means that the world is not a distraction from seeking God, but the very place where God has promised to be found. And that is the dilemma. We have several other perfectly accurate ways of speaking about such a relation to the world. It seems unnecessarily confusing to call it prayer. JATR returned to the subject in *Exploration into God*, in a chapter entitled 'The Journey Inwards' which begins: 'In the last analysis the way of exploring into God is the way of prayer' [EIG, 111]. It would seem therefore that 'Prayer is meditation'. Once again, is this not a way of describing meditation?

JATR acknowledges that if the God of theism is dead for many people, it is not surprising that prayer has gone dead on them. As a starting-point he tells us that 'prayer has to do with life at its most personal' [EIG, 113]. In this case prayer is a way of describing a particular view of reality. Or again, 'Prayer is opening oneself to the claim of the unconditional as it meets one in all the relationships of life' [EIG, 114]. Prayer here is the name for a kind of life lived in the acceptance of transcendence. But in all of these cases prayer is something else, never itself – or at least never what it has always been taken to mean in the past and in the present by the vast majority of people.

Apparently it is now time to bite the bullet: 'It is entirely natural that the reality of God should be *expressed as* the grace and claim of another Person. As a myth, as a projection, the description of God as *a Person*, encountered and addressed in prayer, is an entirely legitimate way of putting it' [EIG, 114]. But surely this will not do. Throughout Part Two JATR was identifying the mythological elements in the Bible. They represented objectifications of religious values and interpretations. Although it was entirely in order for people living within the first-century world-view to use such expressions, it would be false for us in the twentieth century to continue to use them. We cannot use them: but we can come to understand them and appropriate their truth. JATR continues the quotation: 'It is the simplest possible aid to the human imagination. Indeed, for most people most of the time (at any rate in the West) it is impossible to conceive of prayer except as talking to an invisible Person' [EIG, 114]. I suppose that there is a personal element here: we have encountered one of those areas in which JATR is still comfortable with the traditional forms. And if so he is not going to subject it to the same level of criticism as other areas which seem to him to require complete revision. But we have to say at this point that he has not been true to himself. Up till now he has consistently refused that patronizing and elitist view that while scholars can believe one thing, the mass of people can make do with the unreconstructed tradition. There are two reasons for this. The first is that the natives are restless. It is precisely the intelligent laity and those outwith the Church who still reflect on these things, who find the tradition makes no sense. As we have noted JATR has an evangelical concern that they should not be presented in the modern age, take it or leave it, with something which is incompatible with everything else in their experience. But the second reason is if anything more fundamental, that the traditional form is wrong. It misrepresents God, Christ, man and the world. His concern was part missionary, part personal. The line of questioning runs through each of us. Now it would seem as if he is deserting his modern questing audience, perhaps because this is one of a small number of issues on which most of him is to the 'right' side of that line of questioning.

Indeed JATR seems to recognize that there is a cost to continuing with the traditional form. In the first instance, 'the highly personalistic theistic model of prayer and worship may subtly become an escape from the very personal reality it is designed to safeguard and express' [EIG, 116]. In the second instance it can lead to evasion of responsibility: 'By thus "turning" to God in prayer it is easy to *substitute* the "Thou" we cannot see for the "Thous" through whom the claim meets us' [EIG, 116]. For these reasons, we might suggest, it is imperative that prayer no less than all other aspects of theology and the religious life be subjected to the same criticism.

JATR ends the chapter with a reaffirmation of the consistency of his position, though we may doubt whether he has been able to carry it through in practice: 'In spirituality as in theology I find myself returning to the utterly personal panentheism of the God dwelling incognito at the heart of all things' [EIG, 129]. JATR was naturally interested in other attempts to deal with the problem of prayer. But since they were seldom well based theologically, he was often critical. In 1967 he published *But That I Can't Believe*, which included an article which he had written for *New Christian* on 'Pop Prayer'. At that time he was struck by an American 'Litany for the Ghetto', written by

155

an Episcopalian priest, Robert Castle. It included prayers such as, 'O God, who lives in tenements, who goes to segregated schools, who is beaten in precincts, who is unemployed . . .' [BTICB, 119]. I believe one of the reasons why it attracted JATR was his own controversial claims that God is in the mean and the ugly, not just in the gracious and the beautiful experiences of life. It could be directly related to JATR's own theology. By contrast he was critical of much pop prayer:

> But even at its best, as in Quoist, there is the sense of talking to a third person, apart from and invisible to the person whose concern engages me. Does this take the other 'Thou' with real seriousness and the fact that the claim of the unconditional must be me *in him and through him* . . .? [BTICB, 121]

But the same indecision is found as in *Exploration into God*. Pop prayer he sees 'envisaging God as a separate "Thou". Is "O Lord" the last remnant of the poetic diction of a by-gone age – or is it unavoidable? And if so can we use rather than stumble at the "myth"?' [BTICB, 121]. But of the two, he prefers the work of Robert Castle:

> The Litany for the Ghetto with its identification of God with the scene rather than the spectator here seems to me to have the advantage. It has provoked the inevitable charge of pantheism. But it is not asserting a metaphysical identity; simply that at the given moment for the subject in prayer this [is] where, and who, God is – and there is no turning aside, not even to Another. [BTICB, 121]

We see JATR struggling here with one of the most fundamental problems for Christian theology in the modern world, and there are some indications that his own position provides him with some clues as to how he might proceed. Perhaps surprisingly, however, there is one area of his theology which is not brought to bear on the issue. He came close to it when earlier he spoke of how prayer is understood, adding parenthetically, 'at any rate in the West'. At the end of Part Two we saw him reach out to other world religions, in *Truth is Two-Eyed*. It was our criticism at that time, that instead of learning from the East, JATR was inclined to bring forward his own position as the honest broker between two traditions. It seemed surprising at the time that he did not deal with prayer, but in retrospect it might have been because he did not have a developed position of his own to offer. But this might be an area in which there could be a genuine dialogue. A non-mythological, non-objectifying form of the spiritual life might be meditation, which seeks not that which lies beyond the world but, in the phrase of Teilhard which JATR likes to quote, 'God dwelling incognito' within the human world. However that line might be developed, JATR at a personal level clearly felt no need to declare the Lord's Prayer mythological.

14 Through the Fire of Atheism

In the previous chapter we saw that for JATR 'Liturgy is the heart of evangelism'. As we turn now to evangelism we must not lose sight of its corporate nature. It is corporate because it is the responsibility of the Christian community as a whole and not simply the clergy. Corporate because it is proclamation bodied forth; the testimony by each Christian – in the words of the Brighton preacher, F. W. Robertson – 'in whom the resurrection begun makes the resurrection credible' [LCL, 71]. And corporate too in the sense that it is addressed to people not apart from their ordinary lives, concerns, occupations, experiences and relationships, but precisely in, with and under such things. But what are the prospects for such communication, whether by the example of the Church or by its message? Perhaps I could set the scene before turning to JATR's answer.

In recent years we have heard politicians whose policies have been roundly rejected by the electorate claiming that there was a breakdown in communication, as though rejection came from lack of understanding. This is a patronizing and distasteful explanation. It carries the implication that reasonable communication is not effective enough in dealing with the average member of the public. The more straightforward explanation is simply pushed aside, namely that the policies have been rejected because they were understood only too well. There is a parallel when we come to discuss evangelism. Why are fewer and fewer people going to church, joining the church or responding to the Church's message? The answer of the laager is that it is because they are hardened sinners who have rejected God's grace and the forgiveness offered in Christ Jesus. While in some cases this is no doubt true, it does nothing to explain the numbers involved. There is no evidence to suggest that this generation is five times as hardhearted as its Victorian great-grandparents.

We could say that this kind of answer is symptomatic of the problem itself, namely that it is a theological account of what *must* be the case. And if the empirical evidence is against the account, we have a fair idea which is going to be dismissed. A less *a priori* explanation is that it is due to a lack of communication. Christians have simply not been effective enough in explaining what the Church is about or getting the message across. And no doubt there is a good deal of truth in that view. And yet there has never been a generation so susceptible to communication as this one. Television has produced a society with the most integrated consciousness in human history; the only-child in a highland croft is a party to events in the capital, while the house-bound pensioner in the inner city shares the excitement and beauty of an Amazonian expedition. If fewer and fewer people wish to join the Church or make any response to the gospel message, then the least likely explanation is a breakdown in communication. The most obvious explanation is that they understand fairly well what it is all about, and intuitively know that it is not for them. If that were true of the most disreputable people in society it might be taken as somehow confirming the Church in the essential rightness of its position, but if it is true of those whose lives are marked by compassion and integrity, those who are thoughtful and concerned about the ills of our time, then surely questions must be raised about the nature of the Church and the form of its message?

The world does not supply the good news but it does at least have the right to say whether the Church's message is good news, or not news at all, or not even comprehensible one way or the other. The world does not supply the new life promised by the Church, but it does have the right to say whether this is the life it has always been waiting for, or a life it is relieved to have progressed beyond, or whether it is, underneath the peculiarities and pretensions, just more of the life it has always had. In other words there are two sides to evangelism, as to any other form of communication, and the indications are that paying attention to only one side will guarantee continued failure. As James Reston said of the US government's decision to open up a new front in Cambodia while still suffering reversals in Vietnam – 'They seem to have let failure go to their heads.' If more of the same is going to have the same result, but cumulatively, then both the life of the Church and its message have to be reformed, with respect to 'the other side'.

I have produced this introduction as a context for JATR's reflections on the Church and the modern world, as illustrated in the chapter entitled 'Starting from the Other End', in *The New Reformation?* Although the repercussions of the sixteenth-century Reformation have been felt throughout the world, it was in its own time, together with the Counter-Reformation, essentially a domestic quarrel within Europe. It was an in-house controversy carried on by those who seemed blissfully unaware of other world religions or indeed of the rest of the world. When JATR issued his first collection of essays and articles, *On Being the Church in the World*, he looked back to the decade of the 1950s from which they were for the most part drawn. It was a period in which JATR was hopeful about the response the Church would make to the new developing secular culture. In 1959 he preached at a Confirmation service that new members were entering the Church at a time when new things were happening. 'I believe that in England we may be at the turning of the tide' [OBCW, 9]. JATR reflected on this ironically ten years later when the book was reissued. 'The tide was indeed imperceptibly on the turn. But 1960 was to represent the high-water mark not the low-water mark' [OBCW, 9]. The time was already over when the Church could reform itself without reference to society around it, or afford the luxury of in-house squabbles about itself and its own concerns.

Yet JATR himself had never shared that view of reform. In an article entitled 'The Social Content of Salvation', which he wrote as early as 1946, just after the completion of his dissertation, he asked the very pointed question: 'What, in terms of his contemporary society, has a man to be delivered from and enabled to become, if salvation is to appear to him a relevant offer?' [OBCW, 30]. Even at that time his concern for evangelism was shaped by the position set out in the dissertation. He called for a re-examination of evangelism. 'It is clear that neither mass conversion nor the saving of man out of and apart from his environment is nowadays possible or desirable' [OBCW, 36]. The same is true of conversion, which 'must be, through and through, a community affair. For a man becomes a person when he discovers himself in the I-Thou relation of community . . .' [OBCW, 36].

In 1964, in the middle of Vatican II, Cardinal Bea, head of the Vatican Secretariat for Christian Unity, declared, 'The Counter-Reformation . . . is over' [NR, 9]. JATR took this to reflect the new situation in which Christians found themselves, in common cause instead of domestic dispute. This would be the characteristic of the New Reformation. In the period after *Honest to God* the ferment was on both sides: not only Christians who were ready for change, but many outside the Church who suddenly believed that there might after all be something here for them.

But the starting-point cannot be metaphysical statements which presuppose a world-view alien to modern people, nor can it be the abrasive take-it-or-leave-it attitude of what Bonhoeffer calls the 'positivism of revelation'. Starting from the other side means starting from the human world, and building from there. But of course this is in any case JATR's understanding of Christology: 'If men are to see Christ, and therefore God, they can only do it through the one who comes to them, in the first instance, not as a messianic figure, but as one of themselves . . .' [NR, 35]. The text for the New Reformation is to be 'He who has seen me has seen the Father' (John 14.9).

Corresponding to this starting-point, so typical of the modern world, is the equally characteristic inductive method. The former method, the deductive, presupposed that the absolute was already known; only the implications had to be teased out. Within that tradition it is necessary to accept a position as a starting-point, which modern empirically oriented people would wish to reach only as the conclusion of an investigation:

> To ask men to believe in the doctrine or to accept the revelation before they see it for themselves as the definition of their experience and the depth of their relationship, is to ask what to this generation, with its schooling in an empirical approach to everything, seems increasingly hollow. [NR, 40]

The Church must therefore become an 'accepting community', not insisting that everything must be confessed before anyone can enter, nor rejecting if individuals do not come to believe everything that has traditionally been expected. The period of the first Reformation was characterized by strict definition of the centre and a policing of the edges, under threat of excommunication. The New Reformation is closer to the Gospels in focusing on entry into the Kingdom rather than the Church.

'Can a truly contemporary person be a Christian?' Those who see developments in the modern world, principally secularization, as a threat may well say, No. But in the succession of Bonhoeffer and Harvey Cox, JATR is convinced that the modern world can make a very positive response to the Christian message, as long as there are no metaphysical, supranatural, mythological or religious prior conditions attached. Indeed so important is this issue that an Appendix to *The New Reformation?* is entitled, 'Can a Truly Contemporary Person *Not* be an Atheist?' If some consider that the modern world is the enemy of Christian faith, others might hope that it is possible to come to some compromise, some *modus vivendi* within which religion can exist in the interstices of a broadly secular life. But this is not positive enough for JATR. He wishes to explore the possibility that certain developments in the modern world have made it impossible to continue with an inherited understanding of religion – but at the same time these very changes open up the prospect of a more profound kind of religious life. On this scenario it might be necessary to go through the fire of the atheist critiques of religion in order to emerge on the other side of atheism with a greatly purified and enriched religious understanding.

This is not an exploration for the faint-hearted, nor, we might add, for those whose faith must be hedged about with the protection and guarantees of objective authorities from the past. We must take the various criticisms of religion on board, evaluating them in a mature and adult manner. It is not an all-or-nothing, fight-to-the-finish, winner-takes-all confrontation. When these critiques become ideologies, when they become so reductionist or materialist in their accounts of things that they contradict the deep things of human experience, then of course they are to be rejected. But when they make points which modern experience confirms, then they must be accepted, even when incompatible with some religious traditions. We ourselves should be guilty of succumbing to an ideology if we allowed inherited forms of thinking to disguise and distort how things really are.

JATR examines three areas in which the criticism of religion has to be largely accepted. The first is the intellectual. It is characteristic of modern critiques of religion that they are not stridently atheistic. They do not begin and end with a denial of the existence of God. Rather they describe how people think and live in the modern world, without the need to refer to any supernatural order. It is a matter of observation, and acknowledging the actual situation, that even religious people function with a secular view of the natural and social worlds: 'Most of us today are practical atheists. The "god-hypothesis" is as irrelevant for running an economy or coping with the population explosion as it was for Laplace's system' [NR, 109]. JATR urges that we should not immediately rush about trying to find a temporary gap within which God can be said to exist – until the next advance in learning. In every other respect we are fully committed to the modern understanding of things: we are contemporary people. Let us keep our nerve. It is neither possible nor desirable for us to preserve the ancient world-view. The understanding of God which went with that discredited world-view will also have to go.

The second area in which religion has been criticized is the emotional. In extreme situations we seek any additional help we might be able to engage. Erica Jong says that she always lets her mother know exactly when she will be flying. Then by virtue of their combined concentration and will-power they get the plane off the ground and into the air. It is of some comfort to consider the stringent safety regulations governing both the production and maintenance of aircraft, as well as the strict licensing of flight staff. But why take a chance: belt *and* braces. The additional will-power costs little and the combination has always worked so far. The popularity of Ms Jong's work is no doubt due in part to the fact that we can all identify with such mild and harmless neuroses. I have added this example because JATR says that when he first flew he 'used to indulge in additional "cover" for those tense thirty seconds of take-off' [NR, 111]. But is 'prayer-power' at such a time not just as much the symptom of a mild neurosis as 'will-power'? We should not resist the criticism that religion can be neurotic, but try to make sure that it is not a means of perpetuating emotional immaturity.

The third area is the moral. In a society where individual and social actions are closely controlled by religious authorities, atheism is often taken to entail the rejection of all moral standards. Yet in the history of the modern world some specific religious beliefs have now been quietly dropped because they are recognized to be immoral. In the seventeenth-century *Book of Common Prayer* an Anglican priest would say to someone who was ill: 'Whatever your sickness is, know certainly that it is God's visitation.' Whether such a connection should ever have been believed to exist, the demise of the belief is due to the new level of moral sensitivity in society in general. Once again we see the positive effect of the criticism of religion: 'One of the liberating effects of secularization is that *this* idea of divine causation has at any rate been discredited' [NR, 114]. Far from seeking a licence for immorality, there are many people who reject religion for the sake of moral integrity.

Can a truly contemporary person *not* be an atheist? The criticisms of religion, which in short form JATR is identifying with atheism, represent significant gains in the development of a civilized society, and it would be a bad bargain if we had to reject them in order to preserve the traditional understanding of God. At first sight this seems to mean that the contemporary Christian must also adopt atheism, but of course we already know that JATR from the time he wrote his dissertation rejected such traditional theism. Christians and atheists might join in declaring themselves unbelievers in such a god. But they have more in common than that. In addition to their unbelief, they might well share some fundamental beliefs. At this point JATR goes back to his dissertation, via a quotation from *Honest to God*:

> Indeed, the line between those who believe in God and those who do not bears little relation to their profession of the existence or non-existence of such a Being. It is a question, rather, of their openness to the holy, the sacred, in the unfathomable depths of even the most secular relationship. As Martin Buber puts it of the person who professedly denies God, 'when he, too, who abhors the name, and believes himself to be godless, gives his

whole being to addressing the Thou of his life, as a Thou that cannot be limited by another, he addresses God.' [NR, 116]

We are familiar, from Part Two, with JATR's distinction concerning different ways of relating to people: instrumental, functional and truly personal. He wishes to transfer this to attitudes towards the universe, to life as a whole. He distinguishes the scientific-instrumental and the humanist-functional approaches. But there is a third experience:

> The man who finds himself compelled to acknowledge the reality of *God*, whatever he may call him or however he may image him, is the man who, through the mathematical regularities and through the functional values, is met by the same grace and the same claim that he recognizes in the I-Thou relation with another person. [NR, 117]

This is a reiteration of JATR's dissertation position. There is no Being over against the world such that his existence or non-existence can be discussed, or that his non-existence would make no difference to our daily lives. There is no gap, and that is why it is possible for even the most sensitive humanist at first to fail to recognize the presence of God. Like the young Samuel in the temple, it is inevitable, at least to begin with, that the call of God is simply mistaken for the voice of Eli (1 Sam. 3.2ff):

> It may come to him through nature, through the claims of artistic integrity or scientific truth, through the enagements of social justice or of personal communion. Yet always it comes with an overmastering givenness and demand such as no other thing or person has the power to convey or the right to require. [NR, 117]

This is not a device by which God is reintroduced, his existence and nature re-established. With regard to the first criticism, the intellectual, it is not a return to the understanding of God which was earlier discredited and rejected. It is not a fearful return to the false security of the old doctrine now left behind, but an act of faith, a going on to explore and discover the God who is ahead of us. 'The one who us superfluous as a hypothesis becomes all too present as a subject in encounter' [NR, 119]. With regard to the emotional critique, JATR can revive Bonhoeffer's theme of a world come of age, the adulthood of modern man. God the Father need not be what we mean by a 'father figure', a symbol of immaturity: 'The Christian faith, so far from seeking to keep men in strings, calls them to maturity, not the maturity of the adolescent revolting *against* a father, but of the "full-grown man" entering into the responsible freedom of the son and heir' [NR, 120]. The religious person is not shielded from the tragedies and suffering of life: God did not spare his only Son. But as JATR has already argued, God is in the tragedy and the suffering, and Christian faith is that not even these things can separate us from the love of God in Jesus Christ.

And finally there is no question of reasserting the old morally offensive position. A God who brings suffering on the young and the innocent would be morally intolerable. But in the dissertation we have already seen JATR's criticism of the traditional statement of the problem of evil. Evil is in the world. God does not cause it, but neither is he separated from it or impassive towards it. He is present in the evil of the cross, and because of that he is able to overcome it. 'The God of the Christian faith, who alone can be "our" God, can ultimately be revealed and responded to only as love which *takes* responsibility for evil – transformingly and victoriously' [NR, 121].

15 Being a Christian in the Third Wave

We have observed that the communication of the Christian message must be a two-sided affair. At one level this is 'answering' theology: the good news must be adapted so that it is addressed to the contemporary situation. But there is still in this approach an element of triumphalism. It is as if the pure gold of the gospel can simply be recast in the mould of the day, to become acceptable currency. But this will not do, for two reasons. The first is that, as we have seen, developments in the modern world have actually contributed to the refining of the Christian understanding of God. Advances in the natural sciences, in the social sciences, in personalist philosophy, and in ethics have all guided religious thought and practice. God is not contained in the religious; the religious is not the only channel of revelation. The second reason is that Christians are also contemporary people. As JATR never tires of pointing out, the line runs through each one of us. If we are not to fall back into an outdated and inadequate form of religion, we must be Christian as we are, as contemporary people. The new form of religion, the New Reformation, is not addressed simply to 'them', but also the 'them' part of ourselves. There are so many positive advances in the modern world that the challenge and opportunity is to be a Christian in a way that has never before been open to any generation. If a contemporary person can be a Christian, being a Christian is going to be different in this situation.

In this our final chapter we must take up the disturbing but exciting issue of 'the difference in being a Christian today'. This is the title of the book containing the Carnahan Lectures which JATR delivered in 1971 at the Union Theological Seminary, Buenos Aires. Although most of his writings presuppose an English or at least north Atlantic setting, in addressing himself to this issue he is very conscious that one of the most significant differences in being a Christian today is the emergence of Latin America and the Third World.

We saw in Part Two that one of JATR's criticisms of classical ontology was its essentially negative view of time and change. In the classical tradition God is immutable and beyond time, and theology is best represented in that which, in the formula of Vincent of Lérins, has been believed in every place, in every time, by every one. Of course there were changes in ancient times, but they happened relatively slowly and normally over such protracted periods that they could be absorbed as things settled down again. But in the second half of the twentieth century two things have happened. The first is that the speed of change has accelerated. The second that there is now no prospect that things will ever again settle down. The most that can be hoped for is that the pace of the acceleration might settle down. JATR was intrigued by a phrase from Donald Schon's BBC Reith Lectures, delivered in 1970, 'the loss of the stable state', and the issue as he saw it could be restated in relation to the title of the book of Schon's lectures, *Beyond the Stable State*. If religion in general and theology in particular have a stake in that which is always the same and unchanging, how is it possible to be a Christian 'beyond the stable state'?

Many Christians have found this to be a time of great confusion and anxiety, as the fixed points of doctrine, morality and structure are shaken by the new environment of constant change. Little wonder that there has been a revival in fundamentalism, which *adversus modernus*, fervently reasserts that which was previously believed, in the way in which it was believed. This has been true within Christianity, but of course the experience is not confined to one religion, and there has been a corresponding revival of fundamentalism in Islam. Indeed the experience is not essentially religious, and the fundamentalist revival can also be seen in political life in which dogmas that derive from the eighteenth century are propounded in an increasingly authoritarian manner.

Just as JATR was seen, quite unjustifiably, as encouraging moral permissiveness, so he was also accused of fostering doubt and uncertainty. Needless to say this was to get things entirely the wrong way round. The uncertainties about doctrine, morality and structure are the symptoms of the new post-stability environment. There is no question of the Church bringing the new situation to an end, any more than the Church can throw back secularization. But in this conception of the problem we see yet another example of what JATR has already identified in several places as a false dilemma. He opposes the traditional doctrine of God, not because it has become unacceptable to modern people, but because it is wrong, it misrepresents God. He opposes the old understanding of morality, not because people today will not observe traditional codes, but because this approach is not truly moral. Now, as we should expect, he refuses to speak against the new situation of constant change, not because he is pandering to the modern culture, but on theological grounds. As we saw in Part Two,

God is a God of change, who meets us in the new and the creative developments of our time. It would be quite false, as well as immature, to turn back to seek God where he was found by our forebears. It would display a lack of faith to believe that God cannot be found in the modern world. But more than that, it would be to reject the new ways in which God can be known. We have already seen that the modern world has assisted in the raising of religious sensitivity in intellectual, emotional and moral matters.

One of the causes of resistance among some Christians to the new environment of change is the unwelcome fact that the Church no longer has a central place within society. It cannot control the situation of change, indeed it cannot keep up with it let alone direct it. But once again, while this is a threat to a former way of being a Christian, does it open up the possibility of being a Christian in a different and more appropriate way? In pursuing this thought we could be assisted to by two letters, one from the ancient world and one from the modern. The first is from the second-century *Epistle to Diognetus*, in a passage which was important to JATR throughout his entire career and which he quotes in several of his works:

> Christians are not distinguished from the rest of mankind either in locality or in speech or in customs. For they dwell not somewhere in cities of their own, neither do they use some different language, nor practise an extraordinary kind of life . . . They dwell in their own countries, but only as sojourners; they bear their share in all things as citizens, and they endure all hardships as strangers. Every foreign country is a fatherland to them and every fatherland is foreign. . . . They obey the established laws and they surpass the laws in their own lives . . . In a word, what the soul is in the body, this the Christians are in the world . . . The soul is enclosed in the body, and yet itself holds the body together; so Christians are kept in the world as in a prison-house, yet they themselves hold the world together . . . So great is the office for which God has appointed them, and which it is not lawful for them to decline. [DBCT, 30–1]

That was the answer to the question, 'What does it mean to be a Christian today? which Diognetus might have given in the second century, when Christians were a minority without power, submerged in the Roman Empire. It was certainly a very different answer to the one which might have been given in the sixteenth century, within Christendom, depending on where it was asked in relation to the Reformation/Counter-Reformation divide. The various alternative answers at that time would have been concerned with drawing lines within Christianity, or rather in attempting to define and identify those who were in and those who were outside. But if the Reformation and the Counter-Reformation are over, so too is this approach:

> But I would urge as strongly as I can that instead of looking only to what can be salvaged from the old identities we must ask boldly whether distinctively Christian existence is likely in future to be characterized by this 'in or out' model, by a body of doctrine, a code of behaviour, a pattern of spirituality, a religious organization, which is peculiar to Christians and marks them off by exclusion from others. [DBCT, 17]

In the second half of the twentieth century we are in some respects closer to the situation of the *Epistle to Diognetus*, and the answer might be expressed more appropriately in a letter written in our own time.

JATR refers to the words of Bonhoeffer, 'To be a Christian does not mean to be religious in a particular way . . . but to be a man . . .' [DBCT, 18]. This seems to reduce Christianity to humanism. And before we dismiss this identification, let us recall the debt which Christians owe to humanist researches. In Part Two we saw that the Christian doctrine of man, as well as of Christology, has been enriched by the findings of the natural, medical and social sciences into the nature of human existence. And in this Part we have seen the contribution of humanist critiques of religion to the purification and enrichment of the doctrine of God. So that if Christianity were more closely identified with humanism, it is far from clear that this would be entirely reductionist. However, that is not Bonhoeffer's intention, as can be seen from the complete quotation, 'To be a Christian does not mean to be religious in a particular way . . . but to be a man – not a type of man, but *the man that Christ creates in us*' [DBCT, 18].

If God's creation is marred by human sin, in Christ the new creation is to make man truly man. It is not to create a religious man quite different from man. We saw in the section on liturgy that the greatest danger is the creation of a separate world of religious people, language, artefacts, rites, actions, symbols, dress, buildings, architecture, values and institutions. The title *The Difference in Being a Christian Today* is ambiguous. We have already noted that being a Christian in the new environment of change makes it fundamentally different from being a Christian in a more stable era. But there is another, perhaps more subtle meaning to the question. In what way is a Christian different from other people, today? It is tempting to define that by attachment to religious things, to the language, actions and rites to which we have just referred. Tempting, but superficial and misleading. It misleads non-Christians as to what is the essence of being a Christian, and it could mislead Christians themselves. If we recall the emphasis in JATR's Christology then the starting-point in answering the question must be man. Not man as he actually is, but as in Christ he can be. A time of change is a time of choice, and the vocation of the Christian today is to be human. It is in this sense that in several of his works JATR can describe himself as a 'Christian humanist'. There is no hint of reductionism here, rather the acceptance of a new responsibility.

JATR took his starting-point from Donald Schon's book *Beyond the Stable State*, and ended with a reference to Alvin Toffler's book *Future Shock*. He was to return to the theme a decade later, beginning this time from Toffler's sequel, *The Third Wave*. JATR's concern was the same, but the perspective was more advanced, as can be seen from his title, 'Religion in the Third Wave: The Difference in Being a Christian Tomorrow' [WTWM, 112–23]. In the grand style bequeathed by Hegel, Toffler is able to identify three great waves in human history, the agricultural, the industrial and the new third wave which is in some sense post-industrial. Although his interests are not primarily with religion, nevertheless the framework throws light on the forms of religious life, thought and organization which correspond to these waves. Or at least they cover the two waves which already lie behind us. JATR's concern is with the form of religion in the third, coming wave.

Briefly, the agricultural wave saw religion in relation to the stable state (no pun intended). Religion was linked to the natural cycle of the agricultural year, 'and in its medieval hey-day the virtues it extolled were the "dependent" ones of poverty, chastity and obedience' [WTWM, 114]. The organization of the Church could assume the coincidence of life and work. The parish church was within walking distance of village and farm. The origins of the second wave lie in the Renaissance and the Reformation. It is a time of growing nationalism, and with national identity emerge national Churches. It is a time of standardization, achieved through centralization of institutions. In religion new creeds and authorized books are issued – or unauthorized ones banned. With industrialization the link between place of work and residential parish is broken. Individual Christians adopt the identity of their denomination.

But now this wave is exhausted and a third wave is rising. The centre-periphery model is collapsing, and there is a threat to authority. As we have already noted, this has produced its own reaction in the form of a fundamentalist revival. But such attitudes, exemplified in the new inquisition, are already out of phase. The third wave is characterized by a loss of control, and the emergence of what Toffler calls a 'new ad hocracy'. The question of Christian identity in such a fluid situation becomes pressing. Previously religious identity arose from the individual's relation to a particular tradition or denomination. It included common beliefs and practices. Clergy were trained in identifiable ways, and laity knew how to relate to them. But now in the third wave all these external and institutional sources of identity are losing their authority. And if all this is true between one denomination and another, then it is true also between religions, as we saw at the end of Part Two. As if Christian identity within the Church or within society were not a daunting enough question, there is the question of 'Christian identity within the cosmos. For the Christ is bigger than any religion – even than Christianity – and he can wear the clothes of any religion' [WTWM, 122].

At the end of this Part we therefore see JATR as an explorer of the present and the future, a Christian well connected with his roots, yet a man more exhilarated than oppressed by new challenges. A citizen of one country, his concern is with issues which affect all. His lectures given in Buenos Aires begin from W. H. Auden's Christmas oratorio, in which those who seek the Christ in order to find the Way, the Truth and the Life describe their exploration: 'To discover how to be human now, is the reason we follow this star' [DBCT, 23]. They end, after discussion of the crises for theology, morality, the organization of the Church and the training of clergy and laity, with this affirmation: 'And I for one – for all my rootage in the past, for which I am constantly grateful – do not bewail the end of the stable state. Many things must be shaken in our day if the Kingdom which cannot be shaken is to be discerned and exposed' [DBCT, 84].

CONCLUSION

The End of Exploration

JATR was above all things a man of roots. His family roots and his roots in the Anglican tradition have been well portrayed by Eric James in his biography. No less strong were his academic roots, from Marlborough and Cambridge. Normally we should expect someone so well rooted to be conservative in all things, including economics, politics and religion. Inevitably this was true in some respects, at least as he began to make his way. For example, JATR was told that he was not invited to contribute to the Cambridge symposium the year before *Honest to God*, because he was regarded at the time as being too conservative theologically. And politically he recollects, 'I was brought up an unthinking Tory' [CFPS, 89] before be began his progression through the parties. But in the various fields he soon began to define his own position, and by the mid-1960s he was being labelled a radical. JATR, who was always fascinated by etymology, reflected on this paradox. The word radical comes from *radix*, 'a root'. How could his roots at once preserve and project him, encouraging him to be true to the past while enabling him to be free for the future?

In Febrary 1963, a month before the publication of *Honest to God*, there appeared in *The Listener* the text of a talk which JATR had broadcast for the BBC, entitled 'On Being a Radical' [CFPS, 1–6]. In it he reflected on the increasing use of the term 'radical', but while it was normally and loosely associated with a particular type of political activity, JATR used a religious example to illustrate its underlying meaning:

> Radicalism represents the built-in-challenge to any establishment, any institutionalism, any orthodoxy; and it is an attitude that is relevant to far more than politics. Indeed, the essence of the radical protest could be summed up in the statement of Jesus that 'the Sabbath is made for man, and not man for the Sabbath'. Persons are more important than principles. [CFPS, 2]

But true radicalism is not simply anarchy, for it knows that the protection of freedom and individuals requires order. Positively it is the pursuit of freedom for, and not just freedom from. When the movement of the Spirit hardens into an institution, then the radical protest breaks out.

He continues to use the example of the sabbath. The reformist

175

works for some modification of the sabbath laws, while the revolutionary proposes the abolition of the sabbath. The radical in contrast to both goes to the roots to ask what the sabbath was originally about, what values it should express and preserve: 'Unlike the reformist, the radical is concerned constantly to subject the Sabbath to man. Yet unlike the revolutionary, he believes in the Sabbath – for man' [CFPS, 3]. The radical must understand and love his own roots, and out of that love denounce whatever threatens and distorts the basis of that tradition. Unlike the revolutionary he cannot be *déraciné*.

The radical protests, but from the inside. He belongs, yet he is 'a bad party-member, an unsafe churchman' [CFPS, 4]. He sometimes finds himself closer to outsiders, in sympathy with radicals of other traditions because of their integrity if not their goals: 'Amid the cross-currents, the radical will find himself afloat in strange company, and yet he carries an anchor and a compass which belie the impression that he is merely drifting with the rest' [CFPS, 4]. But JATR understands that this is a common integrity, the response to the unconditional call. For some it is no more than that, but, as we have seen, for him humanism, in this case radical humanism is rooted in the love of God made known in Jesus Christ:

> But I have the utmost respect for the integrity of the radical humanist. Or perhaps it would be truer to say that, because I am a Christian, I *am* a radical humanist. For that, I believe, is the quality and direction of life to which Jesus referred when he said that the Sabbath was made for man, and when he summoned his disciples to be salt to the world. (CFPS, 5]

JATR was to return to this subject in the Selwyn Lectures, delivered in 1979 in St John's College, Auckland, New Zealand. They provided the title for JATR's collection of writings from that decade, *The Roots of a Radical*. By that time the fundamentalist backlash of which he had written in the early 1960s was already well in evidence in religion and morality as in politics:

> Symbolic of the seventies are what I call my 'three M's', Malcolm Muggeridge, Mary Whitehouse and Margaret Thatcher. Though I have nothing against any of them personally, and indeed admire them for the courage of their convictions, I can never make up my mind which most represents all that my soul abhors! [RR, 4]

The response to this reaction must not be a slipping back into reformist modifications, nor a wild revolutionary sweeping away. The motto for the 1980s must be: '*Twice as rooted, twice as radical*' [RR, 5].

Although some people found him increasingly conservative, for example in his *Redating the New Testament*, which we examined in Part One, this would be a superficial view of JATR's development:

> I believe in the centre, both biblically and doctrinally, because I am convinced there is every reason to do so *on critical and historical grounds*. But by the same token I am always open to follow the argument wherever it leads (even recently on the Shroud of Turin), and this makes me a frontiersman, alike in terms of theological freedom and of social responsibility. [RR, 5]

JATR sums up his writings by reference to our three fields, the biblical, theological and social. Naturally his radicalism is not the same in each, but our presentation of his main writings confirms his own view, namely that there is an internal consistency in his writings which comes from his distinctive allegiance to his roots and the freedom which he gained from them. We observed in Part One that JATR is not radical in the way in which the term is normally used in biblical studies. But that is a very loose usage. Indeed it is closer to his understanding of *déraciné*, which is not radical at all. It is not derived from roots; it cuts roots. In this case, through undue scepticism about the historical value of the sources, this kind of scholarship brings to the texts unjustified assumptions about what could or could not be written at that time, by such people, in that place. We said that JATR's motto in biblical studies might well have been 'To the texts themselves'. It is this rooting in the texts which gives his work its true radicalism. His understanding arises from the texts, not from the imposition of extraneous assumptions and constraints. But having said that, the person who is rooted is then free to move. This is the paradox of experience. Having gone to the texts themselves JATR can come to conclusions which on specific issues seem conservative. But there is a world of difference between the two. In this context the conservative is not at all free. His position does not arise from the text any more than the *déraciné* radical. It represents an understanding of the text which arose in the past – of the more recent past than is generally acknowledged. But in conserving that position it has no freedom. It is determined not by the texts, but by a now dated reading of them.

In Part One I not only presented JATR's views, but was quick to criticize him when he was not consistent in his own approach. In Chapter 1 he could refer to the Gospels as a 'record' and as giving access to the 'bedrock tradition'. In the examining of evidence of the Shroud of Turin he was guilty of inconsistency and halting between two ways. In Chapters 1 and 2 he was willing to accept the highly mythological passages on the temptations, baptism and the testimony of John the Baptist as if they were purely historical accounts. In Chapter 3 he failed to complete the hermeneutical task which he set for himself, substituting one metaphor for another without leaving the thought forms of the ancient world. And in Chapter 5 he treated the relationship between facts and faith in an almost pre-critical manner, ending up by hailing muddle as one of the great virtues of the English nation. But these criticisms have one thing in common, they indicate points at which JATR failed to follow his own method. It is when he is true to his roots that he is most radical; when he is at his most radical in his own terms then he is most liberated and creative. And this is true also of his theology.

At first sight the positions adopted by JATR in Parts One and Two seem to be diametrically opposed. If in the biblical field he appears to be an ultra-conservative on many issues, in theology he is considered a raving radical on all matters. However, on more careful inspection his position is exactly the same in both, if we take the trouble to use the terms consistently. He is perceived as a radical in theology on many grounds, yet ironically, if he is a radical it is on entirely different grounds. His image of being a radical was based on the commonly held view that he rejects many fundamental aspects of the Christian faith, including belief in God and the divinity of Christ. But after our examination of these issues in Part Two it will be quite clear that this is a complete misrepresentation of his position. He cuts off nothing: that would not be radical. He is rooted in the Christian faith, and there is no question of rejecting its fundamental elements. If he is radical, it is because of his roots, not in spite of them.

But as we have just noted in reviewing Part One, it is the paradox of experience that it is the person with roots, the radical in this sense, who is free. Rooted, but not rooted to the spot. It is the conservative in doctrine who is rooted to the spot and who is therefore not free to move. He is attached to the surface, to the expression of Christian faith as it took form at a particular moment in the history of the Church, or more often of a particular denominational tradition. But if there is one thing that ecumenism teaches it is that emphasizing denominational characteristics does not take us deeply into the heart of the faith. In JATR's terms it is the revolutionary who sees nothing in Christian doctrine and sweeps it all away. The conservative is wedded to the preservation of the doctrine at a particular stage in its development. It is the true radical who is so convinced of the truth of Christianity that he is able to penetrate through the tradition to ask what it was attempting to express.

JATR's radicalism cuts off nothing, but brings everything into question. We considered his biblical studies first because it will have become clear that the Bible is one of his most important roots. It is all too easy to read the Bible from a perspective brought to it, whether of scepticism or of a particular tradition. This is to use the Bible to legitimize positions of the past. The true radical begins from a fundamental re-examination of what the Bible actually says. This provides an important criterion in reinterpreting Christian doctrine. Thus we have seen that his theology is founded on the rejection of the imposition of classical Greek ontology on the Bible and Christian doctrine. He concentrates on the will of God rather than on the divine being, on the living God rather than the divine attributes. He begins from the biblical affirmation about Christ, that it is in this man that God has chosen to reveal himself. This takes place not through an unhuman physiology characterized as two natures, with all its inherent docetism, but through a relationship, expressed in the word *Abba*.

As in Part One, so in Part Two we made certain criticisms of JATR's work, but once again they were instances where he failed to be true to his own position. He did not maintain his distance from the older scheme of two-nature thinking when he attempted to use his new philosophy to answer old problems. He failed to indicate that he did not share the philosophical premises of linguistic philosophy when he was dealing with its treatment of God-language. He did not provide a proper introduction to his own position at the beginning of *Honest to God*, giving a misleading impression of cultured relativism. Nor in that book did he make sufficiently clear the distinction, fundamental to his dissertation, between biblical mythology and classical ontology. By his deference to other theologians he encouraged people to assume that he had no distinctive position of his own. But in each case these criticisms amount to pointing to a failure to be consistent in his own radicalism. He is at his most radical when most closely in touch with his own roots. The same points can be made of his social concerns, considered in Part Three.

In Part Three we dealt with two broad areas in which JATR is considered to be radical, and in each we can make the same judgement as before, namely that he is indeed radical but for very different reasons from the popular perception. The first area is that of morality. As we have seen, he was regarded by some as if he had created, unaided, the new morality. He was regarded as having given his blessing to the permissive society. Inevitably attention focused on sexuality. The subject is dealt with by JATR appropriately and with great seriousness and insight, but public interest did not take its lead from this treatment. It was guided as usual by a mixture of the inherited obsessions of a previous culture in which celibate males pronounced on matters of sex, together with the tabloid voyeurism characteristic of contemporary culture. We have seen in our discussions of previous subjects, such as Christology and adoptionism, that it may be necessary to question the terms associated with the debate because of the assumptions from which they arise. The term 'permissive' is another such example. 'Are you for or against the permissive society?' There is something wrong with the choice, and it has to do with the idea of permitting.

JATR raised this matter in an article on 'Obscenity and Maturity', republished in *Christian Freedom in a Permissive Society*. His subject was censorship in society and he declared that such laws were 'a hangover from the paternalistic society' [CFPS, 69]. The call for their withdrawal is taken to be evidence of the permissive attitude, but who is it who 'permits'? 'The word "permissive" suggests that there is a right inherent in society, or in the leading individuals in society, to exercise control over us and that they are failing in this duty, insomuch as certain activities are "permitted" which ought not to be "permitted"' (CFPS, 71]. He went on to argue that we must pass from the paternalist and permissive society to the mature society. He then set out a very careful analysis of the relationship between the erotic, the obscene and the pornographic, to illustrate how our as yet immature society might develop.

This example indicates how JATR is radical on moral issues. He is not radical in the sense of rejecting all social controls against evil and exploitation, nor is he radical in accepting any form of behaviour. These would not be proper uses of the word radical. His position can be distinguished as usual from conservatism, especially in its authoritarian form. This represents an attempt to tell people what they should and should not do, according to some objective moral code. But if it has any interest in morality, it is counter-productive. People who are coerced into particular forms of behaviour are prevented from becoming moral. JATR's radicalism is to begin with persons and personal relations, and to ask how we can encourage people to be responsible. The discussion on obscenity is a good example of this approach. The erotic is good, and seen to be good in many other cultures and religions, the pornographic is bad. Not bad because it is not permitted, but because it destroys the erotic by perverting sexually and dehumanizing those who are influenced by it. As we have seen in the earlier discussion of morality, this does not preclude safety nets or dykes against evil.

The second broad area in Part Three in which JATR is thought radical, though for the wrong reasons, concerns his relationship to the modern world. It is sometimes thought that he simply goes along with what people today will or will not accept both in terms of belief and moral behaviour. Once again this really has nothing to do with radicalism. Some 'radical' theologians may have fostered a certain image of themselves by appearing to be ultra-modern, vying with each other as to who believed least and who acted in the most secular and irreligious ways. But nothing could be further from JATR's position. He is not conservative in all things, as if this were the responsibility of the Christian. In doctrine, structures and behaviour conservatism normally relates to a particular period, tradition or social class. What it takes to be timeless is quickly dated and therefore dateable.

JATR's relationship to the modern world is much more complex than that. It is neither acceptance nor rejection. Its basis is neither cultural nor psychological, but theological. We have already covered this in the appropriate places, but I think it could be related to two aspects of his work in particular. The first is that we meet the Thou in the thous. God is experienced in the modern world, not in turning away from it. But how he is experienced may be new. This is entirely in keeping with what is said in theology, though too often no implications are drawn. There are new things happening for the first time in the modern age: God is to be sought in them. The second concerns the ambiguities of the age. It is not necessary in all this to 'accept' the modern world, as if everything that happens is positive and worthy. But it is necessary to be aware of what is happening since, as we have seen in the previous chapter, there are many points at which the modern world can make a positive contribution to the enrichment of religion. God is not in the modern world because it has some special virtue. As we have seen, God is in the evil and the suffering as much as in the good and the pleasant. In all ages he is to be sought where he has said he will be found – in, with and under the conditions of life today. With this assurance JATR is free to seek God responsibly without making what people do or do not believe in any sense a condition of his explorations.

As in the other two Parts, we had cause to criticize JATR when he was not faithful to his roots. He wrote in conventional terms about the arms race and prayer. He shared traditional views on priesthood, ministry and ordination. In *Honest to God* he probably fostered the view that he took as his starting-point what people today could or could not believe, when in fact his own starting-point was his dissertation and its critique of classical theism. But in all of these examples the previous truth is confirmed, that he is at his most creative and most radical when he is most sensitive to his own distinctive roots.

In the Parts and in the whole we therefore see JATR exhibiting a radical dialectic, in an image which he used throughout his life, the interaction of the centre and the edges. For all his explorations, he felt he could identify with the title of John Knox's biography, 'Never Far from Home'. And in this metaphor of the returning explorer there is the most important element in his entire work, the affirmation that reality is personal.

> But I suppose that all my deepest concerns both in thought and in action – and I cannot separate the theological, the pastoral and the political – find their centre in a single, continuing quest. This is to give expression, embodiment, to the overmastering, yet elusive, conviction of the 'Thou' at the heart of everything. [EIG, 15]

We have seen in our review of the three Parts that there were certain unresolved ambiguities in JATR's work, and that he was at his most radical when he was most consistently tapping the resources of his roots. But in closing we might pay more attention to the unresolved tensions, for I believe that they were not simply aberrations or loose ends. They reflected a deeper tension of which he may well have been aware, but which he was either unable or unwilling to resolve. As we noted at the outset of this chapter, JATR was above all a man of roots: born in the cathedral close, Canterbury, in the innermost room of the innermost building of the Anglican tradition; educated at one of the great public schools of England and at perhaps the greatest college of the greatest university in that land. Few people could have been as conscious of their roots or more grateful and appreciative of all that they bestowed. At first sight it seems inconceivable that he could have mistaken his roots.

Everything that JATR said about roots and radicalism and about *déraciné* radicalism which does not deserve its title, is true. He was a man of roots, and all his sermons, lectures, articles and books illustrate this claim. But which roots?

The roots to which I have just alluded were his inherited roots, which formed him and brought him to the point at which he could begin his own growth. These were great roots, and old roots, and their resources never failed him during his entire life. But these old roots were not peculiar to JATR and they set many before him on a similar course. If I may say so, my own admiration for JATR coincided with those aspects of his life and work which seemed least to be the product of the old roots. Inspecting my copy of *The Roots of a Radical* I see that I have found almost nothing of interest in the Selwyn lectures. They were in part autobiographical and at times anecdotal. The old roots did not produce the radical.

The roots of the radical were by comparison new roots, his own roots. Anyone who wishes to understand JATR must read two works. They come at different ends of his career. *The Priority of John* is the end product of a life of scholarly reflection on the Bible, the New Testament and the Gospels. In Part One we examined its historical-critical arguments, but it had for JATR a more profound significance than that. It was *the* text in the New Testament which expressed and confirmed his deepest religious experiences. But in that sense it was not a root; his position was already established. The real roots of his intellectual life are to be encountered rather in the first work which he produced, his dissertation *Thou Who Art*. Throughout his career JATR continually learnt from other writers, and gratefully acknowledged their assistance. In his dissertation he readily acknowledged the writers who most influenced him at that time, including Barth, Kierkegaard, Farmer and Temple, but most of all Martin Buber. JATR saw this to be the root of his philosophy and theology. It was a new root, but was it the most important?

It was new in the sense that the existentialist, personalist tradition does not obviously run through Canterbury. It was a new and strong intellectual root. But therein lies the further question, because in writers such as Kierkegaard and Buber philosophy is not simply an intellectual activity. It is only valid and credible if it is a philosophy which arises from life and produces a new kind of life. This is why it is always engaging with the deepest dimensions of religion. To say that *Thou Who Art* is the root of JATR's entire theology is true, although few have been in a position to recognize the fact. But what is the root of *Thou Who Art*? What made personalist philosophy credible to JATR, for it was certainly not part of his inherited roots? The answer, as we have seen from the last quotation, is his affirmation that reality is personal. But far from being an explanation, this seems to be another form of the same question.

It may be that the answer to this question, if there is one, goes beyond the material available to us in JATR's published works. It lies in JATR's own life, and to that extent Eric James's biography is an important source. It is one of the strengths of the biography that its author, a close friend of JATR for over thirty years, felt able to paint a realistic picture which did not attempt to cover up any shortcomings in his subject. He describes how JATR was not socially at ease in one-to-one situations, and had various devices which he used to survive them. A good example is found in the context of the family home in Reigate: 'The house opened immediately on to the Downs. It was ideal for walks – for both John and Ruth, and for "pastoral" walks and talks, in every sense of the word' [EJ, 193]. I smiled to myself when reading this description, because I had been taken on such a walk when we first met. JATR had invited me to 'Fort Lodge', but instead of a conversation in his study, he proposed a stroll up Fort Lane to the open Downs. Presumably in this way he would not have been trapped if for any reason our meeting had not been comfortable. I mention this incident because it confirms to me that JATR was a most unlikely person to have formed the view that reality is personal. Indeed this could be a scenario for a sequel to Sartre's play *No Exit*. In this case the subject would be a man who could hardly cope with another thou, being condemned to live in a universe which was not only populated by thous, but was itself one great Thou! Although JATR never became entirely at ease with individual encounters, the most important influence on his life must have been something – more likely someone – which nevertheless enabled him to come to experience reality as personal.

Because I came to this matter as an academic problem, the experience which made personalist philosophy credible, I was struck by JATR's insistence that we encounter the Thou in the thous. But the academic puzzle was only resolved by one who was better acquainted with JATR's life. I therefore felt my initial understanding of the situation confirmed when I read the following passage in Eric James' biography: 'His "I-Thou" thesis, which he had worked at in 1943/4, and which had at first been an intellectual perception, had been earthed and deepened when he fell in love with Ruth (and had been taken deeper still in and through their marriage)' [EJ, 90].

I was therefore convinced that the roots of the radical were not the old roots but the new. JATR's own recognition of the fact is evident from the last of the theological works in his 'continuing quest'. It is clear from two points in *Truth is Two-Eyed*, which at least in this direction represents spiritually, philosophically and culturally the farthest reaches of his journeying. The first is his quotation from Eliot's *Four Quartets*, concerning exploration. The second is his description of the way in which he has travelled, intellectually and spiritually: 'For my wife and I have come to where were are today via a little book . . . Martin Buber's *I and Thou* . . .' [TTE, 9] When they were students together at Cambridge, setting out in life together, John and Ruth visited Little Gidding in June 1944. And almost forty years later, after so much constant exploration in so many fields, they returned there when JATR's cancer was diagnosed, to the place from which they began [EJ, 282]. Great though the impact of JATR's thought was on millions of people throughout the world, I do not believe it proceeded simply from the intellect, but rather expressed the most profound experiences of his life. In the words of Eliot's poem *Little Gidding*, which meant so much to him:

> We shall not cease from exploration
> And the end of all our exploring
> Will be to arrive where we started
> And know the place for the first time . . .

In matters biblical, theological and social, in the things of liturgy and life, those who are most rooted in the knowledge and love of God in Jesus Christ are most liberated for the challenge of change.

Index of Subjects

Index of Names

Index of Biblical References